AF269461

The Templars at War

The Templars at War

The *Beauceant*

Zvonimir Grbasic

Pen & Sword
MILITARY

First published in Great Britain in 2022 by
Pen & Sword Military
An imprint of
Pen & Sword Books Ltd
Yorkshire – Philadelphia

ISBN 978 1 47389 840 0

A CIP catalogue record for this book is
available from the British Library.

Typeset by Mac Style
Printed through Printworks Global Ltd, London/Hong Kong.

Pen & Sword Books Limited incorporates the imprints of Atlas, Archaeology, Aviation, Discovery, Family History, Fiction, History, Maritime, Military, Military Classics, Politics, Select, Transport, True Crime, Air World, Frontline Publishing, Leo Cooper, Remember When, Seaforth Publishing, The Praetorian Press, Wharncliffe Local History, Wharncliffe Transport, Wharncliffe True Crime and White Owl.

For a complete list of Pen & Sword titles please contact

PEN & SWORD BOOKS LIMITED
47 Church Street, Barnsley, South Yorkshire, S70 2AS, England
E-mail: enquiries@pen-and-sword.co.uk
Website: www.pen-and-sword.co.uk

Or

PEN AND SWORD BOOKS
1950 Lawrence Rd, Havertown, PA 19083, USA
E-mail: Uspen-and-sword@casematepublishers.com
Website: www.penandswordbooks.com

Contents

Prologue

The sufferings of Christian pilgrims in the Holy Land on the way from the Mediterranean coast to holy places spurred a group of French knights to found a monks' community to protect the pilgrims. In the beginning, the knights could hardly imagine that they were laying the foundations for a famous knightly friars' order whose military path creates strong emotions among lovers of history and fiction even today, almost 900 years later.

However, just as pilgrimages did not first start in the early twelfth century, pilgrims did not face dangers in Palestine alone. In early Christianity, pilgrimages were a rare exception. This changed during the rule of Constantine I (Constantine the Great, 306–337), the first Roman emperor to have accepted Christianity, allowed free profession of the Christian faith and eventually declared Christianity as the official religion of the Empire.

At the age of 80, Constantine's mother Helena went on a pilgrimage to Jerusalem, where she undertook what can only be called archaeological research, looking for relics connected with the martyrdom and death of Jesus. According to Gelasius[1] and Rufinus,[2] at a hidden location she found the remains of the three crosses on which Jesus and the two thieves had been crucified. The story goes that a miracle helped her to determine which of the crosses was the one that had held Jesus himself. At the spot of his mother's excavations, the emperor ordered the construction of the church of the Holy Sepulchre[3] where the relic, considered to be the holiest such artefact of Christianity, was eventually housed.

News of Helena's achievement spread among the faithful throughout the Empire, and pilgrimages began while the archaeological excavations were still going on. Places connected with the life of Jesus, such as Bethlehem, Nazareth and Jerusalem as well as the River Jordan, topped the list of pilgrims' destinations. In the following years, church authorities supported the pilgrimages and their numbers continued to grow, which in turn spurred the construction of monasteries and hospices in Jerusalem and its surroundings in order to host, care for and treat the pilgrims; in the early fifth century, there were already around 200 such places. We would say today that religious tourism was undergoing strong development.

Pilgrimages were also undertaken to places connected with the lives of other early-Christian saints and martyrs, almost all of whom came from the East. Church authorities spurred the belief that the content of the saints' graves could produce miracles and, in time, pilgrims and merchants started bringing smaller relics to the West. Stories of their beneficial effects were spread by word of mouth. Thus believers tried to see and touch these relics, further strengthening the religious fervour and the need to visit the places from which the relics originated.

Pilgrimages from Europe to the Holy Land necessitated a difficult, long and uncertain journey taking at least a year. For centuries, such journeys were a private matter until, in the year 910, Count William I of Aquitaine founded the Benedictine Abbey of Cluny in Burgundy. The abbey's doctrine supported pilgrimages and provided practical aid to pilgrims. At first, the entrepreneurial abbots of Cluny completely controlled the pilgrims' travel to Spain and later, they started organizing voyages to Jerusalem.

Travelling from Europe to Palestine has always been expensive, and became extremely difficult and all but impossible to most European pilgrims after Arab conquests of the Mediterranean cut many of the former trade routes. Few people in the impoverished West could afford such a journey; only extremely brave and adventurous pilgrims, facing numerous dangers and with much effort, managed to reach Jerusalem. Prior to the start of the journey, many pilgrims would sell all their property in order to finance it, while others simply renounced their worldly goods with the intent of ending their days in the Holy Land. Travel took place both individually and in larger or smaller groups. It was a good idea to join a nobleman's group with an armed escort. Regardless of political circumstances, travellers faced numerous dangers: robbers and wild beasts on remote highways; infectious diseases and food poisoning in inns; calamitous weather; shipwrecks and so on. Additional problems arose from sea voyages, always dependent on favourable winds.

If pilgrims reached the coast of the Mediterranean at the wrong time of year, they had to spend months waiting for a ship bound for the Holy Land. Usually they sailed from Venice or Bari to Alexandria, Tripoli or Constantinople. Ships also travelled across the Adriatic Sea, from the south Italian port of Bari to Durrës in Albania, after which travellers followed the alternative land route, the ancient Roman Via Egnatia, through Thessaly to the Bosporus.

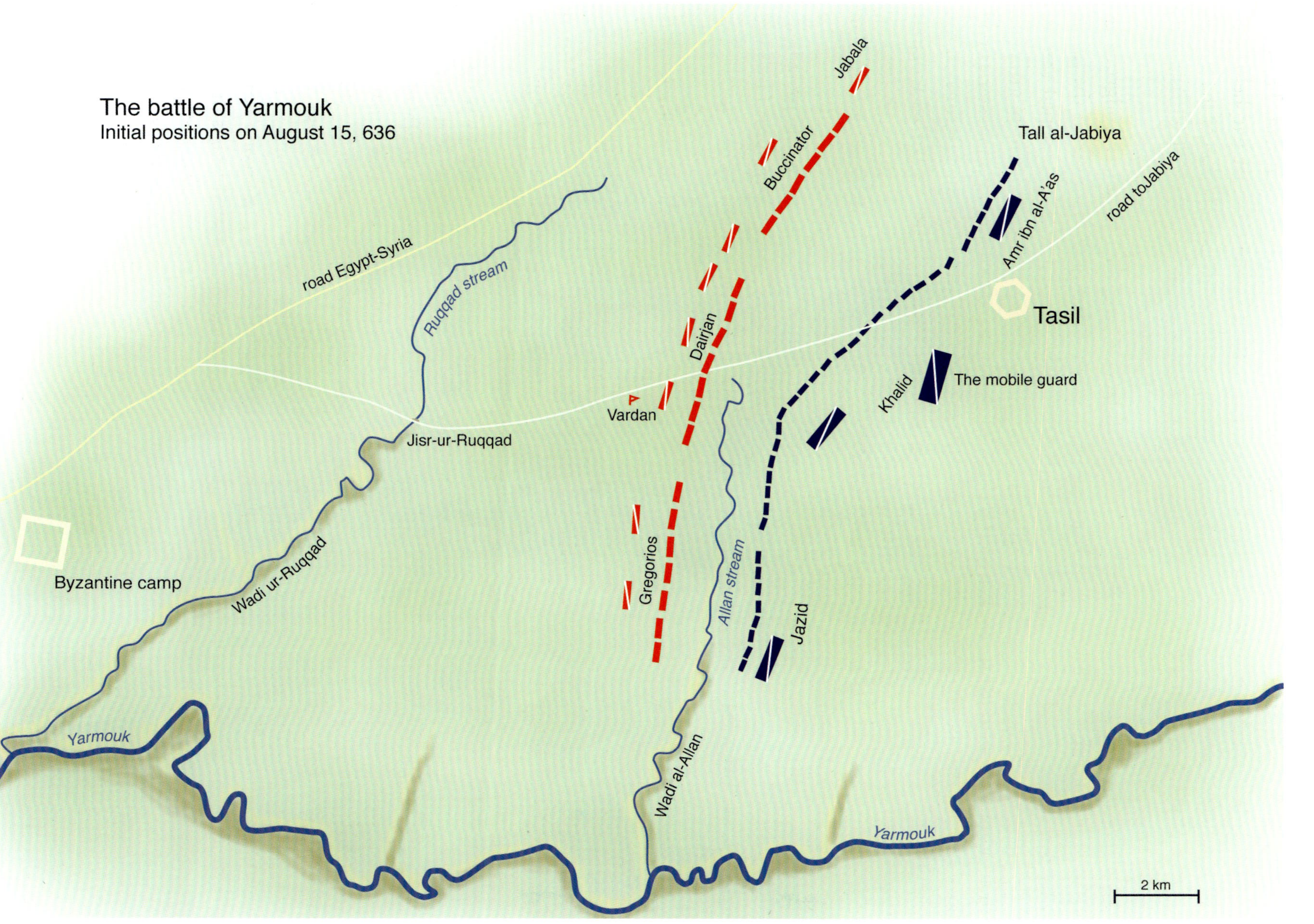

Yarmouk battle initial positions on 15 August 636.

Pirates preyed at sea, particularly after the Arab conquests in the seventh century. In addition to the Muslim pirates, threats were doubled by the appearance of even more dangerous sea-robbers: Viking longboats trading in furs and lumber but not averse to dealing in slaves. When Hungarians – a mixture of Ugro-Finnic and Turkish tribes that settled in Pannonia – converted to Christianity in 975, a land route opened, following the River Danube to Belgrade, then on to Sofia and Adrianople, all the way to Constantinople. Byzantium only gained full control over Balkan roads from the border with the Hungarian kingdom after the year 1019, when this particular route became safe for pilgrims. It was of particular interest to large groups of pilgrims that could not find passage on ships. Northerners travelled either around the western coast of Europe and then through Gibraltar, or else across the Russian steppes down to the Bosporus.

Once travellers reached the coast of Asia, they had to traverse the land route to Jerusalem and other holy spots. Along the pilgrims' routes, the number of inns and hospitals for travellers started to grow. The Hospice of St John, one of the most famous inns (for completely different reasons)[4] was founded as an inn and hospital for the pilgrims in Jerusalem by traders from the southern Italian republic of Amalfi.

Regardless of who held control over Jerusalem and its surroundings – Byzantium or Persia – there were no political or religious obstacles for Christian pilgrims. Although engaging in territorial wars between themselves, the Byzantine Empire and Sassanian Dynasty[5] were both multicultural states allowing freedom of religion, so Christian and Jewish cultures entwined throughout Asia. Not even the great changes in the first half of the seventh century had any important influence on religious coexistence in the Holy Land.

In the year 611, Persia conquered Byzantine Mesopotamia, Syria and Anatolia. The following year, Heraclius[6] chased the Persians from Anatolia but was defeated in 613; after this, the Sassanids conquered Palestine and Egypt by the year 621. This was the Second Golden Age (498–622) of the Persian dynasty. On 12 December 627, near Nineveh, Heraclius reached a decisive victory over the Persians and the Sassanids agreed to return all occupied lands.

In the meantime, Arabia saw the spread of the influence of Mohammed,[7] who was preaching the new religion of Islam.[8] While in Medina, around the year 622, he concluded an agreement with the leading local families and tribes, regardless of whether they were of the Muslim, Christian or Jewish faith. The agreement, known as the Medina Charter, creates freedom of religion in Medina as the centre of faith; it prohibits the carrying of weapons; guarantees safety to women; secures peace among the tribes of Medina; introduces war taxes and guidelines for the creation of political alliances; guarantees security of the individual; founds courts and regulates payment of remuneration instead of blood feuding. This document, which offered coexistence and security, together with Mohammed's preaching of a religion very similar to their own, quickly induced numerous Christian and Jewish believers to convert to Islam, thus becoming part of a religious movement that promised them a better life, and paradise, should they die for Allah. Growing in numbers, Arab Muslims spent eight years fighting with the surrounding pagan Arab tribes. The enmities ended with the Muslim taking of Mecca, destroying pagan shrines and uniting most of Arabia. After Mohammed's death in June 632, Abu Bakr[9] crushed the rebellion of several dissenting Arab tribes and united the whole of Arabia as the first Muslim caliph.[10] By the following year,

Muslims had already taken over Persian Iraq. What followed was the invasion of Byzantine Syria. In June 634, at an unknown location in today's Israel, Arabs defeated the Byzantine army, after which, in September, Damascus fell too. Muslim conquest did not stop at that; because of this, in the year 635, an alliance was created between Persia and Byzantium, strengthened by the marriage between the Persian emperor Yazdegerd III and Heraclius' daughter or granddaughter. The new allies decided to start a joint offensive against the advancing Muslims.

In early 636, Muslims penetrated into Palestine from the south over trade routes, conquering Tiberias, Baalbek and Homs. In mid-July, by Antioch in northern Syria, Heraclius gathered a large army composed of Byzantines and numerous mercenaries: Slavs, Franks, Armenians, Georgians and Christian Arabs. He divided them into five columns and, under the command of the son of Constantine III, sent them towards Homs. In the field, the army was commanded by Theodore Trithorios and Vahan, whose Armenians were in the reserve and were supposed to approach Homs from the direction of Hama. Buccinator, the duke in command of the Slavs, was tasked with reaching Beirut by coast, taking the city and then starting towards Damascus, which was to cut off the majority of the Muslim army at Homs. Jabalah ibn al-Aiham[11] held the command only over Christian Arabs. His marching route led from Aleppo over Hama to Homs. Gregorius, commander of one of the European contingents, was ordered to attack the Muslims' right wing at Homs from the north-east, while Dairjan and the second European contingent were to approach from the west and attack the enemy's left wing. As commander-in-chief, Heraclius oversaw the entire operation from Antioch.

Muslim commander Khalid ibn Al-Walid[12] found out about the Byzantines' intentions through prisoners. He pulled his forces away from Homs and concentrated them at Jabiyah, where the plain allowed for cavalry charges and reinforcements from the south could arrive quickly. However, this was Ghassanid territory, so Muslims were exposed to possible attacks by local Christians and, in the case of battle, the strong enemy garrison in Caesarea would represent a threat at the Arabs' back. Thus, Khalid moved further east, south-east from the Sea of Galilee, to the plains north from Yarmouk, a tributary of the River Jordan. The grassy landscape and proximity of the watercourse provided safe grazing and water for Arab war horses, an issue of special concern for Khalid, who was an extraordinary cavalry commander. The coast of Yarmouk is steep in this area, reaching heights of 30 metres or more. In the west, the plains end with the ravine Wadi-ur-Ruqqad, more than 200 metres deep, connecting with the bed of the Yarmouk. The only west-side passage through the ravine was possible in one place only: over the ancient Roman bridge of Ayn Dhakar. Some 7 kilometres east from Wadi-ur-Ruqqad, the plains are also cut, by a length of around 7.5 kilometres, by Wadi al-Allan, another ravine, this one shallower and shorter. In the north, the plains were crossed by the road to Jabiyah. In the plains, a single hill rose to around 100 metres and from that hill, known as Tel al Jumm'a, the Muslims controlled the environment. Khalid deliberately chose terrain favourable to cavalry manoeuvres and good for the battle the Muslims could not afford to lose.

Muslim sources estimate Khalid's army from 25,000 to 45,000 people, mostly veterans, while both Muslim and Byzantine sources agree that Christian forces were more numerous but mostly inexperienced warriors. Khalid took up the front line of a full 12 kilometres. The left wing leaned on the bed of the Yarmouk, and the right on the hills under the road to Jabiyah. The core of Khalid's army, as was the case with all early Muslim armies, was the infantry armed with 2.5 metre-long spears or 2 metre-long bows. They carried short swords similar to the Roman gladius and protected their bodies with large wooden or woven shields. Arab long-bow archers had a killing range of up to 150 metres. The infantry was divided into thirty-six defensive formations. Behind the centre, left and right wing, in order to provide support for the infantry and counterattack, were situated cavalrymen armed with 5.5 metre-long lances and Sassanid long swords. The mobile guard (*Tulay'a mutuaharikkah*), an elite light cavalry unit of 4,000 men, stayed in reserve under Khalid's direct command, prepared to intervene in the critical decisive moments of the battle.

A few days later the Byzantine vanguard arrived, consisting of light Arab cavalry and camel-riders. Their attempts to reconnoitre Muslim positions were prevented by the mobile guard. After the incident, nothing happened for a whole month, except for the Byzantines constructing fortified military camps west from the Wadi-ur-Ruqqad ravine. The Byzantines formed their fighting line in the plains, 7 kilometres east of the ravine, about 1.5 kilometres behind the Wadi al-Allan ravine. They leaned the right wing, under Gregorius, to the bed of the Yarmouk; the centre was commanded by Dairjan and Vahan, and the left wing by Buccinator. Vahan had a tall observation point built behind his contingent's position so he could supervise the events on the long front line. The Byzantine left wing was unprotected in the plain, not far from the first slopes towards Jabiyah. While arranging the army, in a failed attempt to reach the first slopes north from the fighting lines and thus protect his left flank, Vahan spread the Byzantine front line to a full 13 kilometres, leaving a gap between infantry units. Following Mauritius'[13] military handbook *Strategicon*, the Byzantines put the infantry in the front, adding regular heavy cavalry in a uniform disposition.

The basic infantry unit was still the legion, established by Constantine II.[14] According to the sixth-century AD source, *Legio II Traiana* numbered 1,100 soldiers, while *Legio III Diocletiana* numbered 1,078. Two *Arithmoi* units, eight centuries each, made up the legion. Sozomen (the fifth-century Byzantine writer) has written that full-strength *Arithmos* numbered 666 warriors, or about 1,500 men in the legion, but that was on paper only. On the battlefield, infantry formed dense crowded units, eight files deep. The basic cavalry unit was 240 cavalrymen: strong *cuneus* composed of six *turmae* with 40 cavalrymen each. As infantry, cavalrymen formed battlefield units eight files deep. Cavalry units were capable to perform complicated manoeuvres, cavalrymen were skilled horsemen, and superior war-horses were carefully bred both for infantry, and for cavalry there was the *tagma*. An infantry *tagma* consisted of sixteen *lochaghiai* with sixteen warriors each. While in the heavy cavalry the javelin-throwers (two-thirds) and archers (one-third) were arranged in separate units, in the guard and light infantry there were no separate units for javelin-throwers and archers. In the battlefield, infantrymen formed very compact units of eight rows in depth with the strength of around 1,000 warriors (*chiliarchiai*). A cavalry *tagma* comprised six *hekatontarchie* of fifty horsemen each, arranged in eight to ten rows on the battlefield. The cavalry was prepared for complex manoeuvres, the horsemen were excellently trained and the exquisite war horses carefully raised. A changing number of infantry and cavalry *tagma* created a *morai* (2,000 to 3,000 people), while three higher units comprised a *turmai* with a strength of 6,000 to 7,000 warriors.

The Byzantine infantry fought gallantly, but without any cavalry support the infantrymen had no chance.

Heavy infantry and cavalry were equipped with a lamellar cuirass *klibanion* (made of iron, leather or horn) covering the body to the waist. The upper arms and body below the waist were protected by leather straps (*pteruges*) attached to the cuirass. In rare cases, soldiers wore a hauberk (*lorica*). Also in use were cotton, leather and wool-padded cuirasses. Forearms and shins were covered by metal, wooden or leather straps connected together. The helmet included a neck-protector. Additional protection for infantry came from the oval shield (*skuta*) of 1.2 metres. Light infantry, heavy cavalry and cavalry archers carried a round shield with a diameter of 75 centimetres. Basic weapons were spears (*kontos*) and swords. The cavalry lance, adopted by the Alani and the Sarmatians, measured 3.5 metres in length, while the infantry used even longer ones. Shorter throwing javelins (*rhipatorion*) were used by both the cavalry and the infantry. They also still used short lead-loaded javelins (*martiobarbulus*) which the heavy cavalry carried in their saddlebags. The double-edged, straightened-to-point sword (*spathion*) with a length of 90 centimetres hung over the shoulder and was carried on the left side. Axes and maces were used as secondary weapons. Byzantine composite bows with a length of 1.2 metres, both for the infantry and the cavalry, probably originated from the Huns. The heavy cavalry, *kataphractoi*, the elite of the Byzantine army, used javelins or bows according to their own choice and strength. Slavic infantry, Arabic cavalry, Franks and other mercenary units were neither equipped nor trained in line with Byzantine regulations. According to Muslim sources, prior to the battle Gregorius' infantry vowed to fight to the death and, as proof of their firm resolution not to retreat, chained themselves together, ten men to a chain. This was done with the intention of stopping enemy cavalry breaking through their ranks.

Different ethnic and cultural origins, lack of familiarity and mutual suspicions led to poor co-operation and coordination between commanders of individual contingents. Jabalah was completely ignored, although his men had the best knowledge of home terrain.

Heraclius demanded that all diplomatic options be exhausted before starting the battle. He was playing for time, expecting the beginning of a Persian offensive in Iraq. Failed negotiations lasted for a month. At the same time, Caliph Omar tried to use negotiations to persuade the Persian emperor to convert to Islam. Omar wanted to deal with the stronger enemy first, so he sent Khalid reinforcements of 6,000 warriors, mostly from Yemen, including 100 veterans from the first battle in Muslim history which had taken place on 13 March 624 near Badr in northern Arabia. The command was for warriors to come in smaller groups so that the enemy would get the impression that the actual number of soldiers was much greater. The deception paid off. Fearing that Khalid's Arabs would gain an advantage in numbers, the Byzantines decided to attack.

The largest battle of the time on Syrian soil started on 15 August 636 and lasted for an incredible six days. Only well-trained units could fight for days, retaining order regardless of the losses they took. The first day was merely duelling and Vahan's attempts to gauge Muslim forces. After not very determined skirmishing, both sides retreated to their camps. Over the following three days, Khalid was successful in his defensive strategies. That was his only option, given the enemy's larger numbers. He used the cavalry masterfully in counterattacks, while the mobile guard spent the three days running all over the battlefield and saving the army in critical moments. Byzantine commanders, on the other hand, constantly kept their larger cavalry as a reserve and barely used these elite units, even when, on the fourth day, they had a chance to win. During the fourth day,

Byzantine cavalry archers stepped into the action. They flooded the enemy left centre and left wing with arrows. Many Muslim warriors lost their eyes in the rain of arrows, so the day is known as 'the Day of Lost Eyes'. While the Arab army retreated and took up new defensive positions preparing for the following day, they were protected by 400 cavalrymen led by Khalid's childhood friend, Ikrima bin Abi Jahl. All of them were killed or seriously wounded. Ikrima died during the night. After four days of unsuccessful attempts to break the enemy's line and many losses, the Byzantines' morale failed. On the fifth day, Vahan asked for a truce in order to start new negotiations. His goal was to gain the time needed to reorganize the demoralized units. Aware that victory was near, Khalid refused. He decided to change his tactics and attack, so he spent the day reorganizing the army. He gathered all his cavalry, 8,000 men, into a strong unit surrounding the mobile guard, ready to attack on the following day. His intention was to completely obliterate Byzantine forces. Victory was not enough; he couldn't allow the enemy to regroup and gather a new army any time soon, as that could be lethal for the smaller Muslim forces. In order to achieve this, he had to chase the enemy cavalry off the battlefield.

Khalid observed the battlefield from Tel al Jumm'a. In front of his observation point, spreading several kilometres towards the south, the infantry prepared for the decisive battle. On his left, 11 kilometres to the south, the deep Yarmouk ravine meandered westward and, almost 20 kilometres away, in the vibrant mist of the summer day, connected with the Wadi ur-Ruqqad ravine. The 20-kilometre ravine cut the plain before him, winding towards the north-east, becoming shallower and shallower, and ended a mere 6 kilometres away, facing directly west. There were several passages through the ravine, but strategically speaking, the most important one was the bridge over it some 12 kilometres away from Tel al Jumm'a, slightly to the south-west from Khalid's position. If he wanted to close the trap, he had to control the crossing.

He ordered 500 Arab horsemen to go around the Byzantines' left wing during the night and take the Roman bridge, thus cutting the Byzantine units' retreat towards their fortified camps. In the plains, behind the hill where Khalid stood, cavalry was gathering. They would attack the right wing the following morning. All they would need would be some fifteen minutes of light trotting to surround the enemy completely. Khalid was satisfied and sure of success. Ikrima, and numerous fallen Muslim warriors, now enjoying their just reward in paradise, were to be avenged.

On the sixth day, Khalid ordered an attack on the whole width of the front line. Kilometres of infantry units started towards the enemy in orderly lines. The plain shook under the hooves of thousands of Arab horses galloping around the enemy's left wing. The majority of the cavalry attacked the left-wing Byzantine cavalry, while the rest charged the infantry from the back. Attacked from the front by Arab infantry, from the side and back by the cavalry, the Byzantine left wing started retreating and then dissipated. Slavic infantrymen tried to save themselves by escaping towards the left centre of the fighting line, bringing disorder. Arab cavalrymen turned towards their main goal, attacking Byzantine cavalry, still engaged with the main body of Muslim cavalry, from the back. The only option remaining to the Byzantine horsemen was to escape northwards.

Muslim infantry on the right wing had no more enemies before them, so they turned left for a side-attack on the Byzantine left-centre, already engaged by the Arab infantry. Vahan tried to gather and regroup the cavalry from the right wing and centre but didn't quite make it. While his heavy cavalrymen were still gathering and regrouping, they were attacked by the entirety of the Arab cavalry from the front and side. After a short battle, all the Byzantine horsemen escaped northwards, abandoning the infantry. Khalid's horsemen again attacked the left centre of the Byzantine line from the back and, under a three-sided attack, the line soon fell apart.

Now the entire Byzantine army started retreating. The cavalry cut off their retreat northwards. The only escape route was over the bridge, but it was held by the 500 horsemen. The Imperial army was completely surrounded. Many died fighting, others fell off cliffs, still more drowned in the river. Still, a fair number managed to escape the slaughter. The Arabs took no prisoners. Trithurios was killed. Jabalah ibn al-Aiham escaped and soon returned to the Byzantine court. Vahan was killed by Damascus; a horrific defeat from which Byzantium took years to recover. Heraclius left Syria, taking the True Cross with him.

In November 636 by Al-Qādisiyyah, another four-day battle took place and was ended by the defeat of the great Persian army, marking the beginning of the end for the Sassanid Empire. Muslims conquered Persian Iraq.

These two battles were of key importance for the geopolitical and religious situation in the world. If Muslims had lost both or at least one of these battles, they would probably never have managed to create a serious force. As it was, the door to Asia Minor and North Africa was wide open. Caliph Omar entered Jerusalem in 638 without any bloodshed. Byzantine Armenia was conquered in 639 and Egypt by 642. The same year, the Sassanids suffered a new serious defeat at Nahavand, and the Muslims conquered the Iranian plateau.

After Arabian conquerors took Palestine, Muslim rulers in Syria and Egypt saw financial interest in providing merchant and pilgrim routes, were benevolent towards travellers from the West, and freedom of religion remained untouched.

Only in the mid-eleventh century did the fanatical Egyptian caliph al-Hakim, from the line of Fatimid, banish Christians and destroy numerous Christian religious objects, including the Church of the Holy Sepulchre in Jerusalem (it was reconstructed after his death). In 1055, it was considered dangerous to cross to Muslim territory or to spend much time in Palestine.

Although pilgrimages never completely stopped, the problem appeared again in the late eleventh century as the consequences of Turkish conquests in the Middle East. At the beginning of the century, the first great Muslim ruler of Turkish origin, Mahmud Ghaznavi,[15] created a state on former Persian Empire territory, spreading from Isfahan to Lahore and Bukhara. As mercenaries, he used the light cavalry from the Turkish clan of Ogura[16] from the Aral Steppes, who called themselves the Seljuks after a mythical ancestor.

After Mahmud's death in 1030, Seljuk princes rose against Ghaznavi's heirs, who were pushed to India after ten years of fighting, and in 1050 Seljuk leader Tughril Bey founded his own state on the territory of Persia and Khorasan, with Isfahan as its centre. Five years later, the Seljuks annexed the Abbasid caliphate in Baghdad.

Tughril Bey styled himself the King of East and West. Over the following decades, under his heirs, his nephew Alp Arslan (1063–1072) and Arslan's son Malik Shah (1072–1092), the Turks conquered almost all of Asia Minor, pushing Byzantium to the coasts of the Marble Sea and the Arabic Fatimid out from Syria. Palestine and Jerusalem fell in 1071. The death of Malik Shah caused civil war between his sons, while the Seljuks' power faded. The Fatimid from Egypt started spreading into Palestine again, while Kurds and Arabs rose in Iraq. It seemed that every city had a different ruler. Travel was still possible so there were Christian pilgrims, although even armed pilgrims found it almost impossible to make their way to the Holy Land through all that chaos and anarchy.

In the eleventh century the highest expression of faith was the pilgrimage, either as an expression of martyrdom or as a form of punishment. The Abbey of Cluny fervently incited pilgrimages to Jerusalem, setting the journey as the pinnacle of spiritual life. Those who succeeded in their intention returned to Europe completely impoverished and robbed. Despite all doubts, the prestige achieved by the troubles suffered during the journey and the visit to the site of Christ's martyrdom, together with the prayers offered there, gave pilgrims faith in redemption. Many religious people from the West were unable to resist the lure of the Holy Land. Thus, church authorities felt that one of their most important tasks was to keep pilgrim paths towards the Holy Land open and secure.

Pope Urban II[17] held the first Great Council of his pontificate in Piacenza in March 1095. Byzantine Emperor Alexius I Comnenus,[18] who had fought successfully against the Turks in Asia Minor but lacked the forces for a final victory, sent a delegation to the council, pleading with the Western Church leaders to use their authority to help recruit the fighters necessary to defend the eastern borders of Christianity. The Pope listened to the Byzantine ambassadors with sympathy. This was a great opportunity to reunite Christian churches under Rome and spread western European influence over Asia Minor.

Information from the trip undertaken by the Pope over France in the summer that same year strengthened his idea of a holy war. During the trip, the Pope met and heard the experience of Spain's holy wars from the fabled military leader Raymond of Saint-Gilles.[19] In the Abbey of Cluny, the head of the church was informed of the complete breakdown of pilgrim roads in Palestine. France was still nostalgic for Charlemagne[20] who had, after taking the crown of the Holy Roman Empire, shown interest in the situation in Jerusalem and the surrounding shrines. For a short while, the Western ruler became the patron and protector of Christians in the Holy Land; subsequent generations of Frenchmen remembered this and claimed the protection of holy sites as their right.

The same year, 1095, between 18 and 28 November the Pope held a new council, this time in the French town of Clermont. Before 300 Church prelates, he held a speech in which he pointed out the suffering of their Eastern Christian brothers under the Turks, who were destroying Christian shrines. The Pope particularly mentioned Jerusalem and the troubles of pilgrims on their way to the Holy City. He called on the West to help the East, on Western peers to stop fighting among themselves, and on everybody, rich and poor, to take up arms and go on a holy war in the name of God. In return, the Pope promised that all who died in the attempt would be saved and absolved of their earthly sins. In the end, Urban II asked that preparations should not be put off and the army was to be ready in the summer of 1096.

Some 200 years earlier, Pope John VIII (872–882) had signed a letter promising salvation to anyone who died fighting the infidels. That was the first promise of heavenly rewards for Christian warriors. Death in the fight with the Islamic enemy led directly to the heavenly Jerusalem, the goal of any Christian soldier. The idea of redemption was connected with the fight against Muslims in general.

Response to the Pope's speech was huge and unexpected. The cause for this can be found in the difficult circumstances of the European north-west. Barbarian migrations and Viking marauding had destroyed the infrastructure constructed under Roman rule, roads and aqueducts had fallen into disrepair, dams were destroyed and fields were flooded. Villages far away from noblemen's castles were exposed to pillage from out-of-work warriors and robber gangs. Many fields remained unworked, while forests were off-limits as protected hunting grounds for the nobility. The growing population suffered from hunger and epidemics.

In the late eleventh century, Western Europe had already lived through the colonization and Christianization of warrior peoples – Hungarians, Vikings and Saxons – as well as the dissolution of the Carolingian Empire, so the lack of new wars resulted in out-of-work professional warrior knights. They kept boredom at bay through internal fighting in smaller or larger numbers, while also killing and pillaging the local population. As the proverbial drop that spilled the glass, in April 1095, a meteor shower struck Europe. For the uneducated medieval population in Western Europe, it was tantamount to the announcement of the Apocalypse, or the return of the Son of God to Earth. Many concluded that the final moment had come for every soul to seek redemption, and what easier way to achieve it than in the holy fight against infidels to free Jerusalem!

From the beginning of 1096, warriors started gathering from all sides: Scots, Danes, Spaniards, Germans, Italians, Normans from Italy and from France. Many pilgrims (at the time another name for the crusaders) came from France, called themselves Franks, and thus it was the name the Muslims used for the crusaders throughout the crusades. It had been agreed for the pilgrims to gather on 15 August, after the end of the harvest, to start towards the gathering-place by Constantinople. Coloman, King of Hungary, was informed of the arrival of crusading warriors and approved the passage of the army through Hungary. The Byzantine Emperor Alexius was also preparing. Along the roads from the borders of the Empire all the way to Constantinople, he prepared supply spots for the pilgrims and deployed militia forces that were to ensure there would be no troubles with the passage of the army.

However, some of the French pilgrims, those led by Walter Sans Avoir,[21] started their journey as early as in the spring. They reached the Hungarian border on 8 May and Belgrade, at the Byzantine border, by the end of May. The Byzantine governors were caught unprepared. Militia forces and supplies had not yet been deployed; furthermore, the pilgrims were not expected to take the route from Belgrade over Nish and Sofia to Constantinople, but rather the alternative route through Durrës, Ohrid and Thessaloniki.

Regardless of the lack of preparations for the pilgrims, this first group managed to arrive in Constantinople by mid-July with no problems. Another group, comprising around 20,000 German pilgrims including many women, children and the elderly and led by the travelling monk Peter the Hermit,[22] started in late April. German knights rode horses, Peter rode his donkey, and the others went on foot. In level and well-kept parts of the way, they could travel more than 30 kilometres in a day. They also passed through Hungary in late May and early June. Trouble started under Zemun, after 20 June. Due to a trivial dispute, an armed conflict developed with Coloman's governor's

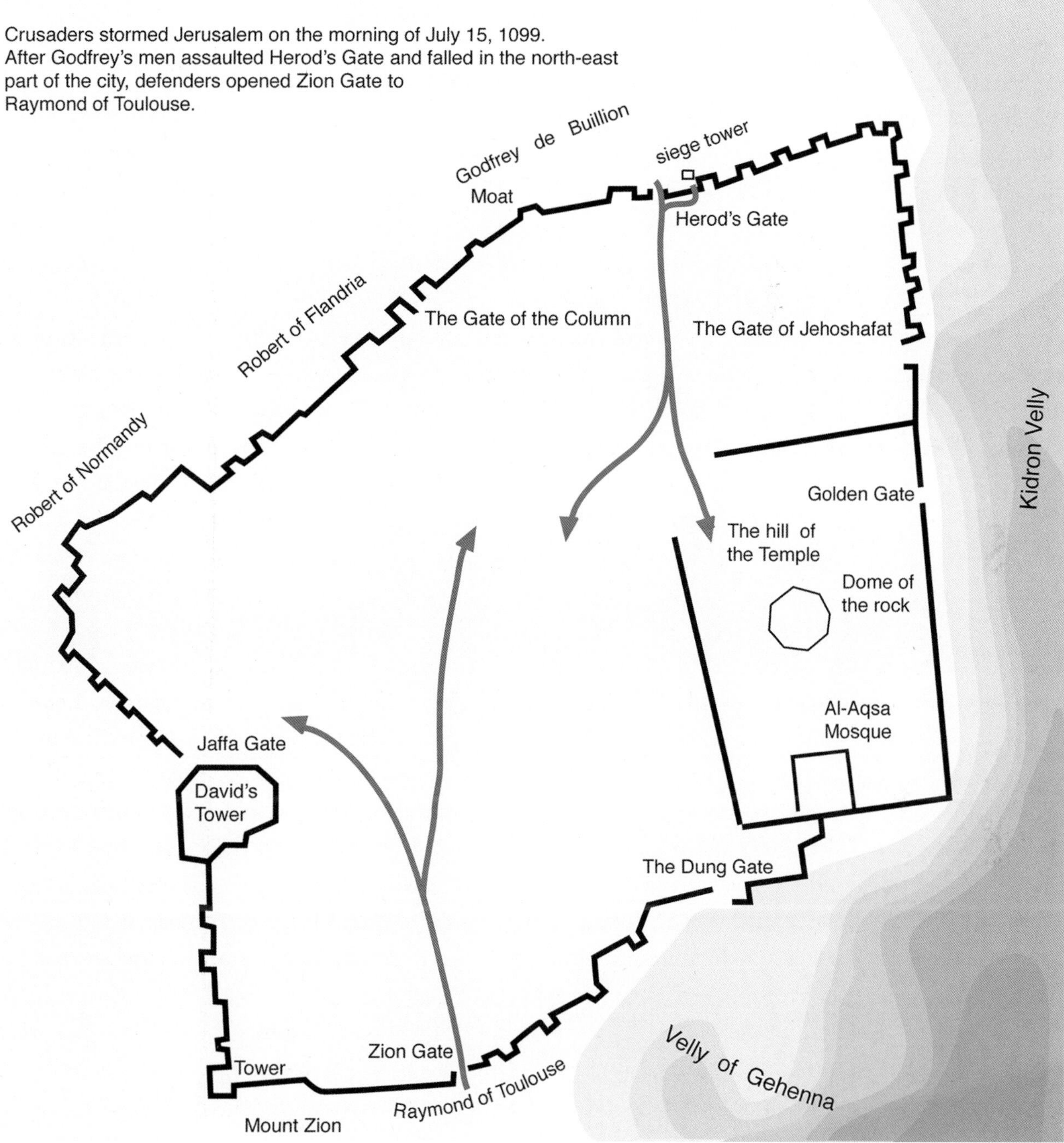

The storming of Jerusalem, 15 July 1099.

men. The pilgrims took over the fortress, killed 4,000 people and robbed the city. Then, fearing Coloman's revenge, they gathered all available wood to make barges and cross to the Byzantine coast of the Sava as soon as possible. The Pechenegs, mercenaries to Niketas, Byzantine governor of Belgrade, tried to control the crossing. Another conflict broke out, the outnumbered Pechenegs retreated towards Nish for reinforcements, the inhabitants of Belgrade ran away and the crusaders pillaged and burned the town.

As the commander of the sector, Godfrey de Bouillon had the honour of entering the city of Jerusalem first, so his Flemish knights Litold and Gilbert led the charge on the city walls.

A new conflict broke out by Nish. This time, Byzantine forces under Niketas scattered the crusaders and Peter lost a third of his men. There were no more conflicts until they reached the gathering-place by Constantinople. Byzantine Emperor Alexius visited the gathered pilgrims – the French under Gautier and the Germans under Peter – and immediately decided they would not be able to survive in an open battle with the Turks. Still, he decided to transfer them to the Asian side of the Marble Sea because the uncouth Westerners' violence was impossible to contain.

The pilgrims were accommodated in the fortified camp of Cibotos, previously used by English mercenaries serving the Byzantine emperor. The pilgrims were supposed to wait calmly for the arrival of the majority of Western forces but they undertook raids, mostly terrorizing the local Christian population until at last, on 21 October 1096, the whole army, leaving the women and children in the camp, started towards Nicaea, a day's walk away, the seat of the Seljuk Sultan Kilij Arslan.[23]

After only a few kilometres' march, the pilgrims encountered a Turkish ambush and, after a short battle, were forced to flee. The slaughter continued all the way to Cibotos. Only 3,000 people managed to escape and reach Constantinople on ships. The others were killed or taken as slaves. This was the end of the peoples' pilgrim army.

In the meantime, in the West, the majority of the forces gathered, consisting of four large contingents. One was led by Godfrey[24] of Bouillon, 36 years old, of middling ability as a warrior but pleasing in appearance and behaviour, which made him well-liked among the pilgrims. Having served well under the Emperor Heinrich IV in the wars in Germany and Italy, Godfrey was rewarded by the Duchy of Lorraine. He gathered a lot of money and equipped a significant force (around 1,000 men in heavy cavalry and 7,000 in infantry) led by the best Walloon and Lotharingian knights.

Godfrey was also followed by his brothers. The elder, Eustace III, Count of Boulogne, who was less than thrilled with the enterprise, gathered a much smaller force, even though he was a very rich nobleman. The younger brother Baldwin,[25] who was to enter the church, had been schooled at the famous academy in Reims and was well-educated but had no property. Following his temperament rather than the family's intentions, he abandoned a career in the church and followed his brothers on the path of war. As he had inherited none of the family property, Baldwin had no secular options in his homeland, so his hope was to win lands in the East.

Normans from Italy were led by Bohemond I of Antioch,[26] who had previously fought against his half-brother Roger over the inheritance of the Duchy of Apulia. Once Bohemond realized that he wouldn't succeed in his intentions, his interest shifted to overseas conquest. He led 500 knights, which included numerous warriors from his half-brother, and his uncle, Roger of Sicily, as well as some French Normans. His army was smaller than Godfrey's but better-equipped.

Raymond of Toulouse was already in his late 50s. He was the ruler of France's richest prefecture, Toulouse, and the equally rich Provence. His wife was Elvira of Aragon, who had connections with the Spanish royal house, so Raymond had participated in fights against Spanish Muslims. He was the one to advise Pope Urban on his way across France. Raymond had hoped that he would get the command of the pilgrim army. He was joined by noblemen from the south of France, as well as the spiritual leader of the pilgrimage, Bishop Le Puy. Le Puy's contingent was the strongest: around 1,200 men in heavy cavalry and 10,000 infantrymen.

The eldest son of William the Conqueror, Duke of Normandy Robert[27] and his brother-in-law Stephen Henri,[28] Count of Blois and Chartres, led the army of French Normans, Englishmen, Scots and Bretons; overall fewer than 1,000 men in heavy cavalry. Robert was in his 40s, courageous and charming but not very capable as a leader. Stephen de Blois never wanted to go to war, but was simply forced to do so by his ambitious wife Adela. With 600 knights, they were joined by Robert II,[29] Count of Flanders, younger than both leaders and a man of strong personality. His father, Robert I, had been in the Holy Land in 1086 and fought against Emperor Alexius' Turks, so his son considered it his duty to continue his father's work. This army was smaller than Godfrey's but, like the Italian Norman force, it was of high quality.

Four armies and even more leaders started towards Byzantium on different routes. After the gathering at Constantinople, the Christian army was an immense force for the period: thousands of knights and many more infantrymen, tens of thousands of servants and camp followers. However, the army was poorly led and poorly equipped. In April 1097, the army crossed the Bosporus with no problems. Turkish Sultan Kilij Arslan was not aware of the full strength of the Western force. He attacked the pilgrims before Nicaea again, and again, he was crushed by the Western knightly cavalry. The pilgrims' path further led them through the dry, hot landscape of Anatolia towards Antioch. On the way, they lost numerous horses and mules, so three-quarters of the knights had to walk.

Baldwin concluded that he had to take action if he wanted any significant spoils and lands. He and his men went to Armenia, where they deposed the Byzantine governor by trickery and Baldwin proclaimed himself the Count of Edessa. It wasn't exactly the Holy Land where he had intended to go, but the constitution of a Christian county on the Euphrates held great strategic importance for the protection of the future Christian state in Palestine.

Before Antioch, a new division took place. Godfrey fell seriously ill, while Raymond and Bohemond hastily raced to conquer Antioch. Southern Frenchmen and Normans barely co-operated during the siege. Antioch, a huge town 3 miles long and 1 mile wide, surrounded by battlements with 400 towers, was taken after a seven-month siege by trickery in June 1097. Although eventually the largest portion of the city was taken by Raymond's men, Bohemond overtook it by deceit. After long quarrels between the two leading princes – Raymond of Toulouse and Bohemond of Taranto, who was the most feared by the Muslim enemy – it was decided that Bohemond would remain in Antioch as ruler of the dukedom.

Representatives from the crusading warriors offered Raymond the position of leader of the whole army, on condition that he organized the march from Antioch. Robert of Normandy immediately decided to start together with Raymond. Godfrey and Robert of Flanders hesitated for about a month before deciding to join them. Antioch was lost to Raymond, but now he had a holy goal before him: the conquest of Jerusalem. Once huge, the crusading army was reduced to around 1,300 knights and 12,000 infantrymen, only a third of its initial force. Rest was necessary, so it was only on 13 January 1099 that the pilgrim army consisting of 1,000 knights and 5,000 infantrymen started towards Jerusalem, led by Count Raymond, barefoot as was appropriate for a true pilgrim.

They arrived under the walls of Jerusalem on 7 June. They were greeted by the magnificent view of one of the most beautifully fortified cities of the time. The battlements had been erected by the Roman Emperor Hadrian[30] and added to by Byzantium, Umayyad and Fatimid caliphates. The eastern wall rose over the inaccessible slopes of the Kedron ravine. Further towards the south-east, the land under the walls drops to the valley of Gehenna and on the western side falls into another valley, somewhat shallower. Only the south-west wall, carved into Mount Zion, and the north wall were approachable to the attackers. The western wall is overlooked by a fortress, David's Tower, an octagonal fortification, its foundations covered in lead, controlling the approach to the Jaffa Gate. Under the white banner of the Fatimid, the city was defended by a strong garrison of Arabs and Sudanese.

On hearing the news of the arrival of the crusaders, the governor ordered orthodox Christians and Christian heretics, the most numerous part of Jerusalem's population, to leave the city. This was a wise and reasonable decision, given that Christians were forbidden to carry arms and were thus useless in battle; supplies would have been wasted on them, and they could not be relied upon to fight against other Christians. The crusaders were not strong enough to surround the entire battlements, so they created camps before the portions of the walls that would be the easiest to attack. Robert of Flanders and Robert of Normandy besieged the north wall and Herod's Gate; Godfrey of Lorraine took the north-western corner of the battlements to the Jaffa Gate, while the western part of the city walls, from David's Fortress to Mount Zion, was besieged by Raymond of Toulouse who, a few days later, realized that he was too far from the wall, so he moved his men to Zion. The inaccessible eastern and south-eastern sides of the bulwark were left unguarded.

The crusaders lost people and animals daily due to the lack of water and food. Time was running out so, as early as 13 June, the first direct charge against the bulwarks was attempted and easily rebuffed by the defenders. At the end of June, news arrived that a Fatimid army from Egypt was coming to help the besieged city. In the meantime, under the command of the brothers Embriaco, two Genovese galleys supported by four English ships arrived at the port of Jaffa bringing some food, nails, ropes and bolts, and some 300 men. Camels brought tree-trunks from the hills of Samaria. The galleys were taken apart to use their wood and, since the ships had brought carpenters as well, the construction of siege towers, ladders and catapults began. During the evening of 14 July, to the amazement of the defenders, siege towers covered in water-soaked ox hide started towards the walls of Jerusalem. On the morning of 15 July, by the north-eastern city gates, Godfrey of Bouillon's siege tower touched the wall. In the steamy inside of the belfry, knights were pushed together, sweating under their armour. Inhaling the sweat-tinged sour air, they whispered their last prayers. The bridge was lowered to the city bulwark and warriors in chain mail, protected from shoulder to calf by their kite shields, rushed the defenders, wielding their swords and battleaxes.

The first to jump to the bulwarks were Flemish knights Litold and Gilbert, then Lotharingian knights and then the Normans. On the west side, Raymond of Toulouse's siege tower could not reach the wall due to a trench but, since Godfrey's men had already penetrated the city, the defenders holding the city gate next to Raymond's tower surrendered. All the Muslim inhabitants were killed, and the Jews, who had sought shelter in their synagogue, were burned alive. In his chronicle, Raymond of Aguilers, chaplain to Raymond of Toulouse, wrote that he had, climbing the hill of

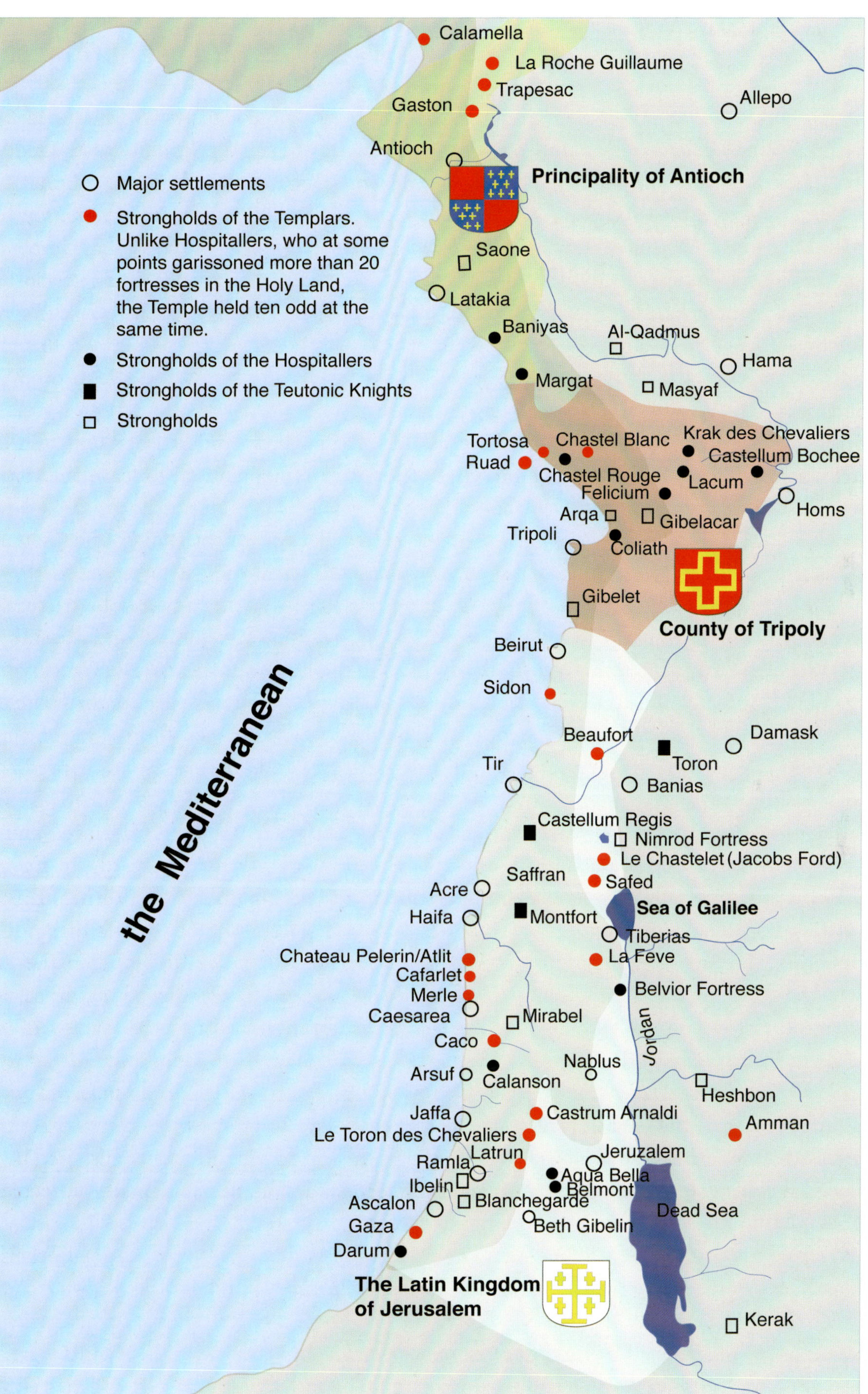

The map of Crusader States and fortresses in the Holy Land.

the Temple, trodden over piles of human heads, arms, legs and blood up to his ankles. Despite the horrible bloodshed, Iftikhar, the Fatimid governor of the city and his bodyguards were spared since Iftikhar bought their free passage by surrendering the city treasury.

On 17 July, participants in the First Crusade organized a procession through the streets of the devastated city to the Church of the Holy Sepulchre. A mass of gratitude was held at the spot of the Resurrection. Pope Urban II died two weeks after the taking of Jerusalem and never learned that the campaign had been successful. The Egyptian army, sent by the Fatimid caliph to help Jerusalem, was destroyed near Ashkelon on 12 August. The winners founded the Kingdom of Jerusalem and three vassal countries: the counties of Tripoli and Homs and the dukedom of Antioch. The leaders of the crusaders' army offered the Kingdom of Jerusalem to Count Raymond, but he turned them down, so they crowned Godfrey, Duke of Lorraine, a jealous and feeble-minded weakling who did not call himself king but 'defender of the Holy Sepulchre'. He was embarrassed to rule in the city in which Jesus had once worn a crown. After his death, Godfrey's brother Baldwin showed less restraint and, at Christmas 1100 AD, he crowned himself Baldwin I, the king of the Kingdom of Jerusalem. Raymond and the two Roberts left Palestine with most of the army.

Only adventurers and those in search of riches remained in poor Palestine, then still forest-covered and full of swamps, with wilderness still ruled by lions. Epidemics – malaria, typhoid, dysentery, cholera, the plague and leprosy – mowed down the European arrivals, unused to personal hygiene. The surviving Muslim population from northern and central Palestine escaped to exile, as did most Jews frightened by the slaughter of Tiberias and Jerusalem. Muslims in the south of Palestine mostly remained in their homes so in that area, Christian fortresses were tiny islands in a sea of Muslims.

To keep his young kingdom, Baldwin I only had a small army of 260 knights (mostly younger sons of knightly families hoping to gain property overseas) and 900 infantrymen, while the neighbouring vassal countries had even fewer warriors. Thus fewer than 1,000 knights, who could only be gathered with difficulty, defended Christian lands in Asia Minor. For the sake of comparison, Baldwin's contemporary, the English King Henry I, son of William the Conqueror, in a kingdom of similar area, could gather around 5,000 knights. Although the Holy Land was now ruled by Christian rulers, travelling without military support from the Mediterranean coast to Jerusalem and further to the River Jordan remained as difficult and dangerous as it had been at the time of the Muslim reign. South from the Dead Sea, the Road of Spices, not controlled by the Franks, was used by Bedouin robbers from the Arabian desert who had connections with Fatimid garrisons in Gaza and Ashkelon which, in turn, provided a passage for Egyptian raiders. Muslim refugees from the north also raided Palestine, keeping to mountain hideouts and robbing unprotected pilgrims and traders. Muslims holding the coastal cities of Arsuf and Caesarea proclaimed themselves Christian vassals but maintained maritime connections with Egypt. Some 300 kilometres of coast north of Haifa, all the way to Latakia, ruled by the Count of Toulouse was in Muslim hands.

In the south, the Kingdom of Jerusalem bordered the powerful Shiite[31] caliphate of Fatimid, able to raise an enormous army. The Egyptians were not particularly good warriors, but they were able to get numerous mercenaries. The caliph, a tolerant ruler and thus a natural protector of Syrian Shiites, also attracted numerous Sunnite[32] Arabs due to their fear of the Turks. Local emirs, led by personal interests and mutual rivalry, did not co-operate well in the fight against Christian invaders. What's more, in order to deal with their neighbours, local Muslim rulers made alliances with Christian dukes. Thus, in October 1108, by Tell-Bacher, Mosul Emir Jawali lined up an army of 2,000 warriors consisting of Arabs, Turks and Frank men under Baldwin Le Burg, Count of Edessa. Opposite him was Redwan, the Seljuk ruler of Aleppo, with 600 Turkish horsemen and 1,500 Franks under Tancred of Antioch. Thus, not all Christian warriors found fighting the infidels the most important thing in their lives.

On behalf of the caliph, Egypt was ruled by the vizier Al-Afdal, an Armenian born in Acre, burning with the desire to put Palestine back under Egyptian rule.

North of the Kingdom of Jerusalem, Bohemond's rich dukedom of Antioch was populated mostly by quarrelling members of different Christian sects, so it was easy for the Normans to control them. In the north-east of Syria, along the Euphrates, the dukedom was protected from Muslims by the much larger county of Edessa, inhabited almost exclusively by Christians and an occasional Muslim city. Count Baldwin Le Burg collected important taxes in the county and was richer even than the king of Jerusalem.

Thanks to the permission of the Seljuk sultan, Baghdad was ruled by a young Sunnite caliph, Al-Mustazhir. The wars between the sons of the late Seljuk sultan, the great Malik Shah, kept them from attacking the Franks at the time. The strongest Seljuk ruler of the time, Malik[33] Kilij Arslan, recruited numerous Turkmens[34] immigrants in Anatolia, preparing to attack Christian rulers. In the town of Sivas, at the heart of Anatolia, the capital of the Danishmend emirate, the reign was held by Emir Ghazi II, yet another Turkish ruler who recruited the Turkmens to wage war on Christians. Between the Turks in Anatolia and the Frank dukedoms in northern Syria, there lay Armenian dukedoms connected to Byzantium and the Orthodox Church, except for the Rubenids, traditionally inimical towards Byzantium. The Rubenids aligned with the crusaders, providing them with protection and provisions on the way to the Holy Land.

The Byzantine emperor looked at the Crusader States in Jerusalem and Antioch with distrust and dissatisfaction. Antioch was important for him because he intended to re-establish a trading pathway towards Asia Minor and, as the supreme protector of the Orthodox Church, he wanted control over the cradle of Christianity. The Fatimid caliphate was a traditional friend of Byzantium and the emperor could not approve of the crusaders' taking of Egyptian lands. He approved of the existence of the county of Edessa because it was a bulwark against the Turks and the Sunnite caliphate.

At first, the leading maritime forces – Venice, Genoa and Pisa – were welcoming to the crusaders because they helped weaken the navy of Muslim coastal towns and provided safe communication between Europe and lands over the seas, but concessions requested by the three states took part of the income from the Frank rulers in the Holy Land.

Jerusalem, Antioch and Edessa needed experienced warriors. The most difficult situation was in the Kingdom of Jerusalem, because the Christian population of Palestine had been forbidden to carry arms since the arrival of the Muslims, thus there were no local warriors. Antioch and Edessa were formed on former Byzantine lands and, as it was borderland, many Christian men, mostly Armenians, were handy with weapons. However, Armenians had shown themselves to be unreliable and disloyal, so it was necessary to offer the commanding positions to Western knights. Antioch was in a somewhat better position as it offered a safer existence to immigrants, while Edessa could only rely on adventurers ready for a semi-marauding lifestyle.

Complex political, economic and religious relations in the area, together with the obvious military weakness of the Kingdom of Jerusalem entwined with numerous Muslim enclaves, gave little reason for optimism to Baldwin I. Frank dukes over the sea, either greedy or fearful, were more of a problem than a support. The Pope's call to Christian warriors to reach the Kingdom of Heaven in the fight against infidels in the Holy Land became more important than ever. Providing a permanent presence of European warriors in Outremer (the Crusader States)[35] was an issue for which Christian dukes needed a quick solution if they wanted to keep what they had conquered.

The Beginning

Count Hugh I of Champagne,[1] one of the most powerful people in medieval Western Europe, ruler of a rich dukedom, richer even than the French king, a known believer, honest penitent and church benefactor, connected two monks, Hugues de Payens and Bernard of Clairvaux, who held a prominent place in the foundation of the first and only exclusively fighting order of monks. The count enabled de Payens to arrive in the Holy Land and was instrumental in providing Bernard with the opportunity of becoming abbot of a Cistercian monastery.

However, we should keep things in order. At the end of the eleventh century, the aforementioned Benedictine Abbey of Cluny was rich and powerful. The money from care for pilgrims in hospices along the way to the shrine of Saint Jacob in Santiago de Compostela, as well as the rent from numerous properties, created a nice nest egg. The church of the Abbey of Cluny was the largest and most beautiful in Europe, while the order's leaders spent more and more time dealing with self-imposed worldly problems and less in alignment with the rule of St Benedict[2] as they had vowed to do.

Robert, the Benedictine Abbot of the Abbey of Molesme, dissatisfied with the serious disruptions of the simple and strict monastery life, founded a new order of reformed Benedictines, the Cistercians, in 1098. The name of the order came from the Abbey of Cîteaux, situated some 15 miles south of Dijon, where the order was founded. The Cistercians discarded the long prayers and litanies of their Benedictine colleagues, links with nobility, acceptance of children in the order in exchange for contributions from noblemen, gave up on servants and worked their properties themselves. In a nutshell, they truly lived according to the Rule of St Benedict. In order to prove the purity of their beliefs, they discarded the black uniform and took up a white monk's habit. The Cistercian vision of monastery life was not particularly popular among the nobility as noblemen intending to take up the habit did not relish accepting ascetic life full of daily work obligations so, at first, only very few noblemen's children decided to join this truly strict order.

Robert, a courageous and honest monk who only thought of faith and not of material goods, shared the fate of two other great contemporaries who passed through Molesme with him. Bruno, who had, at Cluny, taught Otho de Lagery, later Pope Urban II, the originator of the crusades, left Molesme, gathered a group of hermits in the mountains of Chartreuse and founded the Carthusians, an even stricter order. Stephen Harding, of Anglo-Saxon English descent, fled before the Norman conquerors to Scotland and then to Rome, where he took up the habit and finally settled in France, in Molesme. At the time of Abbot Harding, Cîteaux saw the flowering of the Cistercian order.

In 1113 Bernard[3] and around thirty of his followers, kin and friends, all from top families, joined the Abbey of Cîteaux. Although his social position allowed him access to the Benedictine order of Cluny, which would have provided him with the future of a high-ranking church official, Bernard chose the harder way, thus proving the purity of his faith and his renouncing of worldly goods. This was even more unusual given that he lived at a time when many were completely indifferent to their fate after death and the church was plagued by corruption and debauchery. According to Bernard's biographer, the monk was a youth whose face was radiant with beauty, of slight build, soft pink skin, lovely red hair and beard, convincing, eloquent and a passionate orator. He stood out because of his fiery and somewhat wild nature, quick mind and dedication to learning, so after only three years of a monk's life he was appointed as abbot in the new Cistercian abbey, some 40 miles east of Troyes, in a forest-covered valley that had previously served as a shelter for social outcasts.

Bernard and twelve of his monks cleared up the forest ground and built a church. They named their abbey Clairvaux ('the Valley of Light') and indeed, spiritual light spread throughout Europe from the abbey over the coming years. In the words of David Knowles, the Benedictine historian, 'For forty years, Cîteaux-Clairvaux was the spiritual centre of Europe while, at the same time, former St Bernard monks included a Pope, the Archbishop of York, as well as plenty of cardinals and bishops.' The Pope was Eugenius III (1145–1153), whose edict *Quantum praedecessores* called on the French King Louis VII to start a crusade.

Cistercians had been given the land by Count Hugh of Champagne. Some ten years earlier, in 1104, the count started on his first pilgrimage to the Holy Land, from which he returned after four years only to start a new pilgrimage in 1114, searching for redemption and spiritual peace. He was now accompanied by Hugues, possibly a cousin born in Payens, around 10km from the count's see in Troyes. Hugues was at least 44 years old at the time of the count's second pilgrimage. It is not known whether he had accompanied the count the first time as well but, according to a document from the year 1113, it is known that, between the two pilgrimages, he married and had at least one son: Thibaud, later abbot at the Abbey de la Colombella at Sens.

After the count started for his homeland for the second time, Payens remained in Jerusalem. He also had seven more knights from his entourage, all of them de Payens relatives either by blood or by marriage. We have written proof of the names Geoffroi Bisot, Payen de Montdidier, Archambaud de St Amand and Roland. They were also accompanied by Godfrey de Saint-Omer, probably a participant in the First Crusade, mentioned as one of the best knights in the Holy Land in general. For some reason, these nine knights came up with a story for King Baldwin II and Jerusalem's Patriarch Daimbert. Their motivation certainly lay in faith and the desire to ensure absolution, which a monk's habit offered with certainty, but more mundane reasons could have been behind their revolutionary ideas as well. Long years spent in the Holy Land without any real source of income probably brought the knights to the edge of existence. Only some of the hundreds of crusading knights were granted properties in newly-conquered lands for their efforts. Most still had to rely on income from properties far to the west, so it was almost impossible to get money for bare necessities, which was the reason why most warriors returned to their countries immediately after the end of the fighting.

Perhaps poverty[4] and the inability to create a sustainable knightly existence in the Holy Land, together with the possibility that they lacked the funds to return to Europe, forced the knights to come up with a new source of income that would not lower their status and would allow them to remain warriors in the service of the Kingdom of Heaven. They were further hampered by the fact that at least some of them, like Payens and Saint-Omer, were no longer at the height of their power but were rather closer to old age than physical fitness as warriors. It is possible that they claimed support from Count Hugh, which helped to gain careful attention from the king and the patriarch of the Kingdom of Jerusalem. Although Count Hugh's role has not been historically proven, it is quite possible that he himself took part in the conception of the revolutionary idea. This is supported by the fact that Count Hugh joined the Templar order during his third pilgrimage to the Holy Land in 1125. With the intention of staying overseas, he discarded his unfaithful wife and son – he believed the latter not to be his – and left any inheritance to his nephew Thibaud. It is possible that, years earlier, in his first two pilgrimages, he had prepared the scenario for him to remain permanently in the Holy Land.

Payens, a God-fearing and decisive knight, and his comrades-in-arms faced the worldly and spiritual leaders of the Kingdom of Jerusalem with a request previously unheard-of in the Christian world. They intended to become monks but, at the same time, to serve their heavenly master-at-arms, as they had done their whole lives, thus dedicating their warrior skills to the armed protection of pilgrims on the way from the sea to the Holy City.

Until then, *miles Christi* (soldiers of Christ) were only monks who, following the Rule of St Benedict, fought for Christ by prayer and mass, and the very fact that they were monks provided them with absolution and the way to Heaven. Worldly warriors could get absolution either by founding and gifting monasteries or by becoming monks themselves. Only Pope Gregory VII (1073–1085) described fighting for Christ as an armed fight of Christian knights in which true *miles*

Bernard of Clairvaux.

Knight Templar escorting pilgrims. Jaffa, a poor harbour of little depth but the port closest to Jerusalem was the initial point on the approximately 100km-long ancient Jaffa to Jerusalem road. A man riding a mule took eight to ten hours to accomplish the route. One major stop on the way to Jerusalem was Ramla, on the intersection of the Via Maris (Cairo-Damascus) with the road from Jaffa to Jerusalem. The first Templars had no uniform or insignia but used their civilian garments. Certainly they did not wear mail shirt armour because it was impossible to ride the whole day completely armed. A helmet, quilted gambeson and shield were quite sufficient defence against attack by local brigands, but a real necessity was using a scarf cover against heat for the helmet and securing enough water for the rider and the horse.

Christi, worldly warriors with weapons in their hands, were at least close to monks. King Baldwin II accepted the idea. Medieval chronicler Michael of Syria even claimed that it had in fact been the king's desire, and that the knights merely wanted to leave worldly life behind and become simple monks. It would not have been strange if it had been the king's wish since the Kingdom of Jerusalem suffered from a chronic lack of experienced warriors, so allowing a dozen knights to leave their weapons and concentrate on meditation was far from being in the king's best interests. Be that as it may, at Christmas 1119, in the Church of the Saint Sepulchre, the Patriarch of Jerusalem accepted the nine knights' vows of poverty, purity, obedience and submission to the Rule of St Augustine,[5] which were in fashion in the monks' communities of the twelfth century. They called themselves the Poor Fellow-Soldiers of Christ, their primary duty being to protect pilgrims on the way from the sea coast to Jerusalem and further to the River Jordan to the place of Christ's baptism; truly a hard task for so few warriors because the way from the Mediterranean ports of Jaffa and Caesarea led through desolate, hilly areas ruled by lions and Bedouin marauders. Most pilgrims were unarmed and thus made easy prey for robbers and beasts; nothing had changed there since the times of the Romans.

The king put the new monks into a part of the palace built on the site of the Temple of Solomon: *Templum Salomonis*. The housing was added to their name, so they became the Poor Fellow-Soldiers of Christ and of the Temple of Solomon, then Knights of the Temple of Solomon, Knights of the Temple, the Templars and Temple. In order to make their lives easier, the patriarch freed them from contributions and the wearing of robes, so they could serve in their own worldly clothes. Immediately the following year, a powerful French nobleman, Fulk, Count of Anjou,[6] on his return from a pilgrimage to the Holy Land, proclaimed himself to be an associate member of the order, gave the Templars a regular income and promised to maintain two Templar knights in the Holy Land every year. The poor brothers also received contributions from other powerful French noblemen. On joining the order, Hugh of Champagne certainly also brought financial aid and gifts of properties in the homeland.

Although a contemporary chronicler wrote that the number of knight-monks was still nine, this is impossible unless one of the founders had died in the meantime since they were joined by at least Count Hugh and then by two more knights who later served as messengers for Bernard. Another source, Patriarch of Antioch, Michael of Syria, claimed that there were around thirty knights. King Baldwin II showed great trust in the Templar commander de Payens, appointing him in 1127 as one of his two emissaries to Europe. Why him? Had the Order already proven itself by their actions? Did the famous Count Hugh joining the Order and living near the king play a role, or was the deciding factor the support of Fulk of Anjou for the Templars? The third option may be the closest to the truth, since one of the tasks set for the king's emissaries was to talk Count Fulk into marrying the king's daughter Melisende in order to provide a male heir for the throne of Jerusalem. Their other goal was to talk the kings of France and England and the Count of Flanders to start a crusade and thus help Jerusalem in taking over Damascus.

On his arrival in Europe, Payens first spent some time in his homeland of Champagne, and then started for Anjou to see the Templar benefactor Fulk, who agreed to the royal marriage in 1128. Before that, Fulk's son Geoffrey married Matilda, the heiress to the English throne, so the English King Henry I also had reason to help Fulk's protégé Payens. Henry donated a significant amount of money, sufficient for Payens to travel through Normandy, Scotland, England and Flanders. Everywhere he went the elderly Templar attracted attention and gained favour. In 1128, the Templars got their first fortress in the Pyrenean Peninsula, the Soure, near Coimbra in Portugal, given to them by Queen Teresa of Castile. Her son Alfonso, confrater[7] of the order, confirmed the gift the following year. Count Ramon Berenguer III[8] of Barcelona took the vows of the brother of the Templar house in Barcelona in 1139 and presented the Templars with the fortress of Grañena de Cevera, near the border with Muslims. In both cases, the order did not put any garrisons in their fortresses, thus refusing the possibility of starting any fighting outside the Holy Land. In two years, Payens gathered significant amounts of gold and silver, gifts of property, horses and armour, and attracted new future monks. He had the greatest success in his own country of France, so, on return, he appointed Payen de Montdidier as manager of the newly-founded Templar province of France and England.

Payens also had another mission, the most important one for the future of the order: to achieve the church's approval for the existence of the order, as acknowledgement by only the Patriarch of Jerusalem held relatively little weight. Payens appeared before the church council gathered in Troyes on 13 January 1129. The event was described in Articles 3 to 8 of the Rule. Church officials were hosted by Count Thibaud, nephew to the now-Templar monk Count Hugh. Chaired by the Papal Legate Matthew, Bishop of Albano, the gathering included the archbishops of Rheims and Sans, bishops of Soissons, Paris, Troyes, Orléans, Auxerre, Meaux, Châlons, Laon, Beauvais, abbeys of Vézelay, Pontigny, Trois-Fontaines, Saint-Denis de Reims, Saint-Étienne de Dijon, as well as Harding from Molesme and Bernard from Clairvaux. The notes were taken by Jean Michel, self-proclaimed in Article 5 of the Rule. Together with Payens, the Templars were represented by Roland, Geoffroi Bisot, Payen de Montdidier, Archambaud de Saint-Amand and Godefroy de Saint-Omer, who managed to talk Father Guillaume, chaplain of Saint-Omer, into giving the Templars the churches of Slype and Leffinge in Belgium. Payens could not be sure of the success of his idea, since prominent church thinkers doubted the morality of monks serving in arms. However, Anselm, the Archbishop of Canterbury and the biggest opponent of the crusades, had died and his teachings were pushed away by the new teachings of Bernard of Clairvaux.

Bernard exchanged letters with his benefactor Count Hugh, and thus knew that a knightly monks' order had been founded in Jerusalem. Although he had wanted Count Hugh to spend his monastic life in Clairvaux, Bernard did not hold Hugh's choice against him and congratulated him on the taking of the vows. At the time, Bernard's uncle, André de Montbard, also joined the knight-monks and maintained correspondence with Bernard. Payens had also written to Bernard prior to coming to Europe, asking him to support the idea of the Templars and to write the Rule that the monks would follow in daily life. He sent the letter with two Templar knights, Godemar and André (the second one is almost certainly Bernard's uncle, sent with the intention of making the abbot more amenable to accepting the request). The well-informed Bernard truly stepped up before the council, eloquently supporting the Templars' interests and the order was accepted almost by acclamation.

Bernard's appearance was not diminished by the fever from which he suffered during the meeting. The only one who – for reasons unknown – voted against was Bishop John of Orléans. Payens described the foundation of the order for the church father and presented the Rule, then checked and amended by the council, which completed the procedure of the acceptance, later confirmed by Pope Honorius II. 'Hounded' by Payens' insistence, Bernard wrote *De Laude Novae Militae ad Milites Templi* (*In Praise of the New Knighthood*) in order to further strengthen the Templars' position. He did not take up the pen lightly and concluded the work before 1136, therefore before Payens' death. Only five of the thirteen chapters of the work deal directly with the issue of the need for the Templars' existence. Bernard used all his eloquence and persuasiveness as the biggest church authority of the time to prove the need to support the existence of warrior monks, spiritually strong, with the task of killing only enemies of the faithful as opposed to killing people for amusement only, as had been the ugly habit of secular knights. In fact, the idea was to make a good monk out of a secular knight; this is why the highly-appreciated monk Guigo, prior of Chartreuse, felt the need to write to Payens (with two copies, so that at least one of them would make it to its destination), asking the Templars to see their calling as primarily spiritual and not martial.

The spreading of the order certainly exceeded any expectations of the godly Payens and his poor companions. At that point it was of vital importance to construct good connections between Templar properties in Europe and in the Holy Land, thus the port of Acre was chosen as the main maritime base for the Templars. The basis of the order was constructed and all doubts of its members regarding the future of the Temple Knights disappeared. By the end of the 1130s, the order had completed its hierarchical structure and become a true military formation, thanks to the efforts of Payens' successor, Grand Master Robert de Craon, an efficient governor from Anjou and a favourite with Fulk. Robert correctly assessed that the order's only chance of success lay in evading the local church authorities and gaining the Pope's direct patronage.

In 1139 Pope Innocent II issued *Omne datum optimum*, addressed to the Templars' Grand Master with the words 'My dear son Robert', prescribing the category of Templar chaplain brothers who were to wear the finest clothes and leather gloves. Gloves had previously only been allowed to Templars as carpenter brothers and only at work. The privilege of fine clothes and gloves and the right to get the first serving of the finest food in fact put the Templar chaplains on the same footing as the highest church prelates, as Templar chaplains were the only monks' confessors directly under papal jurisdiction. The Rule also gave them greater absolution rights than the archbishops. They could grant absolution in only five cases: if a Templar killed a Christian; if he physically assaulted another Templar; if he physically assaulted a monk from another order or a priest; if he renounced the holy commandments he'd vowed to follow on entering the order; or if he'd joined the order in a state of sin.

Adding the order's own chaplains, answering exclusively to the Pope, meant that the Templars were no longer responsible to local church or laymen dignitaries and were completely autonomous in their actions. Financially safe, freed from paying taxes, acknowledged by the leadership of the Catholic Church and autonomous in their decisions, Knights of the Temple could now completely dedicate themselves to the defence of Catholicism from any and all enemies. Although their warrior services reached undreamed-of proportions, the Templars never stopped performing their original task of protecting the pilgrims.

Chapter Two

La Règle du Temple

Saint Bernard wrote the original Rule in seventy-three clauses, speaking almost exclusively of the monastic aspects of life in accordance with the church's intention to make the brothers monks first. The Rule was created at the time of the Council at Troyes and represented a compilation of already existing practices of the order, based on the rule of St Augustine and the changes written in Bernard's hand, according to Cistercian custom; thus according to the rule of St Benedict. The Rule was translated to French during the time of the Grand Master Robert de Craon, definitely after the Council of Pisa in 1135, where a list of holy days and fasts was adopted which was incorporated in the French translation in Clauses 74 to 76, yet almost certainly before 1147 when the Templars were allowed to wear the red cross on their robes, which wasn't even mentioned in the first translation of the Rule. On the contrary, in Article 18 the brothers were forbidden to wear any sign on their clothes. Translation to French, the official language of the order, was necessary because the Templars did not learn Latin like other monks but were permitted to remain ignorant in that sense.

Afterwards, the Primitive Rule was amended by Hierarchical Statutes (Clauses 77 to 223). This probably happened around 1165 and definitely before 1187 because they mention the commander of the City of Jerusalem – a function that lost any meaning in the latter year with the loss of Jerusalem – and the keeping of the True Cross, a relic lost near Hattin that same year. At the same time, additions included the Penances (Clauses 224 to 278), Conventual Life (Clauses 279 to 385) and the Holding of Ordinary Chapters (Clauses 386 to 543). As the Temple grew in the military sense, there developed a need to create a chain of command, divide the duties and prescribe disciplinary measures, which were necessary for the safe action of such a massive military organization in conditions of peace or war. Together with the Hierarchical Statues, military issues were also dealt with in the Conventual Life as Clauses 366 to 385 speak of discipline in the field.

The chapter known as 'Details on Penances' (Clauses 544 to 656) was only added between the years 1257 and 1268. This is understandable since it contains examples of penances used for years; something like a handbook for similar cases in future generations. Additional to the Rule is also the chapter 'Reception in the Order' (Clauses 657 to 686). The whole of the Rule contains a total of 686 clauses. The Primitive Rule was available to the general public, while the additions, particularly the Hierarchical Statutes, were exclusively an internal document of the order, which is again completely understandable since the statutes contain basic information on the organization and military activities of the Templars and were thus a military secret.

It is necessary to point out certain articles that define the Temple as a military organization. In Clause 1 of the Rule Bernard writes:

We speak firstly to all those who secretly despise their own will and desire with a pure heart to serve the sovereign king as a knight and with studious care desire to wear, and wear permanently, the very noble armour of obedience. And therefore we admonish you, you who until now have led the lives of secular knights, in which Jesus Christ was not the cause, but which you embraced for human favour only, to follow those whom God has chosen from the mass of perdition and whom he has ordered through his gracious mercy to defend the Holy Church, and that you hasten to join them forever.

In Clause 2 he warns 'This knighthood despised the love of justice that constitutes its duties and did not do what it should, that is defend the poor, widows, orphans and churches, but strove to plunder, despoil and kill.'

It is immediately clear what is expected from the Knights of the Temple: submission, defence of faith and a return to the basic values of knighthood. In order to achieve that, the order had to rid the warriors of all thought of worldly goods, of vain but in the military sense meaningless rivalry in the decoration of arms and equipment, and to impose strict discipline. The most important are Clauses 57 and 58, giving Templars the right to own land and collect taxes in European provinces, which provided a permanent source of income for the equipment and maintenance of the Order's military force in the Holy Land. The right to own land pertains to the Order, but not to individuals within the Temple.

Perhaps the most important sentence of this part of the Rule appears in Clause 41:

We command by common consent that in this Order which is ruled by God, no brother should fight or rest according to his own will, but according to the orders of the Master, to whom all should submit, that they may follow this pronouncement of Jesus Christ who said: '*Non veni facere voluntatem meam, sed ejus que misit me, patris.*' That is to say: 'I did not come to do my own will, but the will of my father who sent me.'

Sounds familiar, doesn't it? Whoever has served as a soldier has certainly heard that theirs was not to think but to obey orders.

At the very beginning, it was written that brothers of the Temple were not to even associate with excommunicated knights, unless they were given a bishop's absolution. From the very start, St Bernard made sure that any connection with problematic types would be severed.

As he had done with the Cistercians, as opposed to other church orders, he forbade the Templars from accepting children into the Order. Logically, only mature men could perform physically demanding military tasks, so it would have made no sense to accept children. Knights who wanted to join the order had to be chaste (i.e. unmarried or widowers), which gave security to the heart and health to the body, without which a brother could not approach God or earn eternal peace. Under certain conditions, married knights were allowed to join the Order, but they had no right to wear white habits. Still, knights could not be completely trusted, not even as monks. Thus, Clause 37 prescribes that, if possible, the space in which Templars sleep at night be lit 'so that shadowy enemies may not lead them to wickedness, which God forbids them.' Bernard also banned the Templars from accepting women in monastic service, associating with women or showing them affection, and even from accepting godfather positions for children. The chaste Cistercian was trying to completely exclude women and children from the lives of the rough warriors, thus preventing any kind of temptation or doubt of the monks in the decision to dedicate their lives to the holy goal. Also, even though he threw women out of the brothers' lives, he left it to the conscience of each brother to deal with possible secret meetings with a woman that would cost them the white habit. In other words, it was a case of just make sure you're not caught.

He prescribed that the brothers should dress in clothes of a single colour, loose, neither too long nor too short, cut so as not to limit freedom of movement, appropriate to their service, without decoration or splendour, and without fur (except for lamb or sheep fur when necessary; i.e. warm but plain). To the brother knights who had left the darkness of worldly life, Bernard gave white habits, both in summer and in winter, as a sign of their purity. All other members of the Order were explicitly forbidden to wear white habits; they were obliged to wear black or dark brown, so that their knightly brothers could always and everywhere recognize a comrade at peace with his Maker. The brothers' appearance had to reflect their modesty, so they were forbidden from wearing then-fashionable pointy shoes decorated with bows, and any kind of jewellery, including silver or gold-decorated belts, horse equipment and spurs, as was the custom among secular knights. Every brother was to accept the clothes and shoes he was given. If he complained about it for any reason, he would be punished by being given clothing of even worse quality. At the time, nobility wore long hair as a matter of fashion so Bernard forbade that too, but he did not forbid beards or moustaches, on condition that they were not too long. Apart from the Grand Master, commanders of provinces

Two Templars in everyday clothes. The Cistercians were the very first Order to wear an unpainted monk's robe, which was not white but the neutral off-white colour of the fabric. It was accepted by the Templars too. It was not permitted to have a hood on the head in the monastery area.

Knight Templar, marching order and sergeant brother. In the field Knights Templar had two white robes, a cloak and a surcoat; all other habits were always of one colour, black or brown. The common rider's garment of the day was a leather jerkin with tails back and front and Knights Templar used to have one (the Rule, Chapter 138). Numbers of authors wrote that Templars did not carry daggers. Wrong! Every Knight brother had three knives: a dagger, a bread-knife and a pocket-knife. On the other hand, sergeants wore black surcoats with a red cross on the front and back (the Rule, Chapter 141).

and houses, Templars were also not allowed to own luggage or bags with a lock. Receiving letters from family or third persons was also forbidden but, with permission, the brothers could have such letters read to them.

Templars were also not allowed to participate in hunting as it was associated with undignified behaviour marked by much noise and laughter. However, they were allowed to join hunts in order to protect the hunters from infidels. Yet once they went hunting it was difficult to control their behaviour, particularly since the Templars were allowed to own their own dogs and take them along.

Due to the violence and opulence prominent in knightly tournaments, Bernard condemned participation in such activities. Still, he let the Grand Master allow tournament duels to individual knights. The Templars' participation in tournaments is confirmed by the following sentence in Clause 315: 'When Brothers fight at tournaments, they are not to throw javelins, as it is forbidden due to wounds it can bring about.' Chess and dice were forbidden to the brothers.

Although Bernard's primary idea was to rid the monks of any and all thoughts of undisciplined, undignified behaviour typical of secular knights, he did allow himself to merely set limits without a complete ban on tournaments. He understood perfectly that strict bans would make it impossible for the Order to comply.

Bernard and the Cistercians refrained from eating meat because they believed that it provoked sexual lust. Since Templars were warriors, they were allowed meat three times a week (with the exception of Christmas, All Saints, Assumption and the Twelve Apostles) and on Sundays, when the knights received two full meals of meat, while their servants and pages received only one. Monday, Tuesday and Saturday were reserved for vegetables and bread. The sick were not bound to fast. A tenth of their food and all leftovers were given to the poor.

The Penances enumerate disciplinary infractions that could incur the harshest punishments: excommunication from the Order, loss of the uniform and being put in irons. Only one reason for excommunication from the Order was of a purely military nature: leaving the standard due to fear of the Saracens (Clause 232). A brother would lose his uniform should he refuse to follow an order (Clause 233), and if the infringement was of a more serious nature, he could end up in irons. Those who struck a brother lost their uniform, and if the consequences of the strike were harder, he would end up in irons and would be forbidden from carrying the Order's banner (Clause 234). The brother in charge of the banner during the battle was not allowed to lower the standard or to hit it with the pole. Otherwise he would lose his uniform, might be thrown in irons and would be banned from ever commanding the fight or carrying the standard (Clause 241). The same punishment awaited the banner-carrying knight who rushed into assault without permission (Clause 242). Slightly more lenience was shown to those who started the assault without permission, without the flag, as they merely lost their uniform (Clause 243). In the chapter 'Details on Penances', written in the thirteenth century, some examples of the Temple's treatment of brothers who had infringed the Rule are shown. Clause 611 explains why the lowering of the banner was subject to punishment. Templars who were not near could not know the reason why they no longer saw the banner; the enemy could capture a lowered banner more easily than a raised one; and the loss of the banner could provoke fear among the warriors and ultimately lead to defeat. The following Clause (612) further explains that the standard-bearer could only take up assault without a direct order if he was surrounded or if his position did not allow him to get permission. Clauses 614 and 615 show that the implementation of the disciplinary measures was not rigid. On one occasion in a camp near Jaffa a turcopolier went reconnoitring and fell into a Turkish ambush. Of the ten Knights Templar from his escort, four rushed against the Turks without waiting for a command, believing the turcopolier to be in danger. One of the knights did not have his helmet. Two of the knights lost horses in the battle before the commander of the unit ordered the others to start the assault. At the council held later, the brothers asked for mercy for their four comrades. The two knights who passed the fight with no loss were not punished by the marshal, while the two who lost their horses were divested. Since the turcopolier could have been killed had the knights not rushed to his aid, the two punished knights were absolved of punishment. Brother Hugue de Monlo described the procedure against the knights as well-led.

Clause 640 describes a different kind of unreasonable behaviour. Brother Baldwin de Borrages commanded the knights in the Château Pèlerin. He had been outside the fortress when scouts returned and informed him of the arrival of numerous Turks. The scouts advised Baldwin to return to the fortress as they were too few to engage the enemy. Baldwin ignored the advice and led his brothers to Mirla[1] where they were surrounded by the Turks. He was left with no option but to try to fight his way through the siege. He lowered the banner's pole and, using it as a lance, started the assault. He and two more brothers fought their way to the coast. The others were killed or taken prisoner and all the equipment was lost. With help from his friends, Baldwin fled overseas and lay low for a while, hoping the whole story would be forgotten. No such luck: he lost all authority in the Temple forever.

There were also drastic physical punishments. Clause 554 mentions Brother Paris who had, together with two other Templars, killed some Christian merchants. They were condemned to expulsion from the Temple and a whipping in Antioch, Tripoli, Tyre and Acre, after which they were imprisoned in the Château Pèlerin, where they died.

Chapter Three

Organization of the Order

We do not know how the Order was organized in the first years of its existence, nor is there any mention of it in Bernard's text. It is probable that, at the time of writing the Primitive Rule, the number of knights did not significantly exceed the original nine, so it is clear there was no reason to develop a hierarchical organization of the Order, nor was it the monks' duty to put together rules of service for elite warriors. It is doubtful whether Bernard and the other founders of the Order could even imagine, in those days, what kind of force this small group of monk-warriors would become. However, the situation changed very quickly and by the mid-twelfth century, the Order of the Templars was numerous and became the richest, largest organization in the West.

William, Archbishop of Tyre, chronicler of events in the Holy Land in the twelfth century, wrote the following about the Templars:

… they are progressing so far that today they have in their monastery (the Temple on the hill of Moriach in Jerusalem) more than three hundred knights dressed in white, with numberless serving brothers. Indeed, their properties over the sea, as well as the ones here, are said to be so huge that there can be no province in Christian lands that is not supporting the brothers, whose riches are equal to that of sovereign princes.

Theoderich, a German monk who made a pilgrimage to Jerusalem in 1170, wrote that Templars were using the former mosque of al-Aqsa as a 'warehouse for their weapons, clothes and food which they always keep in readiness to protect and defend the province'. Further, he wrote that, under the mosque, there were Templar stables for 10,000 horses. William of Tyre and Theoderich's texts are the best witnesses to the strength of the Templar garrison in Jerusalem, centre of the Order's command, besides which they also had other important fortresses in the kingdom. Such a large number of knights in permanent service could hardly be seen at the court of any European prince. In addition to that, the Kingdom of Jerusalem alone also held at least 1,000 sergeant brothers, associate knights and turcopoles, and light horsemen from Syria as well as infantrymen. In order to manage such large human and material resources, the organization of the Order was conceived in detail, which is confirmed by the appearance of the Hierarchical Statutes. These statutes, Clauses 77 to 223, are the part of the Rule prescribing the organization of the Order, duties, equipment, animals, escort and behaviour during campaigns, as well as the election of the grand master. This part of the Rule deals almost exclusively with the knights and heavy cavalry; warriors without which any halfway serious European medieval army was inconceivable. All other formations of the time were so underrated that, for example, infantry isn't even mentioned in a number of documents, even though it is well-known that infantrymen shared the fate of the knights in most battles.

The Templars had tied their warrior mission exclusively to Outremer, so properties in Europe had no military function within the Order. The Templars mostly kept to this. Templar properties were divided into thirteen provinces and three of those were in the Holy Land: the Kingdom of Jerusalem, Tripoli and Antioch, where the Order fulfilled their mission of defending Christianity. Ten provinces were in Europe, providing the warriors in the Holy Land with new men, horses, equipment, food and money: Apulia and Sicily, upper and central Italy, Portugal, Castile and Leon, Aragon, Germany, Hungary, Greece, France and England (which separated from France and became an independent province only in the thirteenth century). Depending on the number, size and disposition of the Templar properties, they formed, within each province, smaller territorial units known as baillie (administrative and economic units of different sizes) housing one or more preceptorate.

Communications between the Western provinces and the three Eastern holds passed over the sea. The Order needed numerous vessels to transport men, pilgrims and equipment but, if we rely on the veracity of the Hospitaller document from the year 1312, Templars had no more than four war galleons and a few other vessels, which would mean that they used rented ships. Every year knightly orders organized regular voyages to Palestine; the Templars' was called *passagium Martis* and the Hospitallers' *passagium Sancti Johannis*, with one taking place in spring and the other in summer, with favourable weather. This fleet of merchant ships, protected by war galleons, transported new brother knights, rented infantry, armed pilgrims, large amounts of money and products from European provinces. The Templar squadron was commanded by one of the commanders of the provinces. He was always accompanied by numerous secular knights who had paid well for transport to the Holy Land. Newly-joining knights, who remained in European provinces between two voyages, prepared for their service in the Holy Land by practising faith and military skills. As the Order grew, abuses happened and knights who had been educated by the Order remained in European provinces, enjoying the opulence there instead of travelling to meet their fate. As the Order's property grew, more and more non-knightly personnel were accepted into it. In order to manage the Order's enormous riches, people who could read, write and deal with arithmetic were needed.

In accordance with the Templars' mission, all high officers of the Order lived in the Holy Land. The Order's command was situated in the monastery of the Temple in Jerusalem, which housed the grand master, the Templars' commander, his second-in-command, the seneschal, as well as the Order's marshal and the command of the Templars' countries in Jerusalem, and the commander of the City of Jerusalem.

Papal edict *Omne datum optimum* prescribed that the grand master had to be chosen from among the already ordained knights. He had to be a knight with long experience of life in the Holy Land, familiar with the local situation and a polyglot capable of communicating with brothers who spoke different languages. He also had to know how to deal with finances and swim in diplomatic waters. It was more of a wish list than a rule when choosing the master. Only very few Knights Templar were of important status in society, their names were not mentioned in the records before entering the order, and those who were recorded were almost exclusively in the status of witnesses to other people's charters. As a rule, the chosen grand master retained his position for life. After the death of a given grand master, commanders of the three Eastern countries would gather to appoint a new commander, who would then lead the Order until a new grand master was chosen. The grand commander would gather a council consisting of chosen monks, who would then choose two or three most esteemed brothers among themselves and one of them would be chosen as the commander of the election. These excellent knights would then have as their task fulfilling an electorate body of thirteen members, representatives of different nations and all the Templar provinces. All relevant members of the Order also had to be represented in the electorate body, so it consisted of eight knights, four sergeants and one chaplain. These thirteen were tasked to choose the best knight among the Templars, with no hurry, by over-voting. The intention was to choose a knight who was already in the Holy Land.

Although the Templars always tried to conduct the election in secret with no outside pressures, at least seven of the twenty-two grand masters were elected under the influence of secular sovereigns. Starting in the 1160s, Templar grand masters commanded great respect among Christian but also Muslim dukes in the lands overseas. The grand master was the spiritual leader of the order and the military commander in battles in which he was present. All Templar brothers followed his orders without reservations, but in key matters, such as proclamations of war or signings of peace, the grand master had to consult the Chapter of the Order, consisting of all high officers of the Templars in overseas countries. The relationship is best described by the sentence closing the chapter on the Master (articles 77 to 98 of the Hierarchical Statues): 'All brothers of the Temple must submit to the Master, and the Master must submit to his House.' The grand master had his personal court as well: one personal servant who carried the master's shield and lance and who was usually taken into service for a limited time, although the master could accept him in the Temple as a knight if he wanted; furthermore, there were two accompanying knights, a chaplain, a clerk with three horses, a sergeant with two horses, a farrier, a Saracen clerk (who served as interpreter), a turcopole and a

Shield patterns of Knights Templar. Flemish maps of the Kingdom of Jerusalem (c. 1170) included the Knight Templar in the battle scene armed with a white shield bearing a red cross (1). *Chronica Majora* I, the work of Matthew Paris, English Benedictine monk (thirteenth century), includes the illustration depicting two Templars on one horse, shields black over white with no cross (2). Templars received Pope Eugenius' approval to use a red cross in 1147. Until that year a black cross on a white field looks a quite possible combination (3). At the San Bevignate church that was commissioned by the Templars in Perugia, Umbria, one of the frescoes depicts a 'Battle Between Templars and Muslims'. We can see a bearded Templar wearing a kettle-hat and carrying a white over black shield, with a black cross in the white field (4). There is no evidence that sergeant brothers exclusively carried black shields with red crosses (5). It is more likely that all patterns were used by sergeants as well. The rest (6-8) are variations based on no. 4.

cook, as well as two infantrymen. In case of war, the grand master would also take five to ten more knights as his escort.

Together with the grand master, the top tier of the chain of command consisted of the seneschal, the marshals, commanders and drapers of the countries. In times of peace, the tasks of the Order's leading men were somewhat different to those in times of war.

The seneschal or major-domo (from the Latin *maior domus*, the highest court official in the ancient Frank state) was second-in-command to the grand master and managed properties, houses, food and equipment of the three overseas countries. He was also entrusted with holding the banner of the Order. The title of major-domo was lost in the thirteenth century, being replaced by the term grand commander. The seneschal had a sergeant with two horses, a turcopole deacon with one horse, a Saracen scribe with one horse and two infantrymen. After the grand master, the next in line was marshal (originally ostler, supervisor of the stables, and then supreme supervisor of the army) of the monastery of the Temple. In peace, his duty was to get and distribute the inventory, and to take care of the military equipment and all the weaponry of the Order except for the crossbows and Turkish weapons, which were managed by the country commanders. The care of riding and battle horses and their disposition was also under the marshal's supervision. Wherever he went, he had the right to command the brothers and dispose them according to needs. The other two Eastern countries were allowed to have their marshals as well, but they were of lower rank. Marshals had the right to a sergeant with one horse (who could ask to borrow another horse if needed), and a turcopole with a horse.

The fourth among the high commanders was the commander of the country of Jerusalem. He was the treasurer of the Order and managed all the Order's goods. He oversaw the pack horses, which he gave over to the marshal when the need arose. The breeding of horses on the farms was also under his supervision, as was the care of other pack animals and livestock. All houses and brothers in the Kingdom of Jerusalem, ships, the shipyard commander and the house of Akko, as the main Templar port in the East, were under his command. As treasurers of their provinces, commanders of Templar countries of Tripoli and Antioch and all Western provinces also answered to him. The commander of the country of Jerusalem was accompanied by a sergeant with two horses, a literate deacon, a turcopole with a horse, a Saracen scribe with a horse and two infantrymen.

Commanders of the countries of Tripoli and Antioch had the same duties as the commander of the country of Jerusalem. Additionally they oversaw the provisioning of the fortresses under their command, aided by the chaplains of the fortresses. According to need, they could appoint and dismiss the marshals of their countries, with the approval of the chapter of the land; the same pertained to the chaplains and drapers. Each of the commanders had a sergeant with two horses, a deacon with a horse, a turcopole with a horse, a Saracen scribe with a horse and one infantryman.

At the Order's see, province commanders were simply referred to as priors (preceptors or masters), while in their domicile provinces they were called the grand priors to distinguish them from lower priors and preceptors.

The high officers also included the draper of the Order, providing the brothers' clothes and bedding except for woollen blankets. The draper was in charge of the brothers' appearance, making sure that their hair and beards were cut in accordance with the rules, their clothing appropriate, inconspicuous and whole. The drapers of Tripoli and Antioch had the same duties in their countries and were the highest officials after the countries' commanders and marshals. On joining the Order, each brother was obliged to leave all his secular clothes except for furs with the draper. Drapers had a man who managed the pack animals, as well as the transport of the dressmaking equipment and tents.

The command of the Order was completed by the duty of the commander of the City of Jerusalem, the first among house commanders. He had direct command over ten knights protecting the pilgrims on the way between Jerusalem and the River Jordan. In the field, within his jurisdiction, he carried the black and white banner of the Order. When the Templars transported a part of the True Cross in their possession on horseback, the commander of the City of Jerusalem and his ten knights protected the holiest of relics throughout the entire journey. In camp, they would keep as close as possible to the Cross and two of the commander's knights kept guard throughout the night. The commander's company consisted of a sergeant with two horses, a Saracen scribe with a horse and a turcopole with a horse. Commanders of the houses could command the brothers from their house, reconstruct buildings, construct new ones with the approval of the country commander and exchange food and pack animals among themselves. Commanders of territorial units' baillie were called a bailli and could have been either a knight or a sergeant.

The third and lowest tier of the knightly portion of the chain of command consisted of knight commanders. They were under the command of the country marshal and, should the marshal be absent, under the country commander. In war, they performed the duties of the officers. The importance of the chain of command for the Temple is exemplified by Clause 575, which says that brothers under threat from the enemy, should they have no commander, should choose one among themselves, follow his orders and follow him in battle as if he were appointed their commander.

All the Templar officers listed were merely first among equals. Noble titles that warriors may have had on ordination had no significance among brothers. All those allowed to wear white were knights, and titles of princes, dukes, counts or lords were forgotten. This prevented the possibility of a less-than-capable warrior gaining command due to his title, which was not a rarity among secular knights. Additional security was found in the obligation of all commanders to consult their Chapters on all important matters, regardless of whether they commanded the Order, province or house. While marching and on the battlefield exchange of opinions was discarded in favour of unconditional obedience to the commander. Monks without the status of knight could not be elected in command positions that would put them in command of knights, regardless of their warrior prowess or another important contribution to the Order. They had to be satisfied with commanding positions with non-knightly members of the Order. A warrior commander of non-knightly origin was known as a turcopolier.

Under-marshals (sergeant brothers) were in charge of all sergeant monks in crafts and other craftsmen. They would distribute the work and provide the necessary tools. They would also give crafting brothers permission to move from one Templar house to another according to need and to celebrate during the holidays.

The standard-bearer held command over pages dealing with the important job of horse-care, as well as caring for the knights' weapons and equipment and assisting their masters in the field. Newly-joining pages received their instruction from him as well in rules and regulations, punishments and acts they had to refrain from so as not to be dismissed from the Temple; he would also listen to their requests and make sure that they were properly paid once their contracted time came to an end. Like knights, the sergeants also had their direct commanders, the sergeant-commanders of houses.

Among the brothers there was also a nursing brother who did not, as one might first think, act as the surgeon but rather took care of the decrepit members of the Order. Templars did not have their own hospital but used outside services.

When needed, i.e. when fighting was likely, the Order would recruit numerous turcopoles and infantrymen. As penitence for the murder of Thomas Becket,[1] the king of England gifted the Templars with the funds to start a crusade. A good portion of these funds was used in recruiting the infantry of the Kingdom of Jerusalem in 1187.

Chapter Four

Knights, Sergeants and Pages

The basis of the Order consisted of knights but also of numerous monks of a lower social status known as sergeants. There was no particular difference in the manner of fighting and usefulness between knights and sergeants. Part of the sergeants acted as warriors, fighting bravely and equally with the knight brothers, but many of them also acted as notaries, masons, blacksmiths, carpenters, dressmakers, scribes and other professions important for the life and survival of the monks' community. The Templar community also consisted of associate members who served for a set time and did not have to follow strict monastic customs, but were in turn forbidden to stay at the monastery and were not allowed to wear the knights' white garments. They could marry, but were obliged to leave a part of their property to the Templars on their death.

Not all monks and associates joined the Order spurred on by religious fervour. Many were punished by a time-limited obligation to serve the Order overseas. Thus Pope Alexander first excommunicated the four knights who had murdered the Archbishop of Canterbury Thomas Becket in 1170 and then, following their appeal, he sentenced them to fourteen years of serving the Templar Order in the Holy Land. Not one of them returned to England.

Clause 337 of the Rule prescribes who could be accepted as a knight by the Order:

Not a single brother, unless he is the son of a knight, or originating from the son of a knight, is permitted to wear the white cape, nor are the other brothers to allow him to do so. But should the father of a worthy man die before he could have become a knight, and if the man is such that he can make a knight, his son should not lose his nobility; to the contrary, he can be a knight and brother of the Temple and wear the white cape. No brother who is not born in legal marriage is allowed to wear the white cape, even if he is a knight, or the son of a knight.

This article, which raises the knights as a warrior caste above other members of the Temple, is typical of mid-twelfth-century thinking; it was a time when feudal relations reached the pinnacle of their development. It was impossible for a sergeant monk to be promoted to a knight, as some contemporary novelists like to romanticize. The French King Louis VI ordered in 1137 that anyone made a knight who had not been born a knight was to see their knightly spurs thrown into the trash. In 1187 in Germany, Frederick Barbarossa banned the sons of peasants and priests from becoming knights. These orders and interdictions had far-reaching consequences, since no one who was not born into a noble family could become a land-owner. The warrior class became a closed knightly caste of professional warriors. In the transition period, non-free people with no land could have become knights if they were born to it, as is explained in Clause 435 of the Rule: 'A knight is not to be asked whether he is a servant or slave to any man because, if he said that he is knight by his father, born in legal marriage, and this is true, he is naturally free.'

In the thirteenth century, the word 'page' is used for noblemen of knightly origin but without their knightly spurs. All secular members of the nobility were warriors but not necessarily knights. Even princes and dukes were merely pages until they reached maturity.

By the type and strength of their weaponry, knights represented the basis of every medieval European army. These heavily-armoured horsemen, on large battle horses and dedicating their whole lives to the skills of war, particularly brave and with a feeling of honour springing from being part of a hereditary class, were the warrior elite of the feudal system. Feudalism, founded half a millennium earlier by Frank kings from the Merovingian dynasty, was characterized by the master-servant relationship and natural economy. The master was a nobleman, a land-owner giving protection and land to his vassal (Latin *vassallus*, *vassus*, 'servant') in exchange for military service. According to Franks, warriors were the only truly free men. Everybody else – farmers on rented lands, servants, merchants and craftsmen – enjoyed only partial freedom, and their primary duty was to work to fulfil the needs of the warrior class, which in turn protected the whole community. This understanding of freedom survived throughout Europe during the Middle Ages.

In the twelfth century, a fief (an estate of land) didn't have a set size, although it was originally conceived so that its size would provide the vassal with income sufficient to get weaponry, armour, battle, riding and pack horses, and maintain his family and servants. Some fiefs were huge, others too small and insufficient to equip a warrior. Centuries earlier, at the time of the Merovingian dynasty, a warrior had the right to enjoy his fief for life and, if he had an appropriate heir, inheritance was allowed. Later, inheritance started passing through requests of users until, in the end, during the reign of the Frank King Charles the Bald (840–877), ownership over fiefdoms became a hereditary right, which significantly strengthened the vassals' social position.

Great demand for horse-mounted warriors in Western Europe was connected to Arab conquests in Spain. In the early ninth century, Charlemagne could gather 36,000 horsemen from his empire. In the early Middle Ages, a well-equipped horse-mounted warrior (Latin *miles*) was called a knight, whether he was a vassal or not. Throughout the Middle Ages, noblemen gathered and kept part of the armoured non-landed horsemen in their courts as a sort of a guard, sufficient to deal with smaller military tasks without the need to wait for vassals to gather, equip themselves and get ready for the same task. Vassals were, after all, only obliged to serve a certain number of days in the year outside their fiefs.

In England, the name knight (from Old English *cniht*) became usual, while in most other languages the word used pertained to horsemen: the German *Ritter*, French *chevalier*, Italian *cavaliere* and Spanish *caballero*. Only in the early twelfth century did explicit differences appear between knights (*primi milites*) who had inherited the title and others, equally or similarly-equipped warriors but without the status of knight (*gregarii milites*), who were then called sergeants. Any rich aristocrat could equip as many heavy horsemen as he wanted and could afford, but that would not have made them knights. Of course, among men who were not from warrior families there were always many who proved equal to or better than noble knights by their courage, physical ability and skill, and some of those were rewarded with property and accepted into knighthood by their noblemen.

No one was born a knight. The candidate, after long years of training and having proven his courage, would be accepted into knighthood only in his 20s, in full adult strength necessary to carry heavy armour and weapons and command a battle horse. Numerous noblemen from hereditary knightly families never gained the title of knight either because they were physically too weak or because they had chosen church service or simply because they did not want to become warriors and preferred the less stressful and less dangerous professions of farmers and merchants.

In 1200, Count Baldwin of Flanders proclaimed that any knight's son who failed to pass the knighting ceremony by his twenty-fifth year would lose his noble status and become a peasant. Apparently there was a lack of professional warriors, so threats were necessary to force some to leave their lands and dedicate themselves to dangerous military service.

The knighting ceremony defined a man's position in society, making the warrior a member of an international, caste-based brotherhood marked by golden spurs and the *cingulum militare* belt on which the sword and girdle were hung. The centuries-old right of knights to include another proven warrior into the ranks through the knighting ceremony was abolished in the twelfth century and limited only to new knights coming from knightly families. In such families, boys prepared for the military profession from a very young age, first training in the family courtyard and then as pages at their masters' courts. The intensity of training in riding and weapon-handling was often individual, but always strenuous and long. One had to learn how to use the shield, shoot the bow and arrow, fight with a sword, jump, hold the lance, sit in the saddle and ride well and, above all, not to flinch in the face of danger. The most important and most difficult training for knightly apprentices was to learn how to use the heavy lance in full assault. The knight's task was not only to hit a target but also to gallop their way through an enemy line. Because of this, the training pole would be fitted with a perpendicular staff that could revolve around the axis. The target would be fixed to one end of the pole, while the other would get a bag of sand as a counterbalance. When the rider hit the target on the run, if he slowed down or stopped, the bag would hit him in the back and throw him off the saddle; a painful and not exactly harmless experience.

The sight of a heavily-armoured rider charging on, covered with a big shield, riding a big horse and targeting with a lance was a nightmare for the onlooker.

Only candidates for knights passed through the whole training process. Medieval infantrymen received no military training, while archers only learned bow and arrow skills. Neither the knights nor the other groups passed through any training regarding the movement and action of a unit, so battles in the Middle Ages were not, as in the time of Imperial Rome, won by disciplined, well-trained and formed units capable of tactically outsmarting the enemy. Elite warriors of the Middle Ages could be described as a group of prima donnas, skilful and courageous individuals whose personal ability and bravery was also emphasized by excellent armour, weaponry and a battle horse, which made all the difference on the battlefield.

In Frank law *Lex Ripuaria*, the value of battle equipment, was specified precisely in numbers of cows. The costliest were the hauberk and battle horse, twelve cows each; a sword with scabbard was seven cows; helmet and greaves six cows each; and a lance and shield two cows each. As armour and weaponry were produced by hand throughout the Middle Ages, these values did not change significantly.

Just as the Franks had prescribed what a heavy cavalryman was to have as equipment, the Order of the Temple also specified the equipment for the brothers. Hierarchical Statutes enumerate the full equipment for a knight in Article 138: hauberk, iron greaves, *chapeau de fer* helmet (a helmet with a rim, more usual for infantrymen), sword, shield, lance, Turkish mace, a padded coat, chain mail shoes, dagger, bread knife and pocket knife. In Article 141, dedicated to sergeant brothers, it is stated that sergeants could have the same equipment as knights, except that their hauberk had to be sleeveless and their socks footless. Sergeants also served as heavy cavalry, although with somewhat more modest equipment, and their feet were not armoured so that, should the need arise, they could fight on foot. In the end, it was stated that for sergeants, the equipment was not obligatory but optional, depending on the house's property.

Whoever had the opportunity to see chain mail or, even better, tried to connect only a few of the metal rings of which such armour is constructed knows how difficult and time-consuming a job that is, which makes it expensive. It should be said that, at the time of the Franks, this kind of armour only covered the torso and upper arms. Only in the eleventh century did hauberks get coifs (hoods) and the upper legs were covered, while in the twelfth century the whole of the arms and hands were covered. The hand was covered in wire, leather or simply multi-layered textile gloves, connected to the chain mail. The whole hauberk could weigh up to 14kg and was put on over the head. This was almost impossible for a single man and help was necessary. Hauberks were very uncomfortable due to their weight and could cause calluses and sores. Because of that, it was necessary to wear a leather coat or multi-layered linen underwear. It was particularly important to be careful of the hair and beard, wearing a cap that covered the ears, since hair caught in wire rings often led to cutting or ripping as contemporary re-enactors know all too well.

In the eleventh century, a chain-mail coif covering almost the whole face of the warrior was introduced, leaving only the eyes, nose and mouth exposed. The inside of the coif was covered in textile or leather. Likewise in the eleventh century, the neck and upper chest were additionally protected by a square iron cover padded with coloured cloth and tied to the coif with bows. It became usual for horsemen to wear additional chest protection, a *plastron de fer* (an iron chestplate), under the hauberk to protect him from arrows. Some knights wore even their swords and scabbards under the hauberk so only the hilt and protector of the sword protruded through the cut on the side of the hauberk. Warriors in movies wear their mail hauberks almost all the time. In real life warriors wore no armour and almost no arms on the march unless there was danger of an ambush. Full arms and armour were put on in sight of the enemy or before a battle. The Chronicle of Battle Abby[1] mentioned that William held up his army at Hechelande, less than 5km from the waiting Saxons, and gave his men time to put on body armour.

The amount of respect warriors had for their hauberks is best illustrated by the fact that it was usual to name them individually. King Harald Hardrada[2] called his hauberk 'Emma'. At the front and back, the hauberk was split to the thighs to allow the knight to ride. Instead of hauberks, some made armour out of ribbon-connected metal plates or plates sewn onto leather or multi-layered cloth coats. In the twelfth century, obviously under Arab influence, some wore armour of one or more hauberks sandwiched between outer and inner layers of padded cloth.

As in Byzantium, the Franks protected their shins with long metal plates on leather thongs, or simply by wrapping them in leather or cloth straps. In the eleventh century, the Normans covered the front of their shins with strap-fixed wire. Additionally, starting from the twelfth century, wire socks were made to protect the knees and shins, particularly vulnerable when cavalry was facing infantry. In the thirteenth century, round or square metal plates fixed by straps to the hauberk or the socks appeared as additional protection for the elbows and knees.

From the times of the Franks and right through to the end of the thirteenth century, helmets were mostly made from iron frameworks to which iron plates (*spangelhelm*) were fixed by pins, sometimes covered by a different metal. Iron plates were in some cases replaced by lacquered leather or bone plates. From Norman times, the helmet acquired a larger or smaller nose protection which was, together with the metal carrier-ribbon, fixed with pins to the lower edge of the helmet. Some helmets were made by hammering from a single piece of metal, which required much more skill from the blacksmith, and nose protectors were either added afterwards or else made in one piece with the helmet. Such helmets were often equipped with a row of holes on the lower edge to allow for the tying of the leather border. Face and nape protectors, popular since the time of the Romans, lost their meaning due to chain-mail coifs and were mostly lost by the end of the tenth century. 'Norman-type' conic helmets, whose shape provided better protection from sword and axe strikes, remained popular until the end of this period.

In the twelfth century, a rudimentary whole-face protector started appearing. The so-called great helmets, which covered the whole head but leaving two slits for eyes and air holes in the face-covering part, also appeared. This was good protection but heavy and uncomfortable as a helmet, with a significant reduction in the line of sight. As early as the ninth century, steel helmets also first appeared, providing additional strength. The overall weight of armour kept growing and reached its peak in the late thirteenth century. The hauberk, helmet, *plastron de fer*, metal ribbons sown into padded cloth that protected the shoulders, arms, knees and legs and were worn under the chain mail had a combined weight of more than 27kg, as much as the full armour of the early sixteenth century.

Cavalrymen's protective equipment also included a shield made of wooden planks, usually three, set one against the other (like plywood) and covered in painted leather. In Frank times, the shields were round or oval, up to 1 metre in diameter. In the middle of the shield an opening would be cut, on the outside covered by a metal protector (umbo) pinned to the wooden base, protecting the hand and the metal handle. The edge of the shield could also be additionally strengthened by a metal band. The thickness of the wood was substantial: 15 to 30mm. As the size of the shield grew, an additional band was added from the inside to slip over the lower arm, which allowed better protection and manoeuvrability of the shield. The umbo was discarded when the manner of holding the shield changed and they were then held by slipping the hand through two bands.

In the eleventh century, the inverse tear-shaped kite shield with a gradual curve in the cross-section appeared, probably following Byzantine models which were slightly smaller. The kite shield was ideal as it provided protection for the whole body, including the feet, which was a great problem with the round form. All we know about these shields comes only from illustrations as no examples survived to the present day. The oldest preserved shield dates from the early thirteenth century and was found in Seedorf, Switzerland.

In the twelfth century, shields changed shape again. Instead of being rounded, the upper edge became straight and the shield itself triangular, since the armour and helmet provided improved protection for the head and neck and there was no need to protect them with the shield. The curvature also slowly started to disappear but, until the second half of the century, the shield remained relatively massive. In the thirteenth century, shields became significantly smaller and the triangular form was retained but the curvature disappeared. All these changes were connected to the additional strengthening of the knights' armour, which made the carrying of a large, bulky shield unnecessary. When not using their shields, warriors carried them over the shoulder or freely hanging on the horse's left side on a strap called the guige. Since shields were covered in lacquered, painted leather which required a lot of time, it was customary to protect them with a wrapper when not in use. Clause 53 of the Rule explicitly forbids this custom for the brothers.

In the late twelfth century, horses started to be armoured as well. In a battle against the French, King Richard I took 140 horses 'dressed in iron'. The first Merovingian vassal armoured warriors were actually 'motorized' infantry and only used horses as transport while fighting on foot according to old German custom, so they were equipped with an infantry spear. The English language differentiates between two basic types: the infantry spear and the cavalry lance. The spear had a lighter pole and a length of around 2 metres as it was used for downward strokes, arm over the head. The Frank spear had one, two or even three crossbars at the base of the spike to prevent it from going too deep into the enemy's body.

The latter type of spear was also used by horsemen until the appearance of stirrups because they had no firm footing in the saddle that would allow them to use the spear for blows. Cavalry lances were longer, seldom less than 3 metres, as they had to allow a horseman to strike before the horse's head. It was made from stronger, thicker ash poles (5cm in diameter) so that the pole wouldn't break on impact, and had a smaller spike made of steel or iron, or steel welded in iron (a late Roman custom) with two or three edges. The lance's spike was fixed to the pole by a cone made of thinly-hammered tin, cut along the length to ease wrapping it around the wood and then fixed with pins; if necessary, it was additionally fixed with leather straps. Clause 53 of the Primitive Rule forbade the brothers from wrapping the spike of the lance for protection. This certainly wasn't Bernard's idea, but was rather included at the request of an experienced crusader. Obviously there had been bad experiences with fast removal of the protection. One should bear in mind that Western warriors overseas fought enemies prone to sudden attacks and ambushes, which were not really customary in Europe.

The weight of such a lance increased to an unbelievable 18kg, but this only happened after the end of the crusades. The first description of a heavy lance can be found in the *Song of Roland* from the mid-twelfth century:

> He grasps his spear, which he calls Maltet;
> So great its shaft as is a stout cudgel,
> Beneath its steel alone, a mule had bent.[3]

Horsemen used the lance in several ways, as shown by the Bayeux Tapestry.[4] The oldest fashion was to throw the lance like a javelin, then a downward strike as in wild boar hunting, and the upward strike, holding the lance under the arm. The first image of a horseman holding a lance under his arm appears in the bible from Rhodes (late tenth or early eleventh century), and this manner of using the lance only became usual in the mid-twelfth century. The *Song of Roland* clearly describes the power of a knightly lance's strike:

> The shield he breaks and through the hauberk cuts,
> His ensign's fringe into the carcass thrusts.

This kind of blow can only be the consequence of a strike from a galloping horse, in which the horse and rider's mass and speed of movement play the decisive role. In order to hold a lance firmly and horizontally on a rushing horse, the horseman had to have two points of anchor. The first one was the fist, which supported the lance from below with great weight falling on the wrist, while the other point was the armpit. This position could not be maintained for long, so assault was usually begun with the lance held raised, leaning on the felt base on the bow of the saddle. Only directly before the impact was the lance lowered. Usually the attack was to come from the enemy's left because then the attacker's shield provided protection and the force of impact was better distributed, lowering the chances of the horseman being thrown off his saddle, which would grow if all the burden were to be transferred to the right side alone. On impact, the lance often broke or simply fell from the hand. In order to keep safe on impact, heavy horsemen used tall saddles, leaned forward and leaned firmly into the stirrups, which was only possible with their legs held straight. There were even examples in which knights tied themselves to their saddles.

Templars strictly forbade their knights and sergeants from shortening the stirrups as was the custom among some secular knights who preferred the option of rising from the saddle on their stirrups in order to strike with a sword. Clause 144 of the Hierarchical Statutes says: 'No brother is allowed to shorten his stirrups, nor his cinch, nor his sword belt, nor his trouser belt, without permission.' Thus, in assault, the Templars preferred lances to sword fights and wanted all the armed brothers to act accordingly in battle.

a) Side by side: an average rider, 170cm tall, on a heavy horse 165cm tall; the same man standing; and the same man on a small horse 155cm tall.

b) A breast strap keeping the saddle from sliding backwards on the horse. Made of leather or linen, it wraps around the front of the horse and then behind the saddle cantle.

c) Longer stirrups allowed a rider to have a firm footing during a lance impact.

d) Shortened stirrups allowed a rider to rise up from the saddle and inflict sword blows from above.

Maces and battleaxes were also customary weapons used by heavy cavalry. Some Western knights, particularly those of high rank, preferred the battleaxe, but the Templars opted for the Turkish mace, perhaps because the battleaxe could easily become dull in battle or simply because maces were easy to acquire in overseas lands.

Once his lance was broken or fighting became too close to use it and if he didn't use the mace, a knight would draw his sword, which was an indispensable weapon for them. It reflected the status and power of the knight; it was also believed that swords in time assumed the strength and courage of their owners and that these characteristics could be transferred to new owners. A touch of the sword was ceremonially the moment when a page became a knight.

Knights named their adored brilliantly-hammered steel swords and, at the time of the crusades, blades were inscribed with religious mottos, proving that the weapon was in the service of the faith. In the time of the crusades, they used one-handed swords with a wide blade, intended to both strike and cut. The length of the blade did not go above 80cm in the twelfth century, but they grew both in length and in weight in the thirteenth century when the warriors' armour grew stronger. The blade length reached 100 to 120cm and a larger, heavier pommel was added to the hilt to maintain balance. To make the sword lighter, throughout the blade full-length grooves were added in the middle on both sides. This weapon was known as the 'battle sword'. In the twelfth century it was not customary for knights to also carry daggers, which are only really small swords. Only rarely do we see knights with daggers in pictures from the era as these were considered an infantryman's weapon. This is why it is interesting that Templar brothers were commanded to carry a dagger in addition to their sword.

Every Templar knight had one or two pages, depending on whether they had one or two battle horses requiring special care. Five sergeant brothers also had pages: under-marshal, standard-bearer, brother cook at the monastery, monastic farrier and the commander of the Acre shipyard. The pages were tasked with caring for the knights' horses, weapons and armour, as well as other equipment. At first, pages were only taken up for a limited time and only later did they become members of the Order as well.

Chapter Five

Horses

The Templar Order had excellent organization. Their warriors would pass their complete knightly training; they were disciplined, with high morality and ideals, and equipped with the best of weapons. The picture was completed by battle horses, without which medieval elite warriors couldn't even be imagined, but a battle horse was no ordinary horse by any means. It had to be a big strong animal, capable of running with a heavily-armed rider on its back and tall enough to get over enemy infantrymen, allowing the knight to strike from above. The horse also had to be brave, capable of taking wounds and resisting panic in the turbulence of battle and a fighter himself, biting and kicking with his hooves. Furthermore, knightly horses were equipped with a cruel bit whose jerks created tiny wounds in the horse's mouth and would enrage it; a hard fate for a noble animal. Horses like these couldn't be found easily, nor would they appear without special breeding. This is why, in the Middle Ages, the breeding of battle horses spread and became a very profitable profession. At the very beginning of knighthood, horses were small and light. In contemporary Western European drawings from the eighth and ninth centuries riders seem large compared with the horses, their feet almost dragging on the ground. Although one can make allowances for artistic licence, these were obviously small animals. It seems that Europe didn't have any large horses at the time, so animals had to be imported, then carefully selected and bred in large numbers.

Breeding horses with specific characteristics was no easy job. Once the breeder managed to find a stud and a mare with the required characteristics, he couldn't be certain that their offspring would also have the desired hereditary traits and not some other unwanted features of their ancestors. When a breeder struck lucky, he had to persist with a series of inter-breeding of the offspring with the desired qualities until he had a sufficient number of beasts with the required characteristics. Then came the first step in the creation of a new breed of horses. Nomadic Asian peoples knew that centuries earlier, in the first century AD, the Arabian Peninsula had no horses. Using the first horses that appeared – and they were the offspring of famous Asian riding horses from the foot of the Altai Mountains – the Arabs developed the world-famous breed of light riding horses. They had two advantages: natural surroundings poor in feeding grounds which did not allow for the production of numerous herds, so breeders only kept the best animals. Furthermore, Arabs mostly rode on mares, so one herd did not have many studs. All surplus and poor performers were removed. In such a closed, strictly-controlled environment, first-rate riding horses were created.

The next step in breeding was insemination: during the three months of the mating season, as many mares as possible from several different herds were inseminated by one top-notch stallion. Thus, his male offspring appears throughout the land and can speed up the insemination of a large population of mares by studs of the desired quality.

Finally, the decisive third step of the breeding was undertaken. A stud and some twenty mares were separated from the herd and enclosed in stables. This was done so that the stud would not needlessly waste his strength and semen on the insemination of lesser-quality mares. Discounting twins, a single mare can have only one foal per year, and only if the foal is separated on time. Quite a few mares are simply barren. Every stud mare was taken to the stud separately in heat, providing ideal conditions for the insemination to succeed. This required large stables and appropriate terrains, which became commonplace throughout Europe in the thirteenth century. In order to breed large strong horses, food is important. Grass needs to be rich in water, and the best grass comes from chalk and limestone terrains, rich in calcium. Also, one had to beware of horses becoming too heavy. According to fourteenth-century data, the horse diet included oats, hay, peas and straw. The largest riding horses at the time were those of heavily-armoured riders and horse armour (the fourteenth to sixteenth centuries). Later, the need for such large riding animals disappeared so other breeds of riding horses were produced.

Since the time of the Roman Empire, the laws of horse-breeding were well known. With the barbarians' onrush, numerous stables were destroyed, some mares were stolen and others escaped and were left to random mates. As a consequence, the quality of riding horses declined. Free animals are quick to take up the characteristics of their ancestors, which helps them survive but they lose mass, height and riding qualities.

Top-notch riding horses came to European soil in 711 with Muslim invaders. According to Ibn Khallikan,[1] at the time 12,000 horsemen crossed the Strait of Gibraltar riding Berber horses. Only twelve of these horses were Arabs. This does not mean much since Berber horses, descended from their Numidian ancestors, much respected at the time of the Roman Empire, were light, durable and solid riding horses, just like the Arab breeds. Some of these horses and their offspring were later captured, particularly after the great Arab defeat at Poitiers in 732. Learning of the quality of the horses from Spain, the Franks started breeding their own riding horses. By the late eighth century, in *Capitulare de Villis*, Charlemagne prescribed that property stewards were to take good care of studs and mares. Mares were to be separated early from their foals, which were to be used to form new herds as soon as they were sufficiently numerous. Foals were to winter in stables. Additionally, in *Capitulare de Mantua*, Charlemagne prescribed that studs, like female slaves and weapons, were never to be sold outside the kingdom. In 864 Charles the Bald threatened his subjects that they would be punished by death as traitors should they give Vikings a single hauberk, a piece of weaponry or a horse.

Several decades later in Saxony, a land known for excellent riders since Imperial Rome, riding horses were bred partially from bought Slav horses but mostly from the offspring of captured Hungarian horses, genetically from the Asian tarpan (wild horses), no more than 14 hands[2] tall. It appears that horses bred in Saxony were neither tall nor strong, so logically they couldn't carry heavily-armoured horsemen. Thus it is not surprising that in German lands, the true development of knighthood as heavy cavalry only happened in the twelfth century, 100 years later than in France. Until then, Germans still used to fight on foot. William of Apulia talks about it when he writes about the Battle of Civitate in 1053, in which German warriors decided to fight on foot, knowing they stood no chance on horseback against Norman soldiers with much larger horses.

The strongest cavalry force coming from the dissolution of the Frank Empire was the duchy of Normandy. Thanks to chalky soil and water-soaked pastures, Normandy is very favourable for the breeding of large horses. This fact was first recognized by the Carolingians, so Viking conquerors arrived to find an existing breeding process. The Normans were not gangs of uncouth robbers. On the contrary, Normandy best preserved the institutions of the Frank state, to which the duke of Normandy attracted numerous warrior adventurers from France and even Germany in 1020. These warriors were attracted to the possibility of battle and earning rich spoils, but also by the large number of solid battle horses available in the duchy. At the time of Robert the Magnificent (1027–1035), Normandy was already famous for its numerous excellent war horses. Norman horses were further ennobled by their mixing with Spanish stallions in the eleventh and twelfth centuries. Gray horses dappled with white on a dark background were particularly appreciated. So Normans and Frenchmen got the best blood from Spanish horses.

By the conquest of Sicily, in the second half of the eleventh century, Normans in Italy gained Arab and Berber horses and whole herds were transferred to Apulia and Calabria. These are excellent breeding lands: the grass is rich in calcium from its limestone basis, and the rocky ground is good for the training of muscles and hardening of foals' hooves. These were not large horses, less than 15 hands in height and up to 450kg in weight; agile and strong, they were excellent for riding but not perfect as battle horses.

Normans were very proud of their horses and were good horsemen. Their Italian knights were considered the best riders, whose cavalry assaults could not be stopped. In addition to their skills, the heavy cavalrymen were also quite numerous, judging by the *Catalogus Baroneum* 1154–1166, which shows that the Norman kingdom in Italy had 8,620 knights. Every knight had at least two and more often three horses. The development of horse-breeding in Apulia and Calabria is further confirmed by the fact that they were capable of exporting horses to France on top of that. The pinnacle of Italian exports to France came in 1296/97 when 2,500 horses were shipped.

Large battle horses, mid-range animals up to 540kg in weight and up to 16 or more usually 15 hands in height became particularly popular in the early thirteenth century and were bred in northern Italy. Merchants imported studs from Apulia and Calabria, and they served larger local Lombard mares. Lombard traders and their large riding horses appeared at the London market for the first time in 1232. The French imported large horses from swampy parts of the Netherlands, Frisia and Denmark.

In the Middle Ages, the standard term for all horses, regardless of their quality and purpose, was simply *equus*. The best and most admired was the knightly war horse (*dextrarius*). It has not been recorded why the war horse was so-named, but it is possible that the name came from the custom of being led on the right side. The sergeants rode horses ten times cheaper (*runcinus*), which were also used in daily life, while infantrymen were only given small horses for riding and not for fighting, worth one-fifth of a *runcinus*. The price of a hunting horse (*cursarius*, *fugator*) ranged from the highest price for a *runcinus* to the lowest price of a battle horse. Appreciated for their speed and agility, they were often used as war horses. The best riding horses (*palfridus*) had the same value as hunting horses. Riding horses were supposed to be beautiful and elegant but also strong, and some could walk using both left and both right feet, which was very comfortable and held in high esteem for riding. Pack horses (*summaries*) were valued at one-fifth of the value of a small infantry riding horse, but still three or four times more than a hackney. The cheapest riding horse was valued at 24 times the price of a peasant's working horse, while the best battle horse was valued at 800 times the price. Due to their softer character and steadiness, mules were often used as riding animals and they could vary in size depending on the mare from which they were born.

The choice of horse was a problem for Western warriors. They were all supposed to be studs, which created great problems regarding the keeping of these noble animals. In order to prevent them from fighting they had to be kept isolated, which required a great deal of space. Teutonic knightly order used geldings (castration of horses was a great rarity until the sixteenth century) which were called 'monk horses' (*Monchpferde*). In addition to being calmer and more obedient, if they were captured by enemies, such horses could not be used for breeding. A double advantage!

The care of horses was of key importance to the Templars. A brother who killed, wounded or lost his horse was punished by the loss of uniform (Clause 255). In war conditions, all horses except for those appointed to the knights were under the jurisdiction of the marshal. Wherever he went, the marshal could buy horses for the Temple – stallions, mares, foals, riding or pack horses – but he had to inform the grand master of the fact when and if he was available. In addition to buying horses, the Templars also bred them on their European and Asian properties.

All horses brought from Europe had to stay together until the marshal could look at them. He had the right to choose one or two horses and give them away. The other horses were distributed among the brothers when and if necessary. The commander of the land of Jerusalem also had the right to buy pack horses and camels as well as other animals needed for his job and could, if needed, request riding horses from the marshal's stables, but was also obliged to return them. He could also replace his tired animals with fresh ones from the marshal's stables, again under an obligation to return them. If a sudden need arose, the marshal could take the loaned horses back immediately and distribute them among the brothers. All the horses owned by the commander of the country could also be commandeered by the marshal but with payment. Only foals bought by the commander of the land of Jerusalem, given to brothers under his command to feed, could not be taken by the marshal unless, of course, the commander agreed to it and was paid. Not even the grand master was allowed to take such foals without informing the commander although, in this case, the commander was not allowed to refuse. If one of the brothers under the commander of the land of Jerusalem wanted one of these foals he could get it with the commander's approval, but this was more of an exception than a rule and could not be abused. Commanders of the countries of Antioch and Tripoli, unless they appointed a marshal for their countries, had to provide food and all other equipment for horses and mules of both sexes in their countries. Also any brother could borrow a horse from the marshal's stable and could also ask to keep the animal. Otherwise, all horses had to be returned.

The knights joined the Order as trained warriors at the height of their strength with complete equipment and horses, which would then become the property of the Temple. An associate member, serving a set time, could get a horse from the Order during his service but had to return it once his obligation was finished, even though he could be provided with a replacement horse if his was killed. Hierarchical Statutes strictly prescribe the number of horses allowed for the knights. The statutes only prescribe the riding horses used by the knight daily. Horses for other needs are not even mentioned, which is understandable since knights would only get them in special circumstances such as a war campaign when the need for additional animals, particularly pack animals, could arise. Every knight was supposed to have two riding horses, usually mules (which could be of both sexes), one for the knight and one for his squire, and a war horse. If the knight had two squires, he also had a fourth horse.[3] One of them was for riding and usually a mule, one was a battle horse and one was a pack horse. If a knight only owned two horses, he could ask for and receive a third one. The grand master, the seneschal, the marshals, commanders of lands and commanders of houses got the right to keep a fourth horse in keeping with their position. The seneschal and the commanders of the countries of Jerusalem, Antioch and Tripoli (and other knights of the Temple) were allowed to replace riding mules with top-notch riding horses (*palfirdus*), while the marshals and the commander of the City of Jerusalem could use the Turcomans, elite riding horses from the Central Asian steppes. These horses – intelligent, fast and durable, and of 15 to 16 hands in height – arrived with the Turkmens and were the ancestors of today's Akhal-Teke horses, nicknamed Golden Horses due to the metallic sheen of their coats. In 1935, a group of Turkmen horsemen travelled 4,000km in eighty-four days. The toughest ordeal was a three-day desert route with no water over a distance of 376km.

The grand master of the Temple was also allowed to keep a Turcoman as a fifth horse and to take two pack animals when going for a trip. The brothers were forbidden from openly demanding a second horse or mule from the marshal. Clause 153 of the Rule says that if a brother had a horse that was headstrong and liked to bite or kick, he should inform the marshal and, if this should prove correct, the animal should be replaced. Should the marshal decide that this was not necessary the brother was not obliged to ride the horse for as long as he kept it, nor could the marshal command him to do so. The importance of the care of horses can also be seen from Clause 146 of the Rule:

> … all brothers are obliged to go to chapel unless they are ill, they have their hands in food, or if the fire is lit in the foundry for the working of hot iron, or if they are preparing a horse's hoof for the shoeing, or if they wash their hair.

After completing their duties, the monks were obliged to join the prayers.

There is no doubt that the Templars had access to the best war and battle horses of their world. In the choice of stallions and mares for their own breeding or in acquiring already bred war and riding horses, the Temple had comparative advantages almost unimaginable in the European framework. They had more money than any Western prince and their properties spread in all the best European breeding areas: Apulia, Normandy, Lombardy, Frisia, Hungary and Spain. Their presence overseas gave them an unfailing source of Arabian horses and Turcomans.

Chapter Six

In the Field

Any medieval feudal army met with similar problems regarding command, discipline, provisioning and tactics. Developing the military organization on feudal bases, European rulers didn't even try to apply some of the rich Roman art of war in half a millennium, even though Vegetius[1] had left a valuable written source which was joined in the ninth century by the work of the Emperor Leo VI.[2] The Romans were masters of training, discipline and tactics. Roman military leaders were primarily officials controlling the state organization in their respective provinces, not professional warriors. In order to maintain order, they had at their disposal disciplined and well-trained units of professional soldiers. Military training was, in Imperial Rome, undertaken as a group, so that each unit would learn to act as a well-coordinated whole, which provided Roman officers with an army prepared to perform complex tactical tasks. The Romans were well aware that discipline in the army could only be achieved through daily practice, with the aim of showing the soldier that his body and soul were in the hands of his immediate superior. They also knew that the power of command springs from the power to punish: it instils fear of punishment and leads to submission as a habit of behaviour in a mass of people with only the will to follow orders unquestioningly. Without this, there can be no real army. Lack of discipline was immediately penalized by the harshest punishments, including death.

With the fall of the Western Roman Empire, the understanding of the warrior service changed completely. German conquerors were tribes of free and equal warriors, individuals with no joint military training or discipline. After settling in the conquered Roman provinces, most of them put down their weapons and took up civil professions. From the few who remained professional warriors, two groups formed by the ninth century: the knights and the non-knightly warriors. What didn't change for centuries was individual training and the non-existence of trained units, which led to a complete lack of discipline among warriors. The difference in the quality of equipment between heavy cavalry and ordinary warriors, as well as the permanent training of the former and almost no training for the latter (except for shooting practice for the archers) led to enormous differences in the fighting readiness of knights and non-knightly warriors, particularly foot soldiers. At the time of the Roman Empire, a single legionary foot soldier was considered completely prepared to fight a single heavy rider.

A millennium later, in 1302, before the Battle of Courtrai, the commander of the French army said that 100 of his knights had the same value as 1,000 Flemish foot soldiers.

In the chain of command, lack of obedience from lower commanders towards the leading officer is always a much bigger problem than lack of obedience among the soldiers. Vows given by medieval vassals to their masters did not oblige them to unconditional obedience, or to accept and execute any command but only those within the master's rights. If the vassal showed disobedience, the only punishment he could face would be to lose his fief, but this carried with it the danger of insurrection and civil war. Not even the presence of a crowned head guaranteed deference. Thus in 1161, under Milan, the ruler of the Holy Roman Empire, Frederick Barbarossa lived to see the Duke of Czechs and Landgrave of Thuringia refuse his orders and leave him to go into battle on his own.

Larger medieval feudal armies consisted of several contingents commanded by peers of equal or similar rank. Every prince, duke, count or lord went to battle primarily because of his own interests, usually connected to gaining new lands but also glory and prestige, which could hardly be achieved without a high-ranking commanding position. Insinuations, envy and hatred on the edge of armed conflict were often seen in headquarters of feudal armies, as was the case in the aforementioned First Crusade.

Annual obligation of service to the feudal master was very limited in time, so it was extremely difficult to organize a successful military campaign well, particularly if it had to reach far-off lands. In the thirteenth century in Germany and Italy, old Carolingian rule was still in practice saying that a fief-holding knight had a duty to serve his master for up to three months a year, when and if needed. In France, a vassal was only bound to serve for forty days outside the territory of his own land. All service longer than the contractual obligation was to be paid for by the master, and even then the vassal was free to refuse further service, so it was logical to resolve any campaigns as quickly as possible.

It was extremely demanding to maintain the army's morale on levels necessary to face the enemy at all. Every warrior's goal was to gain some spoils and, at the same time, preserve the most valuable property: horses, armour and weapons. Thus they were primarily interested in passing through the campaign with as little risk as possible as loss of horses and equipment could devastate them financially. Even the highest-ranking officers were also knights and thought in a similar way, so wars of the era were endless, while battles themselves could almost be counted on the fingers of one hand. Every year armies were gathered repeatedly, with the intention of striking a decisive blow against the enemy with negligible losses for oneself. It was rare for both sides to be inspired to fight at the same time. It could be due to hopes of pillage on both sides, or both commanders of the opposing parties could assess that they were holding the advantage, or one of the sides could get cornered and have no option but to accept the fight. Otherwise, things would devolve into lengthy manoeuvring and waiting and, if neither commander decided that they held the upper hand, the armies would be dissolved until the following year. Lack of action, funds for salaries and provisions or a seeming lack of opportunity for pillaging caused daily defections and some vassals would simply decide it was time for them to return to their properties. All in all, it was always easier to find motivation to return home than to start a risky battle. Knights and other warriors could always vent their frustration over lost opportunities regarding glory and spoils by mistreating the civil population, pillaging along the way, hunting or starting internal fights.

Daily camping brought another problem. Potable water was not always available, so it was customary to carry barrels of wine and beer. Warriors killed time by gambling and emptying the barrels. Already in 811, Charlemagne prohibited mutual toasting by a personal edict: '… that no one in the army should call their comrades or other people to drink.' Whoever was caught drunk was allowed to drink only water until they learned to control themselves. The great emperor and king was able to bring order among his warriors, but many warlords didn't know how to do it or simply weren't able to impose discipline, so military encampments of the time often looked more like village fairs.

Since the time of Charlemagne, European medieval armies usually only had about 5,000 to 6,000 warriors and that includes only the horsemen. There was no point in gathering a larger force because that would make it almost impossible to march. Individual contingents of a larger force would travel separately with several days' gap and, if possible, by different routes.

Let us look at the composition, tactics and chambers of a single feudal contingent in the size of a Templar army, i.e. around 1,000 heavy horsemen equipped like knights. Every warrior had servants and peers had an entire entourage. This made an additional 2,000 people minimum and almost certainly rose higher. It can be supposed that every or almost every servant had some kind of a weapon and could serve as a warrior in some circumstances: defending the camp, helping their masters in battle, gathering food or besieging a fortress. After the First Crusade, in feudal armies the number of light horsemen and infantrymen increased: according to contemporary sources, javelin-throwers, archers and crossbowmen made up to 90 per cent of the army (Raymond of Toulouse in the First Crusade: 1,200 heavy cavalry and 9,000 other fighters). We can add a modest assessment of another 4,000 people. The army was followed by groups of warriors' women, entire families, numerous travelling monks and priests, their servants and clerks, craftsmen, merchants and women of easy virtue. This adds 1,000, even though a number five or six times higher does not seem impossible. All capable men, as well as warriors' servants, participated in battles if needed. Even with a very conservative approach, we have arrived at at least 8,000 people, of which only 5,000 were professional warriors.

The comparison between a common knight and a Knight Templar with retinues on the march. What we must bear in mind is that Knights Templar did not carry food. That was a task of logistics.

Knighthood was characterized by a highly-developed sense of personal honour. For every knight it was important to win, but that wasn't the only thing: they always wanted to provide the maximum contribution to a victory, to stand out and gain glory, which was the ideal and meaning of their lives. A warrior with such a great desire to push himself forward is an individualist for whom discipline is a great burden. Only a few men like these are enough to produce total anarchy, so it is clear that discipline had no importance in this kind of army. On one side, great individual fighting will and élan were an advantage, but at the same time resulted in lost battles due to insubordination and obstinacy. Leaders, for they could hardly be called commanders, had very little authority and the execution of their orders was always uncertain, so they tried to command as little as possible. Once the battle began, no commands were issued and even the peers of the highest rank were merely knights in the fight. No sound signals were used because knights did not learn to behave like a cavalry unit that had passed through training and in which, on the gathering signal, horses start towards the place from which the signal is heard. The only signal that had any weight was the banner that marked the place where the leader was, and even that was used only to know that the leader was still alive and there was therefore still a reason to fight.

On the battlefield, tactics were not of much concern. Battles took place on spacious, very level fields because that was the best fit for heavy cavalry. In fact, many battles engaged only the horsemen. The heavy armour and weapons they used brought them advantage only in open spaces and on hard ground. The weight and depth of military formation primarily depended on the number of horsemen and the width of the battlefield. Knights and other knight-equipped horsemen tended to take up the front line (*en haye*), because that was the only way to put their primary weapon, the heavy lance, to good use. If there were enough horsemen, another row would form slightly behind them. The second-line horsemen would have to wait a little and then jump in where needed, whether they noticed a hole in the enemy line or saw a weakness in their own ranks. There were no reserve troops in knightly armies. There was no custom of leaning the wing against a natural obstacle because, due to shallow formation and the skirmish created after the impact, any kind of front or wing within the formation would disappear so that, even if one were to hit the enemy flank, there was no one there to attack.

The front line was usually divided into three parts: centre, left and right wing. The infantry, javelin-throwers and archers would remain behind and away from the knightly cavalry, divided into groups. Knights in the line did not ride stirrup-to-stirrup in the manner of organized cavalry units. According to a French cavalry handbook from the time of the Napoleonic wars, a front of 1 metre per horseman was prescribed, even though, in practice, a single horseman would take up less than the 1 metre, so twelve horsemen, riding stirrup-to-stirrup, created a front line of 9 to 10 metres, 0.75 to 0.80 metre by horseman. Medieval heavy horsemen kept this distance for a number of reasons. Knights were primarily individuals whose way of fighting demanded enough space to manoeuvre the lance and large shield in a first assault, and then use a sword, battleaxe or mace in the skirmish. Their horses could also not be pressed one against the other, as it is in the nature of stallions to kick and bite each other. The front had to be a minimum of 1.5 metres per horseman and was probably wider than that.

If we return to our contingent, which could have been one of the wings or centre of a larger army, and if we divide the horsemen in two lines of 500 men multiplied by 1.5m, we get a front line of as much as 750m in width. Finding a field wide enough to deploy only 1,000 horsemen is not easy, let alone three such groups, so lines were drawn in several rows. A wide front brought another problem: it became impossible to control warriors who were self-absorbed in the first place. So it was quite usual for a knight or two to leave the battle line and thus provoke the same reaction from the enemy, so several duels could take place between two armies as a sort of overture to battle. It was not unheard-of for a single warrior to draw out more than one enemy, even a whole group, which would mean that the whole army had to follow their example unless they wanted to get in an inferior position. Once the assault started, at first the movement was slow to spare the heavily-burdened battle horses, to speed up only near the enemy, but even then, full gallop was not used as was the case with cavalry units of the nineteenth century. Such a speed was too dangerous because the knights might find themselves thrown off their saddles due to the power of the impact. Still, this kind of fighting line would fall apart during an assault because there was no training in group riding, and the braver or simply crazier ones would start with more decisiveness, while some would ride off towards a self-imposed goal instead of the one directly in front of them. Once the impact happened, the battle would become a multitude of duels. Everything came down to individual hand-to-hand fights. Everybody fought in the manner they liked best, so it was not unusual for some knights to simply get off their horses and fight on foot. This was often done by the ones who had no room to retreat, so they felt safer on foot than they would on a horse that could be killed or taken down. Knights often spared each other's lives, sometimes due to the feeling of caste solidarity but more often out of pure greed and desire to collect a ransom for the prisoners. Ordinary warriors were ruthlessly killed.

Infantrymen would enter such skirmishes as aid for their horsemen, and then the battle would become a mixture between cavalry and infantry. There was no other way to use the infantry. In normal conditions, they had no chance in open battle with knights. One must bear in mind that foot soldiers did not have unit training and lacked even individual training. A single man on foot against one heavy horseman had a chance in open space, where he could avoid the assault and hit the horseman from the side, but in the assault of a group of knights against a mass of infantrymen, the latter simply had nowhere to escape and would just end up trampled. The only possibility of holding out against an assault of knightly cavalry was to take cover behind an obstacle, a trench or a fence. Archers could hit the horse or the horseman and disable them completely. They could also let off several arrows before the horsemen reached them and at lesser distances they could be deadly accurate, but archers never waited for horsemen to come close because any horseman reaching the archers meant a certain end for them. So they would usually shoot arrows only from a safe distance with no particular effect and would withdraw immediately.

Battles were often very short. The weaker side would give up and start running, sometimes even before the clash. In such cases the winners had almost no losses, while the losers could meet a very ugly fate, but usually the victors would stop to gather spoils, not thinking about chasing the defeated, so a decisive victory would not take place. Infantrymen and encampments usually took the brunt of the defeat.

Since the time of Charlemagne, it was customary for warriors to drag along everything they needed for the entire campaign. In Roman times, each legionary carried 14.5kg of weapons and armour, another 12kg of other equipment and tools, and food for sixteen days; a total 41kg of burden. In the eleventh century, the weight of the knight's armour reached around 20kg. Tents, cooking utensils, tools, food and drink completed the cargo. By our accounts, 1,000 horsemen had to take a minimum of 45,000kg of food and equipment for sixteen days and that's without including drink or food and drink for the knights' pages and servants. Battle and riding horses also needed a lot of food transported. A 450kg horse needs 11kg of dry food per day and 38 to 45 litres of water; if working, even more. Only three or four weeks of campaigning required the dragging of hundreds or thousands of tons of cargo. Every heavy horseman needed a cart because not everything could fit on the back of a pack horse; a cart was additionally expected to transport any possible spoils. The carts had two or four wheels and were towed by two or four animals. This required thousands of towing horses or oxen. A medieval carthorse could drag around 250kg, while an ox could pull double the weight. The largest cart and team would take up 15m of length. Oxen-towed carts couldn't travel at more than 2km per hour, even on the best of roads. Rounding a middle value of 10m of length per cart, the 2 km of road would accommodate only 200 carts.

On summer days, with sunrise at 4.00 am and dusk around 9.00 pm, 2,000 carts could barely make it over 16km. The first carts would reach their destination around noon, while the last was only starting to arrive at sunset. This would be a day of marching; a full eight hours. Our 1,000 contingent of horsemen, with 4,000 men on foot and 3,000 other personnel would probably drag at least another 100 other carts along; livestock herds as well, since they were used as a source of fresh meat. Such a caravan of up to 20km in length could daily cover only around 10km or had to travel over several parallel roads, which were not easily found in the Middle Ages. The caravans were not trained in joint marching. Where there was enough space, several carts could use the road and its surroundings in parallel but, in places where the trail was all there was such as over bridges, jams would be created and everything would slow down. Also parts of the caravan could fall behind, so the whole thing could stretch over several kilometres. If the enemy was not close the army could march faster with carts and livestock herds coming behind but, on enemy territory, the caravan had to be protected, so the army would spread throughout as well. One also has to bear in mind that highway gangs would lurk along the way, waiting for an opportunity to make a strike on unprotected carts.

There was no trained movement in file. Those of higher rank, their families, escort and equipment went ahead where there was less dust or mud. When the army wasn't moving through enemy territory, women and children would be sent ahead a day early to make the army's movement easier. Behind them would go knights on riding horses, accompanied by pages leading the battle horses. Wire armour and helmets, shields and lances were carried by pack horses or transported on carts. Battle horses and armour were always in view of the knights as these were their greatest treasure.

Knights kept their swords at their belts and a mace or war axe hanging on the saddle, always at hand. Only if there was a possibility of a skirmish would the riders put on the heavy, uncomfortable equipment and ride like that. Completely according to their own whims, knights would leave the

In file the knight seated on a battle horse: in front of him stood the page holding his lance and shield and at the back, other pages rode on spare battle horses.

file, individually or in small groups, and go riding in the environment looking for hunting prey or starting fights with the local population.

Behind the knights, the infantry, javelin-throwers and archers, their equipment helter-skelter, some barefoot or with rag-wrapped feet, mixed with long files of carts carrying the battle and camping equipment, food and drink, and finally the livestock herds. Every group of warriors was followed by masses of non-fighting people.

The air would fill with the shouts of cart-drivers and shepherds, accompanied by whistles and whip-cracking. Certain horsemen would ride along the file for one reason or another. By the side of the road, there would be carcasses of recently dead animals but also people. Dogs would run around and bark, always ready to start a fight with the local guard dogs, while overhead flocks of crows would circle, hoping to profit from the remains of food and dead bodies. Those who were sick, wounded or simply too tired to keep up the pace would drag themselves along in groups or individually far behind the main group in the hope that, by the end of the day, they would reach camp. Such groups often fell as easy prey to brigands or revenge by the locals. On sunny dry days, everything would be covered in dust and the endless file would be hidden in the miasma of transport of people and animals, while the stench spread around. In lengthy rains, the roads became almost impassable quagmires. Either from dust or from mud, after a week or two of marching, one could hardly see the colours. The marching army had no concept of formation, nor were the warriors always prepared for battle. There was no need for much caution, since all European armies were of a similar composition and behaviour so there was no fear of sudden attack.

These were the habits with which Western warriors started towards the Holy Land. The image of the pilgrims' army was no different from the contingent just described. However, the enemy who waited for them forced them to change many of their customs.

The Templars' Hierarchical Statutes offered the solution to many problems with which European knighthood did not deal particularly well. In the first place, the Templars solved the issue of command and discipline where they had the help of the prescribed monks' discipline. Monastic life kept the brothers in a peaceful, quiet life filled with prayer, as well as restraint in food and drink; a complete opposite to the daily life of secular knights. The knights, filled with an honest conviction that they were warriors of God, were much easier to command. Independently from any secular or church official, the grand master was free to decide when the Order would go to war, so Templars did not participate in every conflict in the Holy Land. Once a state of war was proclaimed, the marshal of the monastery would call all members of the Order to take up arms. The first and most important steps in the transfer from monastic life to wartime behaviour are described in Clause 103 of the Rule:

> Once the call of war is sent, commanders of the houses are to gather their horses and join together with the Marshal's squadron, and are not to leave it without permission. And all the sergeant brothers are to go to the Turcopolier, and are not to leave him without permission. And all knight brothers, and all sergeant brothers and all armed men are under the command of the Marshal, for as long as they are under arms.

The armed men included knights, sergeants, footmen and pages serving on contract, either as associate members of the Order or as mercenaries. Commanders of the countries of Tripoli and Antioch had the option of appointing marshals for their countries if they felt they were needed. In that case, the monastery marshal was still the supreme commander of the Order, but had no other marshal authority in these countries.

If the Templars' army was great and could file two squadrons of knights for battle, one of the squadrons would be commanded by the marshal and the other by the commander of the country. In times of war, the Order's chain of command was completed by the commanders of ten knights. One of the leading roles was held by the commander of the City of Jerusalem, and under his banner marched all secular knights associated with the Order. In the marshal's absence, the commander would also issue orders for all brother knights living in Jerusalem or simply travelling there.

In the chain of command, the turcopolier held the highest authority after the marshal. All armed sergeants and all turcopoles were under his command. Clause 172 of the Hierarchical Statutes explicitly prescribes the behaviour of the sergeants:

> Sergeant brothers armed in wire should behave under arms as it is prescribed for knight brothers, and sergeant brothers not in arms, should they show themselves well, God and brothers will thank them. And if they should see that they cannot fight, or if they are wounded, they are allowed to retreat, if they should so wish, without permission and without damage to the house.

One of the turcopolier's duties was reconnaissance, performed by the turcopoles. The turcopolier transferred the information gathered in the reconnoitring to the marshal of the monastery, who then issued the necessary commands. Of all the men in arms, only the knights were not under his direct command, although, in some cases, knight brothers also had to follow his orders as explicitly stated in articles 170 and 172 of the Hierarchical Statutes. In case of need, the turcopolier himself joined the turcopoles in reconnaissance as stated in Clause 170:

> And when the Turcopolier joins the scouts and five, six, eight to ten knights are added, they are under the command of the Turcopolier; and if they are ten, and one of them is the commander of ten knights with a white-and-black banner, the Turcopolier is under his command.

So this was one of the situations when the turcopolier commanded the knights. The other was when armed sergeants were filed for battle, as described in Clause 172:

> If the brothers are set to command sergeants under arms, they are not to go on assault or leave for another reason without permission; but if the Marshal or brothers are on assault, they are to lead the sergeants in attack, filed near the knights, as best they can, so that, if brothers should need them, the sergeants can be of help.

As the brother sergeants were in a squadron under the command of the turcopolier, it is clear that this pertained to the brother knights in the same squadron. The Rule says nothing about who

A Temple squadron beginning the charge. Behind the knights, the squires ride spare horses provided as a remount if a charger was wounded or blown. The sergeants formed a third rank to assist or rescue the knights.

commanded the infantry, but it is quite possible that, as warriors of non-knightly origin, they too were the turcopolier's responsibility.

Logistic support was led by the under-marshal of the Order who, on the marshal's orders, took care of the maintenance of the warriors' equipment and the knights' supply of weapons, saddles and other smaller equipment and dispatched available pages to care for horse caravans and protect the camps. In a campaign, the Templar army was also joined by the Order's draper, whose men provided replacements and repairs for the warriors' clothing.

Commanders of the countries of Jerusalem, Antioch and Tripoli supervised the use of pack animals and livestock herds in times of war. All war supplies – leather, iron and steel, wine and food for men and horses – requested by the marshal were to be sent on pack animals by the commanders of the three overseas Templar countries. Theirs was also to provide sergeant sentries for all Templar fortresses in their countries. As Templar fortresses were under their supervision, all Turkish weapons and crossbows, used primarily by the sergeants, were at their disposal. All weapons and armour gained as spoils in a campaign were immediately given to the marshal, while other spoils including livestock, pack animals and slaves went to the commander of the country. In the whole, well-conceived chain of command, not even the pages were left to their own devices. Every one of their tasks was completed jointly, under the watchful eye of the ensign.

When marching, the Templar army had strictly prescribed disciplinary measures and a schedule. When the monastery was preparing to march, the brothers were not allowed to saddle their horses or load the pack animals, get in the saddle or leave their places without a command from the marshal. Prior to the command, they were allowed to load only tent hooks, empty bottles, cam axes, ropes and fishing nets onto the pack horses. If they wanted to speak to the marshal, the brothers had to go to him on foot and then return to their places. Once the marshal issued the order to ride, the brothers were first supposed to carefully go over the camping site so that no part of the equipment would be left behind, and then they would quietly get in the saddle and join their troop at a walking pace. Their pages followed them with the equipment. In the forming of the marching file, a knight would take his place but, if he couldn't find room for himself and his equipment because another brother was already there, he had to ask the brother taking up the position to relinquish it, which the other brother could but wasn't forced to do. Once all knights had their place in file, each knight would let the page with pack and battle horses precede him. The head of the file was taken by the ensign, followed by the banner carried by a page or another man entrusted with it. The ensign was to lead the warriors and the logistics along the way as commanded by the marshal.

If a brother joined the already moving file, he could only let another brother do the same before him, never behind. If it was at night, the file moved in silence, speaking only the necessary commands. When brothers wanted to talk, the one in front had to join the one behind, while their pages and equipment were to stay before them. Once their conversation was over, each had to return to his place. If someone wanted to ride alongside the march for one reason or another, they were only allowed to do so downwind so that their dust would not bother the file. If for any reason a brother was unable to return to his place in the file, the closest brother had to give him the place before him until daybreak, when the lost brother had to return to his squadron quickly and safely. The same applied to pages. No one was allowed to ride alongside the file to talk or for their own pleasure, either alone or in the company of one or more colleagues. For the sake of rest, the file stopped in the morning.

Horses could not be watered without permission. Only in peaceful surroundings were horses allowed to be watered without permission, but while taking care not to break up the marching file. Even on reconnaissance, watering horses was only allowed with permission or when the ensign did so. On the move, when the horses were grazing or in ambush, the brothers were not allowed to remove their horses' saddles or halters without permission.

Semi-desert and desert terrains through which they marched dictated the use of pack animals instead of carts for equipment transport. Numerous Templar fortresses and properties throughout all three crusaders' countries overseas allowed the Order to deploy wartime supplies along their lines of movement, so there was no need to drag along everything they needed for the whole campaign from the start.

Going back to the total of 45kg of cargo per horseman for sixteen days, let us add another 15kg of food for the page and another 10kg or so in weight for the tent. This gives a total of 70kg, with food and water still to be added, so the cargo would reach 200kg per single warrior. The Templars did not carry their food and wine supplies individually, nor were they allowed to keep them in their tents during camping. That was the job of logistics, so the knight and his men had one thing less to carry and worry about. A single pack horse could usually carry cargo up to around 30 per cent of its body weight, so 100kg is optimal for a horse of around 300kg. Therefore, two pack horses per brother (knight or sergeant) were enough. That means that 1,000 brothers needed 2,000 to 3,000 pack horses, the number of which went down significantly if camels were being used as they could carry from 150 to 300kg of cargo. If camels were used for cargo, this resulted in certain complications since camels had to be led separately from the horses. Such a file took up significantly less space per ton of cargo than in Western feudal armies, so the files were much shorter.

There were no women and children and therefore no equipment and food for them. If Templar cavalry was the only unit marching, the knights, sergeants and turcopoles, with pages and servants also on riding animals, they could march quickly. According to the study of French General Jarry from the time of the Revolutionary Wars, horsemen could cover 3km per hour on a poor road if the horses were walking. If they marched non-stop for eight hours, they would travel 24km, a full 8km further than the feudal army transporting equipment and food on oxen-pulled carts. The presence of men on foot slowed them down. Again according to General Jarry at the time of the Revolutionary Wars, infantry could cover 2.3km per hour on poor roads, so in an eight-hour march they would cover 18.4km. There is no reason to think that medieval infantrymen could not move at the same speed, which would mean that a Templar army including infantry still covered 2.8km more than the average feudal army.

In addition to the task of leading the brothers on the march, the ensign also determined the place where they would camp. The erection of the encampment could only begin after the shout, 'In the name of God, gentlemen brothers, make camp!' The first to take place in the camp were the tents for the grand master, marshal, chapel, canteen and country commander. Around these tents, which formed the centre of the camp, a rope fence would be set up. The command crier (who would raise the alarm) and the officer in charge of the grain were situated next to the ensign. Then

A Templar colour party consisting of a marshal holding the banner, a commander of ten knights carrying a wrapped reserve banner and ten knights as escort.

GRBASIC

the brothers arriving in squadrons were allowed to choose places for their tents and the entourage around them. Once the command was given, the knights were allowed to send their servants to get firewood and take horses grazing. If grazing and wood could be found close to the encampment so that an alarm would be heard from there as well, they were allowed to do it without waiting for the command. The pages who led the horses to and back from grazing were led by the ensign with the banner deployed. The saddles removed from the horses had to be covered with blankets, and it was forbidden for brothers to request their war saddles without prior permission. Whoever had two or more pages always had to keep one close by to assist him in case of necessity. The brothers were allowed to leave the camp for fun only to a distance from which they could still hear the alarm call or bell. Either in war or in peace, they were not allowed to ride away further than a league[3] without permission, nor to ride out in daytime between two meals or to ride away without their boots.

Brothers received food and wine from the commander of provisions, who had to take care that all meals were distributed justly and in equal amounts. At meals, the first to be called was the master's sergeant, who would take the best for his master. Meat was divided in such a manner that a measure for two knights was sufficient for two poor men to be fed from the remains. The two-knight measure served three turcopoles, and a two-turcopoles measure was intended for three sergeants. Two brothers received five measures of wine, four measures in fast; two turcopoles received three measures of wine and also one measure of oil. This indicates that the turcopoles received larger rations than the sergeants, which confirms how much the Templars appreciated them as warriors.

If an alarm was raised during the march, the ones closest to the place of shouting would mount their battle horses, take up their shields and lances, and then calmly wait for further commands from the marshal. The others would ride to the marshal, awaiting his commands. If the alarm was raised while they were in camp or at another overnight settlement, they were not allowed to leave the place without permission. When the alarm was raised from somewhere within the camp, the closest men were allowed to mount and take up their shields and lances, while all the others were supposed to go to the chapel tent where they would hear their orders. If, on the other hand, the alarm was raised somewhere outside the camp, no one was allowed to leave it without permission. Once the banner was out, everybody was supposed to follow it as fast as possible.

On the battlefield the brothers also followed very strict rules. Depending on the number of the knights of the Order and their associates, the Temple would form one or two squadrons. There is no exact information on how many knights went into a squadron or how it was filed. It all depended on the momentary ideas of the squadron commander. As this was not a tactical cavalry formation trained in joined manoeuvres, they didn't have to fear that too great a size would make changing and retaining the formation difficult. A squadron was simply a temporary group of knights ready for battle under the command of the marshal, the master, country commander or, if they were absent, another official of the Order. The goal of creating such a squadron was merely to provide the commander with control over the knights and the knights with the opportunity to hear commands and see the banner. No one was allowed to leave the squadron and go to the next one and, in order to be allowed to mount a battle horse and pick up a shield and lance, a knight had to await orders.

Once in file, the knights sat on battle horses, in front of them stood the pages holding their lances, and at the back other pages rode on the knights' spare battle horses. Waiting in the squadron, the knight was not allowed to turn his horse to fight or yell. A knight was allowed to ride out of the file in order to check whether his saddle and saddle-blanket were well fixed, after which he was supposed to return to the file in silence. Still, he was not allowed to take up a shield and lance without permission. Every knight was allowed to put the wire cap on his head, but was not allowed to take it off without permission. The knights could not leave the file or start the assault without permission. Only if a Christian was attacked nearby and the brother decided that their help would be of use was the knight allowed to assist the one under attack and then again return to file quietly. Any disrespect of this rule or a self-initiated assault was punished by the biggest offence a knight could imagine. They had to return to camp on foot, with their armour and weapons confiscated.

Before leading the Temple brothers in assault, the marshal would take the banner of the Order from the under-marshal, who went under the command of the turcopolier unless the marshal decided to keep him by his own side. Then the marshal would select a group of five to ten knights who were to be his bodyguards during the battle. If the marshal was killed, wounded or otherwise prevented from leading the squadron during the assault and the banner was lost, his position would be taken over by the commander of ten knights from his escort. He would then deploy the reserve banner of the Order, which he normally carried wrapped while riding next to the marshal to mark the point of gathering for the squadron. Under no circumstances was the banner to be lowered or its pole used as a weapon. Other knights attacked to the left and right of the marshal and his escort. While the marshal's bodyguards could not leave him under any circumstances, the other knights were allowed to attack the enemy everywhere around, always bearing in mind that they should stay close enough to be of help to the marshal's group and protect the banner. The commanders of any additional squadron of the Temple behaved in the same manner. None of the officers leading the squadron's assault, including all commanders of ten knights, were allowed to go to attack or leave the squadron without permission from the master or his replacement, even if their lives were in danger or they were faced with the danger of being surrounded. Otherwise they were punished and their monk's robes taken away.

During battle it could easily happen that a knight or group of knights might get cut off and be unable to return to their banner. In that case, they were to fight their way to the closest Christian banner, preferably of the Order of St John under which they were to fight quietly until an opportunity arose for them to return to their own banner. If it happened that the Christian army was defeated, the Templars were not allowed to leave the battlefield as long as their own banner or the Hospitallers' banner or any other Christian banner was deployed. The punishment was, again, expulsion from the Order.

A wounded knight was not allowed to leave the battlefield without permission and, if the wounds were so severe that he was not able to request it, he was to send another brother to ask permission for him. The Temple's battle line and procedure in starting an assault were carefully prescribed. In the front there were the squadrons of the knights. At this point they would hold their shields and lances in their hands. Behind them, on reserve battle horses, were the pages. Even further behind were the sergeants under the command of the turcopolier, who was helped by the knights appointed to lead the sergeants and the brothers commanding ten sergeants. Behind them all, the squadron's ensign gathered the remaining pages on the knights' riding horses and mules. At the marshal's command, the squadron (or squadrons) of the knights started the assault, first at walking speed and then speeding up. They were followed by their pages. When a knight lost his horse in the assault, he would be approached by his page and helped to mount a reserve animal so he could continue. Then the sergeant squadron would start the assault. Further behind them, the ensign deployed his banner to lead the remaining pages behind the heavy cavalry. These pages were not expected to participate in the battle; they were expected to help their masters in trouble. The turcopoles and infantrymen are not even mentioned, just as there is no mention of them in any feudal army. Light horsemen were of more value in reconnaissance and skirmishes with similarly-equipped enemies than they could be in a real battle, while the infantry only entered the battle as support for the heavy cavalry; i.e. after the conflict had already started.

If we now compare the average feudal army and the Templars, it is clear that the former were a more or less undisciplined group of warriors with no clear organization, additionally burdened by numerous non-fighting followers. They moved in long, disorganized marching files, dragging along all the necessities on numerous carts and pack animals. In moments of rest, they were prone to uncontrolled behaviour and drinking. On the battlefield, their behaviour was completely unruly. They did not strictly follow even the most basic of commands; they were prepared to leave the file, assault out of control and leave the battlefield of their own will. They had no chain of command, nor were there any punishments for the breakers of discipline.

On the other hand, the Temple had high officers and meticulously specified their authorities and duties. All members of the Order, whether they were monks or paid to do their jobs, had their commanders in times of war and nothing was left to chance or chaos. Their logistics were marvellously organized and efficient. There were no surplus men or any women and children. The Templars marched and camped following strictly-set rules of conduct, following orders. All they needed was transport by pack animals, which allowed them better mobility and shorter marching files. All the tasks were completed in silence, ensuring that commands were heard clearly and understood correctly. They did not eat or drink to excess, making sure that all the men and animals were provided for justly and on time. Although the knights' monastic vows compelled them to unquestioning obedience, on the battlefield their wilful nature was additionally taken into account. By prohibiting them from taking up the lance and shield until the last moment, they were also prevented from undermining the battle line-up by individual actions. During the battle, there was also a marked difference between the secular armies and the Templars. The former moved over the battlefield on a whim and left the battle at will, while the latter always had to stay close to their banner and fight as long as they could see it.

Hierarchical Statutes were, in fact, a rule of service which, within the framework possible at the time, provided the organizational foundation for the best feudal army, prescribing the chain of command, logistics, behaviour in the field and equipment of the warriors. The only unresolved problem remaining was one that marked all feudal armies: that was the lack of joint training and the non-existence of permanent units.

Chapter Seven

Fraternal Knightly Orders in the Holy Land

Christian states overseas held a narrow strip of land by the Mediterranean Sea, of which a good portion was taken up by desert and mountains. Christian rulers had only a limited area of potential fiefdoms for their vassals, so the number of vassals was too small to protect the Holy Land. The few hundred knights were undoubtedly much fewer in number than the surrounding infidels, except during the time of the Western crusaders. Any loss of territory also meant a significant drop in military force for the Kingdom of Jerusalem, Antioch and Tripoli. The help of European sovereigns was, understandably, weak and untimely. It depended on political circumstances in the West, the state of kingly treasuries and, in the end, on the motivation and response of the peers and secular knights. If there was no chance of winning rich spoils, gaining new lands and killing, interest in fighting in a faraway land was almost non-existent among secular knights. The long and uncertain journey to Palestine did not help the Christians either.

Knightly orders were in a completely opposite position from that of the secular rulers in the Holy Land. The orders' infrastructure in Europe was safe. They constantly received donations in the form of money, equipment, weaponry, horses, tax relief and larger and smaller properties. Already in the 1120s, the Hospitallers had a network of properties in the West, and the Templars followed their example. The largest donation for the Templars and the Hospitallers came from King Alfonso of Aragon. As he had no children, he left his entire kingdom to the Templars and the Hospitallers. After his death in 1144, problems in the execution of the will dragged on for ten years. Finally, a compromise solution was found: the Templars received six fortresses, a tenth of the kingdom's income, release from payment of taxes and one-fifth of the enemy properties they might conquer, which forced them to participate in the Reconquista.

Thanks to power, wealth and the trust they had earned by honesty and good judgement, the Templars and the Hospitallers held great political influence both in the Holy Land and in the West. The leading men of both orders were gladly used by popes and kings as counsellors. New knights kept coming, inspired by the achievement of warrior glory in the defence of holy places, and took the monk's vows. Young knights were also attracted by the opportunity to travel to the Holy Land, which they would never otherwise see, and some simply joined the ranks in Palestine because they'd spent all their money to return from a pilgrimage and had no better choice. It was often the case that numerous members of the same noble family joined one of the orders. However, orders lost many warriors in battles, to illness and exhaustion so that, despite so many voluntarily taking their vows, it was still necessary to fill their ranks with punished and excommunicated knights like the murderers of Thomas Becket. Sovereigns of states in the Holy Land but also those in the West soon realized that the knights in monastic communities were prepared to fight for Christian ideals where secular knights were unable, unwilling or insufficiently numerous to do so. Voluntarily sacrificing themselves for the spreading of true religion in the service of the church, the monk knights waged a preserving war against the infidels, even when there were no crusades. The political power, wealth and popularity they enjoyed in the West allowed the knightly orders to always keep strong armies overseas; without this, the crusaders' countries would certainly not have lasted this long.

The merchant republic of Amalfi is first mentioned in the sixth century, soon becoming a maritime force thanks to sales of grain, salt and wood for Muslim gold dinars, which they then used to buy Byzantine silk and sell it in the West. It was during the time when European trade was still based on pure exchange of goods. Amalfi's merchant ships were privileged in Muslim ports. In the early ninth century, Amalfian traders received permission from the Egyptian Caliph Ali az-Zahir to reconstruct the hospice, chapel and monastery of St John the Baptist in Jerusalem, demolished by az-Zahir's predecessor Al Hakim in 1005. The reconstruction of the buildings in Muristan, south of the Church of St Sepulchre, was completed in 1023. They founded a refuge for the poor, sick and wounded pilgrims devoted to St John the Baptist. The refuge was served by Benedictine monks and sisters. In the late eleventh century, a merchant or warrior Gerard Thom arrived in Jerusalem; he was probably of Amalfi origin and was appointed the *praepositus* (provost) of the male part of the hospice. He was the founder of the independent Order of St John, acknowledged by Pope Paschal II in 1133 by the edict *Geraudo institutori ac praeposito Hirosolimitani Xenodochii*.

The Hospitallers abandoned the teachings of St Benedict and chose instead the teachings of St Augustine. Already in Gerard's lifetime – he died in 1120 – the Order received numerous properties in the Kingdom of Jerusalem and equipped numerous inns at pilgrim routes in Europe where the Hospitallers introduced an administrative structure later imitated by the Templars. Gerard's heir, Raymond du Puy,[1] a French knight who remained in the Holy Land after the First Crusade, widened the hospice in Jerusalem, providing accommodation for 2,000 people and 600 knights, and founded a hospital near the Church of St Sepulchre and also other hospitals throughout the Holy Land, particularly in ports where pilgrims usually came to land. Soon the monks extended their activities from providing hospital care to offering armed escort for pilgrims on their way from the coast to Jerusalem, and the protection of their Red Cistern hospice on the way to the River Jordan, indicating that Raymond thought similarly to de Payens. Raymond also won the charter allowing him to raise armed forces for the defence of the Order, its hospitals and hospices. Now the previous monastic organization was no longer sufficient, so in 1126 the position of the constabulary of the Order was created, indicating that a permanent mercenary unit probably existed. Furthermore, there is mention of twenty monks in charge of guarding the tomb of Christ. The prior of these monks also received oaths of guarding the tomb from secular warriors.

Starting in 1136, the Hospitallers received some of the key fortresses in the Holy Land: the first was Gibelin in the Kingdom of Jerusalem, then two in the county of Tripoli in 1139, including the magnificent Krak des Chevaliers. That means that, as early as 1136, the Hospitallers were capable of raising a strong military force to defend the given fortresses. Unlike the Templars, the Hospitallers left no information on what exactly was the position of the knights serving the order; i.e. whether they were mercenaries or held the Hospitaller fiefs with the obligation of military service. After the tremendous Christian defeat near Hattin in 1187, the Pope concluded that military engagement of the Hospitallers was necessary, even though he still maintained that the Order should primarily be active in its primary function. Only in 1206 was the Hospitaller Statute written, allowing the monks to be warriors so, from that point onwards, all important military functions within the Order were in the hands of the marshal, answering solely to the grand master.

Since then, the structure of the Order of St John included two groups of monks: brothers and sisters still dealing with their primary function; i.e. caring for exhausted, sick and wounded pilgrims, and knights, with sergeants, who fulfilled their monastic call, like the Templars, by fighting for Christ. Until then, the knights and sergeants were merely associate members as it was possible in the Temple for warriors who did not take vows. In the early thirteenth century, the Hospitallers' properties and military force were so strong that they became rivals to Templars. In the Holy Land alone, they had around 600 knights. The Templars and the Hospitallers made up half of the overall number of knights in overseas lands.

The Hospitallers' hierarchy in the Holy Land, going from grand master, marshal, hospitaller, treasurer, quartermaster and turcopolier, was identical to that of the Templars. In Europe, the Hospitallers had provinces similar to that of the Templars called priories and divided them into houses (*comturias*). The priorates were gathered in larger territorial units, great *comturias*, which in the late thirteenth century formed seven 'tongues'. Unlike the Templars who mostly spoke French, the Hospitallers chiefly came from the Spanish- and Italian-speaking areas until the Temple was banned, since when the French language has prevailed among the Hospitallers as well.

Brother knights were allowed to have four horses and two non-fighting pages, and were under the command of the marshal, like the Templars. The sergeants had two horses and, starting in 1302, a page. At least some of the pages were in arms that year, since the position of military page, a commander of armed pages, was introduced. In the 1120s, Hospitaller warriors wore white surcoats with red crosses and probably white robes over their armour, and their banner was white with red spots, symbols of holy blood. In 1130, the Pope prescribed that fighting for the faith was to be undertaken under a red banner with a white cross. At the time, Hospitaller warriors

Knight of St John and a sergeant brother. Knights of the Hospitaller Order were almost exclusively hired, not members of the Order, so they were allowed to wear their family insignia on shields. Long-sleeved black surcoats were in use until 1248. A sergeant brother, fitted out for fighting on foot, wears a common black surcoat of the Order over a sleeveless mail shirt and gambeson (quilted jacket), cattle-heat helmet and buckler shield, very popular among foot soldiers.

Teutonic knight and sergeant brother. This late-thirteenth-century knight wears an off-white coat of plates over mail armour for the whole body. Teutonic sergeants wore a grey surcoat with the tau cross of St Anthony, a long-sleeved gambeson with reinforced high collar and metal plates fastened on a padded base as knee protection.

were wearing standard black monastic robes with a white Latin cross since black was the colour of both Benedictine and Augustine monks. At their request, in 1248 Pope Innocent IV allowed Hospitallers to wear red surcoats with a white cross in military campaigns. It is no wonder that the knights requested different clothes from the monks since they were only associate members without monastic oaths; i.e. without the obligation to behave and dress like monks. The permission pertained only to the knights, while sergeants remained in black surcoats, as was the case with the Templars, but not for long. In the statute of 1278 it was prescribed that all brethren at arms should wear red surcoats and black mantles.

In the second decade of the twelfth century, a third knightly order was already founded in Jerusalem. Underneath the northern city wall there lay a lepers' hospice held by the knights of St Lazarus, whose primary duty was, of course, caring for the lepers. According to legend, at first they were a part of the Order of the Hospitallers as their head was the master of the Hospitallers. According to Templar and Hospitaller rules, all their monks who contracted leprosy had to join the Order of St Lazarus. By the mid-twelfth century, the Order had built its own monastery and church, and then acquired houses in Ashkelon, Tiberias, Acre, Beirut and Caesarea. At the same time, they equipped a never particularly numerous group of armed brothers, who fought bravely side by side with grand knightly orders.

During the Siege of Acre, 1189–91, the chaplain of the dean of the English Cathedral of St Paul treated the sick and the wounded. When Acre fell, Richard I gave the chaplain the funds to construct a small chapel and hospital. The chaplain gathered monks with the task of treating English pilgrims and warriors; they followed the Rule of the Cistercians and called themselves the Knights of St Thomas. Their seat was in England, in Thomas Becket's birthplace. They received gifts of land in Cyprus, on Sicily, in Greece and in Naples. The Bishop of Winchester gave them a large sum of money in 1231, ordering them to follow the example of the Templars and fight infidels with arms; the monks, however, stuck to their primary duty of caring for the sick and wounded. Since most English warriors joined the Hospitallers, the Order remained small and their fighters participated in battles without playing any significant roles.

In 1189, the great emperor of the Holy Roman Empire, Frederick Barbarossa, started a crusade that was expected to fulfil all the hopes of the Christian world. Barbarossa managed to lead the grand German army through the Balkans and to Asia Minor with no losses or problems. In 1190 he cleared Anatolia of Turks and entered the mountains of Cilicia on his way to Syria. This is where bad luck struck. Instead of leading the combined forces of the West (English and French kings were already besieging Acre with their armies), the red-bearded emperor drowned in the River Saleph within the Armenian kingdom of Cilicia. He couldn't be bothered to cross the bridge jammed by his men, so he tried to cross the river on horseback. The stream pulled them and the weight of his armour cost the emperor his life. Most of his vassals immediately started for Germany to witness the election of Barbarossa's successor, fearing a possible civil war. Others fell before Turkish assaults and only 5,000 men from the once-grand army joined, under Barbarossa's son Frederick VI of Schwabia and the Hungarian Prince Géza, the English and French forces under Acre. The English King Richard the Lionheart hated to receive the vassals of a Hohenstaufen, who had chased and disinherited the Duke of Bavaria and Saxony, Henry the Lion, husband to Matilda, sister of Richard I. Richard didn't hold back; he used every opportunity to insult his German allies. This irritated French King Philippe, so the French, together with most Germans, simply left the siege and returned to Europe.

During the siege, the Germans suffered great losses due to heat and infections. The northern men were simply not used to such a climate with hordes of insects, eastern food and lack of water. As with any siege, sanitary conditions were disastrous and the dead were so many that there were no funerals; bodies were simply thrown into the moat under the city walls. The Hospitallers holding the warriors' infirmary took care primarily of their compatriots, the French and the English, while the Germans were mostly left to their own devices. Desperate, German warriors from Bremen and Lübeck decided to constitute an order to care for the sick and the wounded in Acre, which met with the approval of Duke Frederick VI Hohenstaufen, Patriarch of Jerusalem, as well as the Templars and the Hospitallers. The monks at first followed the Rule of the Order of St John the Baptist. By 1191, another new large group of German noblemen and knights arrived overseas and, under their influence, the Order adopted the Templar Rule, given to the newly-elected master in written form by the grand master of the Temple.

The Rule of the Teutonic Order is written in German, shorter and clearer than the Templar version. Its basis was the same: a vow of poverty, purity and obedience. Under the name of the Order of the Infirmary of St Mary of the Germans in Jerusalem, the monks performed the same duties as the Hospitallers. Pope Celestin III acknowledged them as an independent order which, in the coming years, spread the chain of their hospices and infirmaries in the Holy Land. Soon, the more popular name 'German Order' became usual or, under the influence of English speech, 'Teutonic Order'.

A new crusading army arrived overseas from Germany in 1197 and found the infirmary and numerous hospices of the Teutonic Order providing German warriors with safe haven, care and all kinds of aid for those who had lost property and equipment in the crusades. The citizens of Bremen again represented a large part of the German army. Many of them gave gifts to the Order, of which they were co-founders. Numerous warriors who had passed through knightly training joined the Order, leading to considerations of possible military actions by the monks in the Holy Land; their defence in those years almost completely relied on the forces of the Templars and the Hospitallers anyway. The Pope's permission for military engagement of the Order was requested and Innocent answered with an edict of approval in 1199. By 1220, Teutonic knights already had twelve houses (*comturias*) in Palestine, Greece, Italy and Germany. By 1230, they were already capable of equipping 600 brother knights, catching up with the Templars and the Hospitallers. However, overseas they never became a significant military force because all the important fortresses and lands were already owned by the Templars and Hospitallers so there was simply no room for another large Order.

In Europe the Order was divided into three branches: the German, Prussian and Livonian ones, of which the latter two had their provincial commanders (*Landmeisters*). The bases of the Teutonic Order in the Holy Land were originally in Antioch and Tripoli, and then in the fortress of Starkenberg, north-east of Acre. Due to the unfavourable situation for the Order in overseas lands, the Teutonic knights transferred the majority of their military activities to the pacification and Christianization of Prussian tribes.

The commander of the Teutonic Order was a master but, since the Order also had warriors in Prussia and Livonia which were also commanded by masters, it became necessary to proclaim the Holy Land master as a grand master (*Hochmeister*) to stress the importance of the role of Teutonic knights overseas compared to the European branch of the Order. In the Order's see in Acre, together with the grand master, there was the grand commander of Holy Land forces (*Gross Komtur*) and Order treasurer (*Tressler*). Each one of them held one of the keys that jointly opened the large coffer of the treasury. Throughout the Holy Roman Empire, there were regional commanders and chaplains for numerous Teutonic fortresses. Teutonic knights also had a marshal (*Ordensmarschall*) who was most concerned with the equipment and training of the horsemen. The quartermaster commander (*Trapier*) and hospital commander (*Spittler*) were his subordinates.

Almost exclusively of German origin, the monks of the Teutonic Order differed from other warrior monks in that they did not live in a monastery. Each brother monk had the right to ten armed men, lower-ranking Order members who served either on a time-limited contract or else for life. They were called half-brothers or greycoats since they dressed in grey, and fulfilled the duties of sergeants or pages.

Unlike the Templars, they were allowed to hunt on horseback as this was the usual way for German knights to keep in shape and hone their riding skills. They could also use dogs while hunting beasts and wild boars, but only if it was necessary and never for amusement. They were supposed to avoid women, but this was difficult to control given that they were not obliged to live in a monastery. The Rule ordered them to stay away from places where alcohol and female company were on offer, and not to talk to a woman on their own, particularly if she was young. The range of punishments was wide, from very mild to very harsh ones. There were even irons, dungeons and whipping. After serving his sentence, the monk could be returned to service or expelled from the Order. There was no possibility of forgiveness for three particular transgressions: cowardice, treason and sodomy. The last one entailed lifelong imprisonment or the death penalty.

Apart from the Templars, all the other knightly orders were founded to provide aid for the sick, wounded and exhausted, while military service was only approved afterwards. The appearance of other orders was also a reflection of the desire by other people's knights to get away from the patronage of the Frenchmen in the Temple.

The Templars were not even the oldest Order since the Hospitallers were founded before them, but the Order of St John was the first to allow monks with swords in their hands in 1206. The activities and growth of the Templars and St John's knights ran in parallel, and this soon led to rivalry between the two leading Orders in the Holy Land which, in turn, often created diplomatic and even armed conflicts instead of co-operation in the defence of Christian interests. At last, in 1258, in Acre an agreement was drafted to resolve the conflict but, by then, so much in the Holy Land had already been lost due to lack of co-operation between the two Orders that this did not improve the situation in any significant manner.

Chapter Eight

Enemies

In 1096 the crusaders came to Asia Minor to meet an enemy whose army was also composed almost completely of horsemen, but with different battle customs. Muslim warriors were also individuals, lacking the discipline to constitute permanent units. Hundreds of years before that, the Prophet gave Arabs the faith in one God and left the believers with the book of laws, the Quran, and one leader (both military and religious, in the form of the caliph) to rule them on Earth. Unlike the Christians who preached peace, Mohammed called the followers of Islam to fight the infidels with a sword in their hand so as to gain an eternal place in Paradise. At the time of his heirs, in the seventh and eighth centuries, faith led the desert warriors and made them a very disciplined army, including even the belligerent Bedouin tribes famous for their disobedience.

At the time of the first caliphs, Muslims started the battle by sending off the *mubarizunes*, elite horsemen proven in duels as excellent javelin-throwers, archers and swordsmen, before the front line; following the ancient customs of Byzantium, Persia and the Arabs, they would challenge the best of the enemy's warriors to duels. The goal was to cut down as many enemy champions as possible before the enemy lines and thus influence fighting morale on both sides. Only the bravest and most confident in their skill dared to ride out and fight without help from their comrades. Such famous warriors were celebrated in their own ranks and provoked awe among the enemy. Their very presence encouraged poorer fighters, similar to the effect that the top players have in sports teams today. One should try to look at it from the position of warriors observing the duel. On the winner's side, a view of the victor rising in his stirrups and swinging his bloodied weapon caused cheers from the warriors, creating even more noise by banging their weapons against armour and shields. Like a crowd in the stands of a sports arena, general elation strengthened the feeling of community and gave faith in their side's superiority and victory. On the other side stood the enemy, quietly watching the lifeless body of their fighter, one foot still stuck in the stirrup of the sweaty horse, with only an occasional sigh, prayer or angry cry rising here and there. The death of a comrade certainly provoked a desire for vengeance in some, but a general feeling of unease and anxiety could certainly not be subdued. If their best warrior had lost, what could those with less prowess in arms, physically weaker or poorer riders expect in the battle with the enemy's champion? If the army was small, everything took place within little space, or if the soldiers were inexperienced, it could easily happen that the whole fighting line took one look at the enemy charge and simply turned their backs, running from the battlefield. By fighting and winning duels, even a stronger enemy could be dissuaded from the real battle.

It is a historical fact that communities that win wars often stagnate in the military sense due to a sense of superiority and security. After numerous conquests, Arabs gradually accepted civilization and left fighting to others. Apart from the border areas, huge territories under Islam were safe from outside enemies. Local enmities of Muslim emirs mostly had no effect on civilian life. In the religious, economic and cultural sense, nothing changed and the civil population was left alone. Being a warrior meant putting one's head in the noose. In the Middle Ages, death in battle was mostly a better fate than being wounded or losing part of one's body. Most of the wounded, even if their wound was slight, died ugly deaths from infections and gangrene. Invalids with no property were condemned to begging and inhumane life conditions. On the other hand, merchants, craftsmen and farmers could live peaceful and safe, if not plentiful lives.

Instead of the faithful, warrior ranks were filled by mercenaries used to the rough life of nomadic warriors, usual for numerous Turkish and Mongol tribes in the vastness of the Asian steppes and deserts. They were not connected to a homeland, had no developed religious belonging or loyalty to a single dynasty; they were not led by faith and the common good, but rather the desire for power and spoils of war. Among the mercenary ranks, particularly famous were the Seljuk Turks, who converted to Islam in the tenth century. Turkish mercenaries quickly infiltrated the whole of the Muslim world, and their emirs proclaimed themselves as rulers of large areas, leaving only the role of the religious leader for the caliphs. As in the West, professional warriors formed only a small portion of the population. Muslim elite warriors can be compared with Christian knights, although the former were slightly more disciplined since traces of a firm connection between the faith and the sword remained.

The aforementioned Byzantine Emperor Leo described Turkish warriors in his work *Tactics*. According to his text, these were horsemen wearing not-too-heavy strong armour, a helmet with a cap and protectors for arms, thighs and shins. Their weapons consisted of two bows, thirty iron-winged arrows, a strong lance with an iron spike, a spear, an iron sword, a two-edged knife, a mace, a two-headed axe and thirty stones in two bags on both sides of the saddle. The emperor mentions no shield, but it is certain that Muslim horsemen used the kalkan, a dome-shaped round shield made of iron, steel, bronze, wattle, leather, bamboo or reed. They rode on armoured war horses with firm hooves and strong chests, necks, and front and back legs.

Of course, this is a description of a warrior equipped to perfection, which could only be attained by those of noble blood and with deep pockets. Not all warriors had all the prescribed equipment or a horse-armour so, according to this, they were divided into completely armoured horsemen, horse javelin-throwers, horse archers and horse spearmen.

Equipment, weapons and the manner of fighting were not significantly different between European and Muslim heavy horsemen, but numerous horse archers on the Muslim side were a complete novelty for Christian warriors. The archers wore no armour because it would restrain their movement and the handling of bow and arrow; they rode light, fast horses who allowed them to get very close to the enemy, shower them with arrows and then run away from the pursuit. With a 180-degree shooting radius, they could hit the enemy arriving, from the side and leaving, and heavy arrows thrown from composite bows pierced the knights' wire armour. The knights' unarmoured horses also fell as victims, since in the early eleventh century there was no particular danger from archers in Europe, not counting the crossbows.

The tactic of Muslim warriors was completely simple and long known throughout the Asian steppes, the horsemen's old country. Archers were sent ahead, with the intention to go around the enemy's flanks and get behind. Always on the move, they showered the enemy with arrows until they were forced to start in pursuit in order to stop the losses or else the rain of arrows forced them to retreat. Now, heavy cavalry would get to the scene to provide the final blow to the weakened and disorganized enemy. The 'hit and run' tactics of the Turkish horse archers was a constant danger for Christian lines of supply too, as well as marching files where again, the towing, pack and riding animals were the most exposed, which slowed the crusaders terrifically and forced them to throw away much equipment, food and animal food. The consequence was that warriors were exhausted from carrying the burden instead of the fallen pack animals, but also from lack of food and water, tiredness caused by constant vigilance and skirmishes, and in the end, it led to the desertion of many panicking warriors and their escorts, who then became easy targets for Muslim horsemen. Since, due to the weight of their armour and the size of their battle horses, the knights were not able to successfully pursue Muslim light horsemen, Christians were also forced to take up mounted archers, the aforementioned turcopoles, where knightly Orders were in the lead.

Abbasid caliphs could not trust the local warriors, more loyal to their nobles, tribal elders and their own families than the rules. This is why, starting in the ninth century, among foreign slaves of the lowest rank, they would choose young men believed to have the potential to grow and be trained into excellent warriors thanks to their physical and psychological characteristics. In Iraq, they usually chose slaves of Turkish descent, while in Egypt they bought Armenians, Turks, Sudani, Georgians and the Cumans. After the young men accepted Islam, their military and religious training started in isolated barracks where they were instructed in faith, courage and nobility, horsemanship tactics, riding, handling bows and arrows and treating injuries. After the completion of the training they were freed, but remained living within their garrison, tied to a master, either a nobleman or the ruler himself. They would still compete in archery and keep up their riding and

A Seljuk Turk heavy cavalryman. They were mostly composed of *Ghilman* (slave soldiers or mercenaries) trained at their lord's expense. Loyal service was granted with freedom. *Ghilman* served as a master's bodyguard and fought in bands for high payment. His head, neck and chest are covered with a long mail aventail hanging loose from his helmet. A lamellar cuirass protected his torso. High boots with protection for the knees are fastened to the waist belt. A *gurz* zoomorphic mace, composite bow and sword are his main weapons. (*Seljuk Rum, Army Museum, Istanbul, Turkey*)

A Mamluk (property) horseman. As *Ghilman* they were slaves during military service. Bonded together, they were a knightly military class, or *fursan* (knights), ideal warriors. As with their predecessors, the *Ghilman*, they were trained to use all kinds of weapons. This archer carries a kalkan shield on the left upper arm which allowed him to use a bow. Persian gaiters, a mail shirt under a long-sleeved garment and a helmet covered with a scarf completed the vision of this desert warrior. Although almost all contemporary Egyptian sources represented warriors with cloth winding over helmets as turbans, for sure riders covered their faces when it was necessary.

fighting skills. They were a military force loyal to their master because they had no connection with the existing political structures.

The Mamluks were marked with a strong sense of belonging to their brotherhood; they spoke Arabic and, in Muslim countries, they were considered guardians of Islam against the crusaders and Mongolian conquerors. The privileges granted to the Mamluks inspired even free inhabitants of Egypt to go into slavery so they could enter the Mamluk corps. The status of Mamluks was above that of the free Muslim population and they could reach high functions of regional governors (*atabeg*), army commanders, and in the end, in the mid-thirteenth century, they founded the Mamluk Bahri dynasty in Egypt. The name was derived from the Bahriya unit consisting of Kipchak Turks and the Cumans, whose seat was on the island of Rodah on the Nile. The Mamluks were the basic military force of the medieval Islam world and in 1291, by conquering Acre, they destroyed the remains of the Crusader States overseas.

All Asian warriors were excellent horsemen on good riding horses. Unlike the European warriors, they rode almost exclusively on mares who obeyed their riders better and were not mutually belligerent, which was of crucial importance particularly for riding archers, providing them with the necessary calm and security in riding and letting their arrows loose.

The Templars adapted to their overseas enemy but, on their path of war, they met another enemy, who turned out to be immeasurably more difficult. In the steppes of Central Asia, with its rough continental climate with long icy winters where winds on the plains can blow hard enough to throw a rider off his horse, in the early thirteenth century the strongest medieval army started forming. Life in a harsh climate resulted in a cruel, somewhat glum and stoic people, prepared to accept pain but also to inflict it callously and to kill ruthlessly. Each man's obligation was to learn riding and using the bow and arrow at an early age. They were perfect warrior material. They lived in tribes divided into patriarchal clans. Each clan had their own habitation or horde (*ordu*), in which every polygamous family lived in their own tent (yurt) made from a wooden frame over which a felt cover was spread. A tribe was led by Khan, his officials were the *noyani*, and the lower aristocracy, similar to European knights, was known as the *bahaduri*. Under the tribe of Genghis Khan who united all the tribes, the people were called Mongolians, even though some Mongol tribes were larger, such as the Naimans, the Merkit, the Kerait and the Tatars. All men above the age of 20 were obliged to answer the call to arms, with the exception of priests of any religion, surgeons and washers of the dead. Mongolian armies consisted not only of Mongolian tribes; they were also filled with conquered enemies or neighbouring nomad tribes who joined them voluntarily for pillaging.

The Mongol army differed from medieval Christian and Muslim armies in the long joint training of their units, which allowed them very precise battle action. Genghis Khan introduced the custom of the 'great hunt'. In times of peace, before winter time, the whole of the Mongolian army in full readiness went hunting as if they were going on a military campaign. Such a hunt lasted for three months. The army would spread into a line of 12 kilometres and, following a sign, they would start forward, driving all potential prey before them. Small animals, deer and does, foxes, bears and even packs of wolves and tigers escaped before the masses of hunters. At night half the army slept under full arms, while the other half, deployed by the officers, made sure the animals did not run. As long as the chase lasted, no animal could be killed, nor could it escape through Mongol lines. If that should happen, the warrior the animal had passed and his officer were both severely punished. As the days passed and the prey accumulated, the army's wings spread more and more before the centre of the Mongolian army, thus preventing the prey from escaping either left or right before the marching warriors. When, hundreds of kilometres further on, the army's vanguard finally reached the goal marked by banners, the wings started one towards the other, thus closing the ring around the prey trapped in the middle. Thousands of distraught animals were surrounded by the Mongolian army. On the last day of the hunt, the Khan would first choose his own prey and then the rest of the warriors could kill. Edible animals were killed for food, while the others could be massacred by a weapon of any warrior's choice. Some warriors died trying to show off and kill a beast with their bare hands. The day of slaughter ended by an old man and a young maiden approaching the Khan, begging him to release the surviving animals. Once their request was fulfilled, the hunt that graphically showed all warriors what they could expect on campaign would end.

The next important difference between the Mongols and other people was their choice of commanders, who were chosen for their experience and loyalty, not by their noble birth and the size of their property. The Khan's confidence in his commanders was such that they had completely free rein in the execution of their orders. The Mongolian army also used to spy on the enemy, long before the start of the campaign, detailed planning was based on gathered information, and strong reconnaissance patrols were sent far ahead (up to 100km) and to the flanks of the army, which gave them an immense advantage over the enemy. Mongols were also the only people who attacked even in the middle of winter, using the weather for fast advances. No one before or after the Mongols managed to take Russia in the middle of winter.

The largest Mongolian unit was a *tumen*, which could be compared to a cavalry division. A *tumen* had 10,000 horsemen, divided into ten *minghans* of 1,000 men each. Guard *tumen* consisted of *minghans* of daily guard, night guard and quiver-carriers, each in different uniforms and on horses of a different colour, and seven *minghans* of the old elite bodyguards in black armour and uniforms on black horses with red equipment. The 1,000 warriors within a *minghan* were divided into ten *jaguns* of 100 horsemen each as in military squadrons, and these in turn consisted of ten of the smallest Mongolian army units, *arbans*, of ten people each. The ten chose their commander and the ten *arbana* commanders in turn chose the commander of the *jagun*. Commanders of the *tumen* and *minghan* were appointed by the Khan himself. These commanders held the rank of *noyans*. The Mongolian army consisted of several cavalry *tumen*, several *minghan* of engineers and throwing devices, commanded by an *orlok*. Each Mongolian army consisted of the left wing (east, *Junghar*), right wing (west, *Baraunghar*) and centre (*Khol*), mostly consisting of the guard (*keshik*) made up of the best units of the sons of *jaguna* and *minghan* commanders and chosen warriors. The army horde (encampment) was served by officers (*yurtich*) whose duty it was to choose the place for the encampment, erect it and provision it.

The tents traditionally turned towards the south, and each *arban* had two tents where food was brought daily. The camps also had places where Chinese and Persian doctors provided care. The camp was visited daily by officers to check the condition of the equipment, and carelessness or loss of a part of the equipment was cruelly punished, just like other oversights in the service. For example, the first transgression among guard units was punished with thirty whiplashes and the

A Mongol heavy cavalryman: peaked segmented helmet with leather nape defence and leather armour reinforced with metal lamellas; spear with the riveted hook for unhorsing an enemy; a sword and two bows, one ready for use, the other one unstrung in the quiver.

next one with seventy. Cruel strictness ensured strict discipline typical of a real army, a complete opposite to undisciplined feudal armies.

During the march Mongols moved in files and they attacked simultaneously and together. They entered battles in five rows of units, of which the first two were heavy cavalry on armoured horses, armed with lances, swords and maces, while the remaining three were made up of light archers and javelin-throwers. Every row was made up of *jaguns* and there were large gaps between them. Once the battle started, the light cavalry *jaguns* would run between the heavy horsemen towards the enemy who would get buried in a shower of arrows and javelins with no direct contact. The rest of the light horsemen would start surrounding them simultaneously on both flanks, trying to reach behind the enemy's back, as in the great hunt. If they were attacked, the *jagun* of light cavalry would retreat and the next one would take its place, keeping the coming enemy under fire. Everything took place in silence, with commands issued by black and white flag signals in daytime and using lamps by night. Once the enemy was sufficiently exhausted and distraught from the onslaught of arrows and javelins, heavy cavalry would step in to deal the final blow. Drummers on the backs of camels gave the signal for assault with their large drums, accompanied by the earth-shattering howling of the Mongol army. After the silence in which light cavalry had thrown their arrows and javelins, the thunder of drums and the howling were intended to completely frighten the already shaken enemy.

Mongols never completely closed off the enemy's escape route, making them think they might save themselves, but it was in vain. Whoever panicked and started running was hunted to exhaustion, caught and ruthlessly finished off. In that respect, the Mongols were also an exception. While other armies stopped the battle, preoccupied by spoils, Mongols did not consider a battle to be over until the enemy was completely destroyed. The Mongols also used catapults to throw buckets of burning tar to create smokescreens, or threw firebombs in terrain where their light cavalry was unable to manoeuvre in order to force the enemy to move from the position. Otherwise catapults, ballistas and engineers remained in the back, as did reserve horses.

Mongolian horses were the successors of ancient Przewalski horses: hairy and sturdy, with wide foreheads, short legs, resistant and brave. When the Mongols conquered Uzbekistan and Turkmenistan, they started crossing their own horses with Arab breeds. A Mongol war horse was 13 to 14 hands in height, somewhat taller than the contemporary Mongol horse, and some could reach a full 16 hands. Mongols rode horses intensively in the first two years of the animal's life, which taught them obedience at a young age. Then they would let them graze for the following three years and afterwards rode them again, while some were prepared for war. They would often organize long horse races to check their stamina. Every warrior took at least three riding horses to war in joint *tumen* herds. In long marches, reserve horses went behind each warrior, so he could change the riding animal in motion without stopping and sleep in the saddle, drinking the blood of the weakest horse instead of taking food. Mongolian warriors rode mares who gave them milk, blood and even meat if necessary. Weak horses were killed for food anyway, and those ridden by messengers sometimes died from exhaustion.

However, those were situations when there was no other choice. Mongols were very careful with their horses, regarding them as their most valuable property. They took better care of them than the Muslim warriors. It was even forbidden to lead a horse with a bit in its mouth. They did not drive horse herds, but rather led them using the mares' instinct to follow the stallions, or stallions and foals following a mare. The war horse that carried a warrior to battle was respected like any other comrade in arms and was never killed for food. A decrepit or old war horse would be released to pasture. If the warrior died or was killed, the horse followed him to death so their spirits could still ride together. Mongols paid special attention to the colour of their horses; many were dappled, and herds were gathered together by colour. White horses were particularly valued and only princes and shamans were deemed worthy of riding them.

There were no important differences between the military systems of the medieval West and East. Both relied on more or less undisciplined horsemen, individually equipped and trained, with a small difference in battle action introduced by Eastern light cavalry archers and javelin-throwers. In the twelfth and thirteenth centuries, the difference was largely removed by the introduction of identical or similar light horsemen to European feudal armies. Only Mongols took a large step in the construction of an orderly army whose strength was based on joint training, existence of units and firm discipline.

From the War Path

What Hugh de Payens and the Templars did in the military sense in the first years of the Temple's existence has not been written down. In the beginning, they probably stayed close to the basic idea of protecting the pilgrims' routes as they built a fortress, a hospice and a chapel by Cisterna Rubea, halfway between Jerusalem and Jericho, and then a tower near Jericho, a fortress and a monastery at the place of the forty-day fast and temptation of Jesus and a fortress on the River Jordan where Jesus was baptized by John the Baptist. The first fortress the Templars got outside the pilgrims' paths was Bagras or, as the Temple knights called it, Gaston, dominating the Aleppo plain and guarding the Belen Pass mountain crossing (also known as the Syrian Gates or the Door of Syria), between Cilicia and Antioch, and later, for the protection of the same crossing, even further northwards, they built the fortresses of Trapessac and la Roche de Roussel.

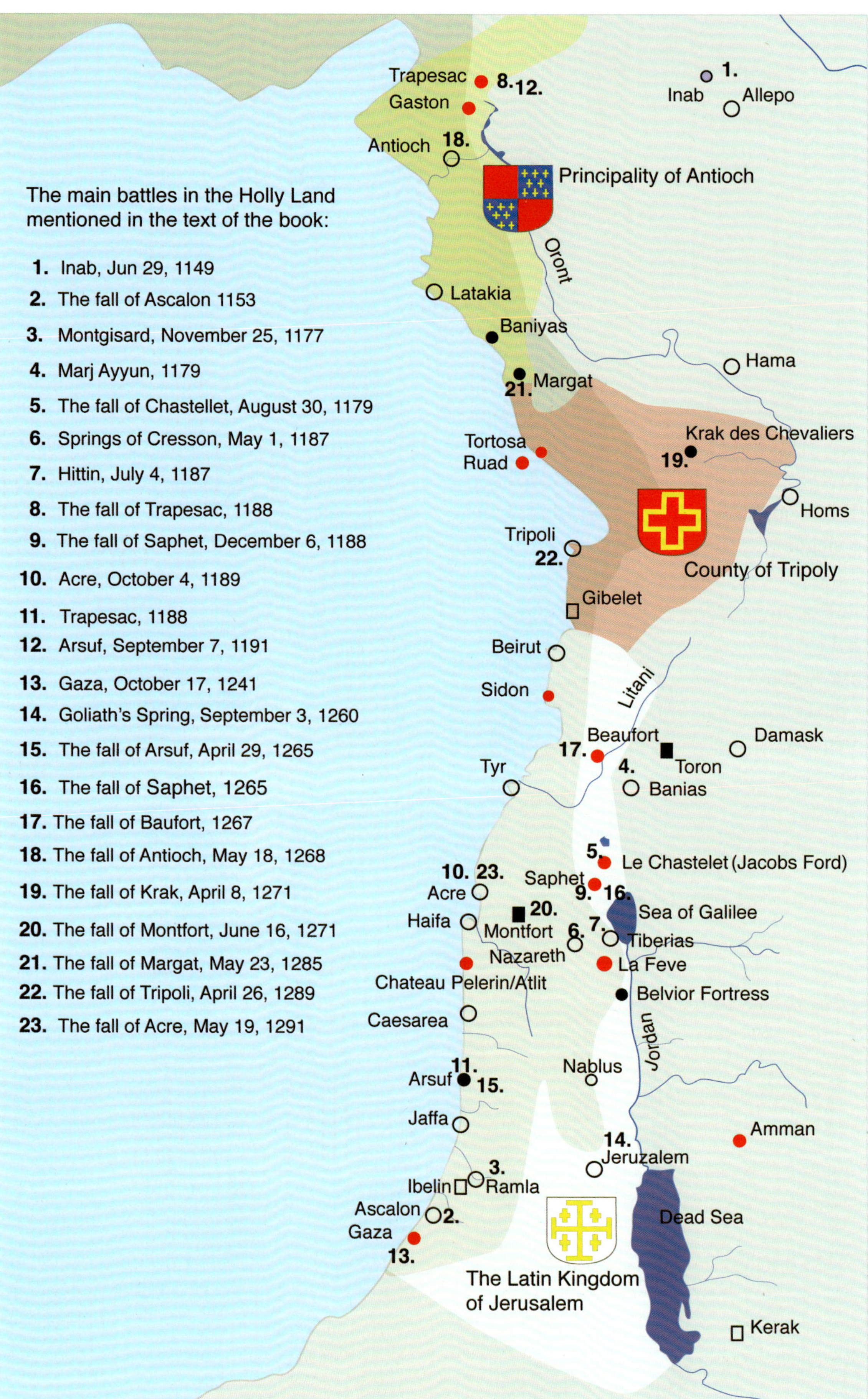

Map of crusader fortresses and major battles.

In 1129 King Baudouin II organized a campaign in Damascus after Hugh de Payens and William de Bures[1] returned from Europe with the requested reinforcements led by Fulk V, Count of Anjou.

The whole army of the Kingdom of Jerusalem, together with help from Europe, started in November under the fortress of Baniyas. They arrived only about 12 kilometres from Damascus with no resistance and camped at the place known as the Wooden Bridge, south-west of the city. Turkish atabeg[2] Taj al-Muluk Buri took up position between the city and Baldwin II. Bures and the European newcomers were in charge of gathering food and materials from the surrounding area needed to besiege Damascus. However, these people cared primarily for pillaging. During one of their forays, some 30km south of the Christian camp they were attacked by light Turcoman cavalry and, despite courageous fighting, the Franks were defeated. Only Bures and forty-five of his men managed to get out alive and return to the Christian camp. Hearing about the battle, Baldwin decided to attack immediately. However, a great storm broke and the plain became a quagmire in the blink of an eye. Any forward movement became impossible and Baldwin decided to give up on the siege. In complete order, his army returned to the fortress of Baniyas, after which it was dismissed. A Templar squadron had been part of this unsuccessful campaign.

Pope Eugenius III, a former Cistercian monk at Clairvaux, addressed the French King Louis VII in 1145 with the proclamation *Quantum praedecessores* asking the king to start a crusade in response to the Muslim taking of Edessa in 1144. The 25-year-old Louis could not attract enough of his peers on his own, so he was helped by Bernard of Clairvaux, who delivered one of his most inspired speeches in Vezalay and then started travelling through Flanders with the same mission. He addressed the English in writing. The response was great, of which Bernard wrote to the pope: 'You ordered, I obeyed; and the authority of the one who had issued the order made my obedience fruitful. Villages and towns are abandoned. You will hardly find one man to seven women. Everywhere there are widows whose husbands are still alive.'

Louis thus became the first European ruler to lead a crusade. Bernard also visited Germany, calling for a campaign in the Holy Land. Here, too, pointing out the possibility of salvation and absolution, he managed to win over the German King Conrad III and his followers. In 1147, the Pope came to France to say goodbye to the pilgrims. Accompanied by King Louis, the Archbishop of Rheims, 4 bishops and 130 knights, on 27 April he attended the council of the Order of Templars at the Temple property near Paris. The master of the Templars invited his best knights from Spain and Portugal for the occasion. Numerous knights in white and many black and brown sergeants of the Temple left a strong impression on Eugenius III. It is believed that it was the occasion when the Pope, inspired by the view of bearded warrior faces in monk habits, flooded by religious fervour, decided to allow the Templars to wear the red sign of the cross over their hearts in remembrance of the red blood of martyrs.

Some 20,000 German crusaders, including the vassal forces of Czechs under King Vladislaus, Poles under King Boleslaus IV and warriors from Lorraine, started in May from Regensburg. The French started from Metz a few weeks later, led by their own king, more religious than the militant Louis. A Templar squadron was also strong among the French crusaders.

Almost 60 years old, sickly and weak, Conrad wasn't capable of keeping his army disciplined. He crossed the Bosporus first, leaving the civilians on the shore under the protection of Byzantium, and went on to Anatolia. By Dorylaeum, his army stopped at a small river. Joining the infantry, the riders dismounted to slake their thirst and rest their horses. All of a sudden they were attacked by a mass of light Turkish horsemen and the slaughter began. The king and only a tenth of his army returned to Nicaea, where they waited for the French. Both kings then started towards Ephesus, but Conrad fell ill along the way and returned to Constantinople. All the way through imperial properties, there were conflicts with Byzantine warriors who defended the lands from crusaders' pillaging. In order to stop the skirmishes, Louis sent the Templar's master des Barres and two more negotiators to arrange a truce with the Byzantine Emperor Manuel Comnenus.

In December 1147, Louis continued from Ephesus towards the Byzantine port of Antalya, where he arrived in early February 1148. The road led the crusaders through high and desolate mountains. Winter cold, thirst and hunger, combined with frequent attacks from Turkish light cavalry threatened to destroy the French pilgrims. In a hilly landscape, among narrow mountain passes, European heavy horsemen, who would have made short work of the enemy in open land, had no chance. The only disciplined unit remained the Templar one. The grand master Everard des Barres divided the whole Frank army into units led by the Templars. Everyone took a vow to follow their orders unquestioningly, after which the Franks resisted the attacks of the enemy archers, overcoming the temptation to charge towards the enemy's pretended escape. They would wait for the opportunity to perform a simultaneous charge at the best moment, so as to jump the majority of the enemy forces. The Templars even managed to align the movement within the marching file so groups of warriors no longer lagged behind, exposed to the danger of becoming surrounded and certainly destroyed. Once they left the mountains, the path became safer because Turks did not dare to attack in the open. Out of Antalya, a smaller portion of the French army was transferred to the port of St Simeon under Antioch by ship. The rest were left to their own devices. After the German King Conrad disembarked in Acre, both rulers arrived in Jerusalem in May 1148. There a new campaign on Damascus was arranged and ended with complete defeat of the crusaders' army on 28 July that same year.

The grand master of the Temple, des Barres, stood down from his duties in 1152 and withdrew to monastic life at Clairvaux. That same year, the German King Conrad died. The instigator of the Second Crusade, Pope Eugenius III, died in July 1153 and Bernard only a month later. As the lives of these four men reached their ends, overseas power relations changed in favour of the Muslims.

The biggest enemy of Christianity overseas was Nur al-Din,[3] a member of the Turkish Zengid Dynasty, and emir of Syria, then a province of the Seljuk Empire. His life's mission was the destruction of the Crusader States in the Holy Land. William of Tyre described him as a persecutor of Christianity, but also as a respectable righteous man, cunning, wise and religious. He directly threatened the duchy of Antioch and the county of Edessa.

In 1149 the duke of Antioch, Raymond of Poitiers[4] and his ally Ali ibn-Wafa, head of the Hassasins[5] and Nur al-Din's enemy, undertook a small campaign (400 knights and 1,000 infantry) against Nur al-Din, who was besieging the fortress of Inab, one of the few Christian fortresses east of the River Orontes. Nur al-Din had at his disposal 6,000 men, mostly horsemen. Believing that the army was merely a Frank vanguard, the atabeg withdrew from Inab. Raymond decided to spend the night away from the protection of the fortress on the plain, near a freshwater spring. When

Nur al-Din realized that this was the entirety of the Frank army, he commanded his warriors on the night of 28 July to surround the Christian camp by the spring of Murad. In the morning, Raymond tried to fight his way out of the surroundings. The weather was against the Christians. The wind carried dust into the faces of knights, who were in a bad position in the first place, riding uphill. Raymond was a huge man and fought bravely, cutting down everyone who dared approach him. After a two-hour battle, Raymond and ibn-Wafa were killed and most of their small army destroyed. The majority of the duchy of Antioch fell into the hands of the Turkish atabeg.

Joscelin II[6] was the last to rule the county of Edessa. When his neighbour Raymond needed help, Joscelin stayed away and he met his just deserts. In April 1150, on the way to Antioch, he was captured by Turcoman highwaymen with the intention of letting him go in exchange for a ransom, but Nur al-Din was faster. His horsemen took Joscelin away from the robbers and took him to Aleppo, Nur al-Din's capital, where Joscelin was blinded and imprisoned. He died in captivity in 1159.

Thus two Christian states, the duchy of Antioch and the county of Edessa, lost their leaders and almost ceased to exist. Antioch would have surrendered to Nur al-Din had not Baldwin,[7] the king of Jerusalem, come to help them with a small escort consisting mostly of Templars. The king's appearance forced al-Din to sign a long-term peace agreement in 1150, according to which Christians only kept part of the duchy, Antioch and the surrounding plains, and a part of the coast between Alexandretta and Latakia. Nur al-Din became a Muslim hero and decided to ruin the Christian states by calling for a *jihad* (holy war).[8]

While the situation in the north was getting out of control, in the south of the Kingdom of Jerusalem the conditions were somewhat better. A Fatimid Egyptian caliphate held the city and port of Ashkelon, from which Egyptian warriors regularly attacked the surrounding area. Jerusalem's King Fulk (1131–42) had the idea of surrounding Ashkelon with fortresses in order to limit the enemy's range of action. First he built the fortress of Ibelin by Ramla, controlling the ancient Roman road of Via Maris connecting Cairo and Damascus and Jaffa and Jerusalem; next were Blanche Garde and Bethgibelin, given to the Hospitallers. His successor Baldwin III finished the fortress on the ruins of Gaza in 1150 and gave it to the Templars to manage, which completed the surrounding of Ashkelon. Now it was possible to attack Ashkelon. In January 1153, the grand siege of the city began, including both knightly Orders: Templars under the grand master Bernard de Tremelay and Hospitallers under their master Raymond du Puy. The problem was in the fact that the besieged couldn't be forced to surrender through famine because the city's reserves were sufficient for the defenders to last up to a year. The city was large and strongly fortified with fifty-three new towers and the number of defenders was greater than that of the besiegers.

The siege lasted, with changing fortunes of war, for a full five months when in May the Egyptian fleet delivered new supplies. The small crusaders' fleet was unable to prevent this. Everything seemed impossible for Jerusalem's army until the night of 15 August when the defenders set one of the siege towers near the city bulwarks on fire. In normal conditions this would have been a success for the defenders but, to their misfortune, the wind changed direction and the flames caught the city walls. Part of the wall broke from the heat and crumbled. As this part of the wall was besieged by the Temple, de Tremelay and forty Templars burst into the city. The defenders surrounded them and cut them down, exposed their bodies on the city walls, sent their heads to Cairo and quickly walled up the break in the bulwarks.

According to the chronicler William of Tyre, the fate that met the Templars was purely the product of their master's greed, as he'd commanded his men not to allow the entrance to other crusaders so that all the glory of taking the city and most of the spoils would go to the Temple. On the other hand, the Muslim chronicler of the siege doesn't even mention the event, so the veracity of William, who never liked the Templars, can be questioned. The fiasco discouraged the besiegers, and it was only the Hospitallers' insistence that prevented Baldwin from returning to Jerusalem, his business unfinished. Four days later, after a lengthy bombing of the city, the defenders decided to negotiate terms of surrender. Defenders and the population were allowed to leave and most of them went to Egypt. Spoils of war and the strong fortress were the grand prize and the pinnacle of Baldwin III's rule. Although they'd lost quite a few men under Ashkelon, the Templars were still capable of patrolling along the caravan road leading from Damascus to Cairo from their base in Gaza. The following year, they attacked a unit accompanying the Vizier[9] Abbas and his son Nasr al-Dina. The two were escaping from Cairo after the murder of the caliph and an unsuccessful attempt at a coup d'état. Abbas was killed and Nasr and large amounts of treasure taken. William of Tyre wrote about the consequences of this event. He claims that, in incarceration, Nasr had learned Latin and was prepared to convert to Christianity, but the greedy Templars decided to return him to Egypt for a huge ransom; there, he was first mutilated by the caliph's widows and then hanged. Whether William was truthful when accusing the Templars of inappropriate greed we do not know, but their behaviour was appropriate for victors of their times.

Both the Templars and the Hospitallers had huge expenses in the upkeep of their fortresses and armies, and any income was welcome. Not even the rich properties and all the income could save the Hospitallers from going bankrupt in the 1170s.

While passing through the valley of the River Jordan in 1158, grand master of the Temple Bertrand de Blanchefort, as well as 87 brothers and 300 secular knights, was captured and taken to Aleppo, where he remained a prisoner for the following three years.

At the court of Baudouin III, Reynald de Châtillon,[10] a knight who remained overseas after the Second Crusade, stood out with his courage, cruelty and attractive appearance. Believing in his warrior abilities, the king appointed him the duke of Antioch, after which Reynald started for his duchy and, with the Templars' agreement, took Alexandretta, which he then gifted to the Temple as a sign of gratitude. Reynald turned out to be a bad and stupid duke. Killing, raping and pillaging the Christian population, in 1156 he joined forces with the Armenian Lord Toros[11] to invade the previously peaceful island of Cyprus. As the king of Byzantium was Baldwin's ally and future son-in-law (the royal wedding between Baldwin and Theodora took place in 1158 in Jerusalem), Reynald had to be punished. Toros fled before the Byzantine army into the Armenian mountains, while Reynald was forced to humble himself before the emperor, Manuel Comnenus. Barefoot and bare-headed, he exited the walls of Mamistra and threw himself in the dust before the emperor, his court and army. After this humiliation and the imposed conditions of forgiveness, he was allowed to go to Antioch as imperial governor, but Reynald had learned nothing. In 1160, he attacked

Syrian cattle-growers and stole a herd of livestock. Upon his return he was ambushed by Aleppo horsemen, who captured him and his ransom remained unpaid for the following sixteen years.

Baldwin III died in 1163 at the age of only 33, respected by his followers but also by his biggest enemy, Nur al-Din. Baldwin's successor and brother Amalric,[12] tall and hairy with an aquiline nose, tending to thicken, stammering and often suffering bursts of noisy laughter, the previous governor of Ashkelon left the defence of the northern borders to his Byzantine allies and decided to take on his old enemy, the caliphate of Egypt himself. With the help of numerous Templar warriors, Amalric started towards Egypt in the autumn of 1163, but a network of trenches and ditches in the Nile delta, which he couldn't cross, forced him to retreat. The following year, he undertook another campaign, also with no particular effect, except for the signing of peace with Vizier Shawar, the regent for the juvenile Caliph al-Adid.

Using Amalric's absence from the kingdom, Nur al-Din attacked the duchy of Antioch and besieged the fortress of Harenc, so the Duke of Antioch, Bohemond III,[13] son of Raymond de Poitiers, rushed to help with a small army of 600 knights including Templars. Nur al-Din retreated from the siege and young Bohemond followed him despite advice to the contrary and the fact that his army was much smaller. He was lured to ambush with the usual Turkish tactics of false flight and was completely defeated. Sixty Templar knights died there, while seven brothers managed to save themselves.

In 1166, the Templar garrison gave Nur al-Din the fortress on Jordan, even though it had been thought impregnable, and King Amalric was on his way to help the defenders. On the way, in anger, he had the twelve Templars who had abandoned the fortress hanged.

Poor leadership of Christian forces among secular commanders and the attitude of King Amalric towards the knights of the Temple spurred the Templars to rely on their own judgement in military issues and use their right to obey only the Pope and not secular rulers. In 1168, when Amalric organized a campaign in Egypt counting on all the available forces of the Kingdom of Jerusalem, most of his vassals and the Hospitallers agreed, but Templars' master Bertrand de Blanchefort openly told him that the Templars would not be part of the campaign. Though a skilled warrior, Bertrand preferred negotiations and launched the Templars' image as guardians, not uncivil warriors. However, in this case the Templars were accused of greed because they co-operated with Italian merchants in Egypt, so it was not in their interests to disturb the situation in Cairo. They were also accused of obstructing the campaign because it had been conceived by the rival order of the Hospitallers, for which this was perhaps the last opportunity to avoid bankruptcy by gaining significant spoils of war. The truth was probably different. The Templars had suffered a difficult loss. They kept forces along the borders of overseas Christian properties and, unlike Amalric's councillor William IV, Count of Nevers, who had only just arrived from Europe, they were trying to resolve conflicts diplomatically so as to avoid a military conflict in circumstances unfavourable to Christians. The conflict between Amalric and the Templars went so far that the king decided to ask the Pope to dismiss the Order, but death was faster than the 38-year-old ruler. Both Amalric and Nur al-Din died in 1174.

Amalric's throne was inherited by the 13-year-old leprous King Baldwin IV.[14] Until he reached his majority, the regent was supposed to be his cousin, Count Raymond III[15] of Tripoli, an experienced and cautious dark-skinned knight with an aquiline nose who had spent years in Muslim captivity, where he learned Arabic and gained insight into the nature of the enemy. The Hospitallers and leading families of the Kingdom of Jerusalem stood with him, while the opposition was led by the Templars and the notorious Reynald de Châtillon. Raymond III was in Gerard de Ridefort's bad graces because de Ridefort had entered the count's service in 1173 and was promised the hand of the first available heiress in the county. However, the count reneged on his promise, giving the girl's hand to a rich nobleman from Pisa for a large sum of money. Gerard joined the Templars and became the Order's seneschal but never forgot this insult.

The leadership of Nur al-Din, a warrior and God-fearing ruler, managed to unite the emirs from other provinces of the Seljuk Empire, showing that it was possible to start a joint holy war against the Franks. During his lifetime in Egypt grew the future ruler of the Middle East, Salah ad-Din Jusuf,[16] known as Saladin, a Mamluk of Kurdish origin. Saladin was shortish, with black hair and dark eyes, a thoughtful, melancholy face, handy with weapons like any Mamluk, but also learned like all the Muslim elite, religious, merciful when it was needed, generous, but also cruel in decisive moments. He tried to be kind towards everybody, except towards those belonging to knightly Orders, who he regarded as his worst enemies and towards whom he showed no mercy at all. Saladin's father Ayub was one of two of Nur al-Din's most trusted warriors. The other was Saladin's uncle Shirkuh, a brilliant one-eyed warrior who best realized the strategic importance of conquering Egypt.

In early 1169 Nur al-Din sent Shirkuh and Saladin with an army of 8,000 horsemen to overthrow the pro-Franks Vizier Shawar and take over Egypt, a mission they completed successfully by March. Shirkuh proclaimed himself vizier and king of Egypt, but died soon afterwards. After his uncle's sudden death, Saladin was appointed vizier, which was to the liking of the youthful caliph and his councillors, hoping that the inexperienced Saladin would be easier to control than one of Shirkuh's leading emirs, but Caliph al-Adid died in 1171. Acting independently and defying his former master, Saladin took over power and, destroying the heretic Shiite caliphate of the Fatimid, renewed Egypt's connections with the Sunnite Abbasid Caliphate of Baghdad. After Nur al-Din's death, Saladin peacefully entered Damascus and took Hama and Homs in the following year, 1175, provoking the enmity of his former masters from the Zengid Dynasty. After militarily defeating them, he was proclaimed sultan of Egypt and Syria by the Abbasid Caliph Al-Mustadi. The Mamluk dynasty that would rule the Middle East by the end of the thirteenth century was constituted. Nur al-Din had been a prudent ruler and military leader, whose actions had constrained the Seljuks' conquering intentions.

Seljuk Sultan Kilij Arslan II[17] used the tumult created by the death of Nur al-Din and attacked Byzantium in 1176. Emperor Manuel's army was completely defeated at Myriokephalon. Anatolia fell forever under Turkish rule, and the crusaders in the Holy Land remained alone and cut off from the Christian world. The Kingdom of Jerusalem could only rely on itself. Baldwin IV and his governor Raymond hoped for a new crusade, but the only one to arrive in September was Flanders' Count Philip and he was there only for the pilgrimage and not to wage war.

The exact number of Christian barons and knights permanently inhabiting the Kingdom of Jerusalem with their families is unknown but, in the best of times, they couldn't have been more than 1,000. The county of Edessa never counted more than 100 knightly families, the county of Tripoli around 200 and Antioch slightly more. Apart from the knightly caste, there were many more sergeants, mostly coming from the Frank infantry that settled on the properties of their masters. John of Ibelin[18] claims that, at the time of Baldwin IV, the Kingdom of Jerusalem could raise 577 knights and 5,025 sergeants. In addition, there were warrior mercenaries and turcopoles, light cavalry gathered and trained following the Byzantine model, whose name comes from the Greek expression meaning 'sons of Turks'. The turcopoles originated partly from orthodox Syrian Christians and partly from converted Seljuks or from mixed families. Apart from serving for reconnaissance and skirmishes for the crusaders, the lightly-armoured turcopoles sometimes attacked in the second assault wave as support for the knights and sergeants.

The numbers mentioned show that the king of Jerusalem could in no way gather a respectable army without the knightly Orders. According to sporadic and unreliable claims which do not mention all the brothers spread out in Templar garrisons, in the kingdom alone the Temple had 300 knights and 1,000 sergeants, plus an unknown number of associate brothers, infantry and turcopoles. The Hospitallers were certainly no less numerous. In the campaign in Egypt in 1158, 500 Hospitaller knights took part. The king's problem lay in the fact that he held no power over the Orders. This was one country with three rulers: the king of Jerusalem, and the respective masters of the Templars and the Hospitallers. The destiny of Christians in the Holy Land depended on the internal relations between these three men.

In 1177 Saladin led his army over the Sinai desert towards the southern borders of the Kingdom of Jerusalem. According to William of Tyre, there were as many as 26,000 Muslim soldiers (8,000 horsemen, 18,000 light infantrymen and a body of camel raiders armed as archers or spearmen). Templars believed that Saladin would attack Gaza, so they concentrated all their available forces there, but he went around them, continuing towards Ashkelon, which forced Baldwin IV to start towards the Muslims. The king's small army entered the city before Saladin's arrival. Knowing that Jerusalem was left unprotected, Saladin left a smaller force to keep Baldwin in Ashkelon and went towards Jerusalem with the majority of his army. He felt safe and allowed his forces to spread over a large territory in pillaging. Baldwin managed to send a message to the Templars to leave Gaza and help him. When they appeared, the king and his men fought their way from the city, and the joint forces started along the coast to the fortress of Ibelin, after which they turned inland, following the careless enemy, who they caught on 25 November in the plains by Montgisard. The Christians decided to attack immediately, while the Egyptians were scattered and tired by the long march. According to William of Tyre, Baldwin had 375 knights, which included the brothers Baldwin[19] and Balian[20] of Ibelin, Joscelin III,[21] Count of Edessa and Reynald de Châtillon, released from his imprisonment in Aleppo a year earlier. The Templars' master Odo de Saint-Amand led around 500 knights of the Temple. There were also several thousand infantrymen.

Before the battle the king dismounted and knelt to say a prayer before the True Cross, having had the relic brought before the army. The warriors all participated in the silent prayer. Then the king rose, met by his army cheering. In the meantime, Saladin was trying to put his force in order and create some semblance of a battle line. Before he had achieved this, Christian heavy cavalry, mostly in white Templar robes, rushed over the sand plains and struck at the still unprepared enemy,

By all means the most magnificent cavalry charge performed by the Knights Templar took place at Montgisard.

inflicting significant losses. It was a magnificent scene, and probably the best-performed Christian cavalry assault overseas. Baldwin fought alongside his knights, hands wrapped in bandages to hide his signs of leprosy. The brothers Ibelin were prominent with their valour. Many Egyptians started fleeing, and a good portion of them threw away their weapons and armour so that they could ride faster. Saladin's Mamluk guard was cut while saving their sultan from capture. Saladin escaped on a racing camel. Jerusalem's army persecuted the enemy until nightfall and then returned victorious to Ashkelon. All the way across Sinai to the Egyptian border, the remains of Saladin's army were attacked and destroyed by Bedouin robbers. Only a tenth of the grand army reached the border with Egypt. Christian losses were also great. According to the report of Roger de Moulins,[22] there were 1,100 dead and another 750 wounded warriors. If Baldwin had had any reserve forces capable of following Saladin to Egypt and attacking Damascus, that could have been the end of the Ayyubid Dynasty. As it was, this was merely a victory that saved the Kingdom of Jerusalem for a short while.

In early summer of 1179, Saladin made camp in Baniyas in north-western Syria and sent units to Lebanon and Galilee with the task of destroying their rich harvest. Baldwin gathered his army, including a large body of the Templars, and called Raymond of Tripoli to join him. Joining forces, they started through Galilee towards the fortress of Toron on the road from Tyre to Damascus. On the way, they learned that one pillaging unit was returning from the coast with their spoils, and decided to cut their way at Marj Ayyun ('Meadow of Springs') between the upper part of the River Jordan and the River Litani. From their vantage point on the hill, Saladin's men saw sheep in panicked flight before the enemy army. Saladin immediately raised his army, intending to catch up with the crusaders. In the meantime, in the valley, the king's men were fighting with the highwaymen, while Count Raymond and the Templars went ahead towards the River Jordan. At the entrance to the valley, they ran into Saladin. The Templars' master Odo de Saint-Amand attacked without a second thought but, outnumbered, he had to retreat. In flight, he crashed among the king's men, causing general havoc. Soon the whole of Baldwin's army was on the run. The king and Raymond found sanctuary in the fortress of Beaufort. A part of the army fled on, but they were cut down before they could cross the River Litani; this group included numerous Templar brothers. Odo de Saint-Amand ended up among the prisoners. He died the following year in captivity, too proud to allow his exchange for one of the captured Muslims. He simply believed that no one was equal to his worth. William of Tyre again blamed the Templars, apparently quite justifiably this time, although for a personal reason: one of his cousins had died in this battle. William accused Odo of adventuring out of arrogance and a thirst for glory, which resulted in the loss of many lives and completely opposed the basic Templar idea of serving the faith humbly and without putting themselves forward. William held it against the Templars that they'd chosen a knight who had previously served in the high secular position of the marshal of Jerusalem as their grand master since this marked him as a man of career rather than one motivated by pure faith.

The same year, in August Saladin won another decisive victory over Jerusalem. In October 1178, Templar Knights began building a fortification called Chastellet Castle at Jacob's Ford on the River Jordan, a key crossing-point on the main road between Damascus and Acre. The finished fortress would cast fear into the sultan's northern invasion. In the summer of 1179 the castle's walls were 10 metres high, overlooked by one tower and in the process of construction. Saladin decided to lay siege and win the fortress before any help could come. His army arrived on 23 August and at once attacked the defenders with arrow showers, depriving them of the possibility of keeping Saladin's sappers far from the walls. Digging a tunnel to the north-east corner of the castle began. In the meantime, the garrison sent runners for help, but although Baldwin was at Tiberias about 10 kilometres from Jacob's Ford, he was not able to assemble his army in the next few days. Not a week passed before the tunnel was finished and miners set a great fire in it, but failed to cause the collapse of overheated walls above the tunnel. So they were forced to put out the fire – a very risky task – and the sultan paid one gold piece per bucket poured over the fire. The re-lighted fire caused a collapse of the walls and the Muslims assaulted through the break and escaladed the walls. By 30 August the castle was captured. This was a great blow to the Templars because they lost 1,500 warriors and experienced workers (800 killed and 700 captured), 80 knights included. Muslims crumbled the whole castle into ruins, but Saladin could not enjoy the victory. The August heat caused the decay of corpses in ruins and a plague killed some of Saladin's major adjutants. Above all, the oncoming winter and spring were extremely dry, sowing produced poor crops and no side wanted military actions to devastate what was left over. In May 1180 Saladin signed a two-year truce with Baldwin's representatives.

On 24 September 1180 Emperor Manuel died in Constantinople;[23] he was the most powerful ally of the Crusader States. The decline of Byzantium in the following years caused by internal unsettled conditions shook the balance of power and imperilled the existence of the Crusader States. An additional threat was the notorious Reynald de Châtillon. At the end of 1182 he undertook pirate voyages on the Red Sea and robbed sea caravans to Mecca, sank Muslim pilgrim ships and attacked the Arabian coast. Even Christian lords cried shame upon his crimes. Saladin vowed that Reynald should never be forgiven and in autumn 1183 the sultan invaded Palestine. Jerusalem assembled the army, much smaller than the Muslim forces. Both armies met at the Spring of Goliath and remained stationary for five days. After unsuccessful attempts to provoke the Christians into attacking, Saladin retired back behind Jordan. In November, the sultan, without success, tried to capture Reynald's stronghold of Kerak. In December he returned to Damascus. Tension between the Christians and Muslims persisted.

A heavy but expected stroke hit Jerusalem in early 1185. The young king Baldwin IV died, overcome by an incurable illness. Raymond of Tripoli, as keeper of the regency, proposed four years of truce to Saladin, who on his side accepted. Thanks to the agreement for a four-year peace between Saladin and the Kingdom of Jerusalem, signed in March 1185, the caravan roads between Damascus and Egypt, passing partly through Christian lands, opened again. Numerous large caravans passed without the danger of being robbed by Frank barons or Muslim emirs.

In late 1186, a huge caravan was on the way from Cairo. The few warriors accompanying it were supposed to protect it only from Bedouin robbers. However, yet again, Reynald de Châtillon showed that he cared not a whit for peace if it went against his own personal interests. He attacked the caravan, killed the escort, imprisoned the merchants and, together with the immense spoils, took them to his fortress of Kerak. Saladin tried to keep the peace by asking Reynald to let the prisoners go and repair the damages. The same was required by the king of Jerusalem, Guy de Lusignan,[24] although his request was lukewarm at best since he was Reynald's friend and

The Battle of Montgisard.

biggest ally. Reynald ignored all demands, and war that would bring certain destruction to the kingdom became inevitable due to the greed and stupidity of one man. Saladin vowed that he would personally kill de Châtillon. Count Raymond of Tripoli and Bohemond of Antioch decided to renew peace negotiations with Saladin and leave the king of Jerusalem to his own devices. Guy saw this as an act of treason and was preparing to start against Raymond. Balian of Ibelin stepped into the fray, warning the king that he would certainly regret giving up on Raymond. The king sent Balian, the masters of the Hospitallers and the Templars and the Archbishop of Acre to Raymond in Tiberias as his negotiators. They were escorted by ten Hospitaller knights. Along the way, Balian turned aside for a day to deal with his own business. At the same time, a Mamluk unit of 7,000 horsemen was passing through the county of Tripoli under the command of Saladin's son al-Afdal, with a mission to explore the situation in Palestine. Al-Afdal invoked the peace agreement and asked for permission to pass peacefully through the county, which was reluctantly approved on condition that he finish his business in one day. Count Raymond sent messengers in the area to prepare the population and travellers. On the evening of 30 April 1187, one of the messengers ran into the masters of Hospitallers and Templars by the fortress of La Fève. On hearing about the passage of the Mamluks, the grand master of the Templars, Gerard de Ridefort, immediately decided to take military action. Master of the Hospitallers Roger de Moulins tried to oppose him, but without success. Gerard called the Templar marshal Jacqueline de Mailly, who was in the village of Qaqun, 8 kilometres away, with ninety Templar knights, to join them immediately.

The following morning they started towards Nazareth, where they were joined by forty secular knights. The unit consisted of 400 infantrymen and an unknown number of turcopoles. They left the archbishop in Nazareth and, as they passed, Gerard shouted out to the population to hurry up and join them to get the spoils. As soon as they climbed the hill above Nazareth, the knights saw thousands of Mamluks watering their horses at the Cresson springs. Roger and Jacqueline prudently advised retreat on seeing the number of the enemy, but Gerard refused to back down and teased his own marshal with the words, 'You like your blond head too much to lose it!' Jacqueline's answer was no more polite: 'I shall die in battle as a brave man. You shall be the one to escape like a traitor!' Provoked by Gerard's cantankerous prodding, the Templars, ten Hospitallers with their grand master and the secular knights rushed downhill towards the mass of the Mamluks. They disappeared in a cloud of dust and enemies. It was simple slaughter. The Templars' marshal and the Hospitallers' master fell next to each other. Roger de Moulins was killed by a spear in his chest. The story goes that Jacqueline was seen last on a white horse, fighting the mass around him with one arm. The gallant knight, respected and admired even by Muslims, slaughtered a number of enemies before he was dead. The surviving knights were taken prisoner. Then the Mamluks dealt with the infantry as well. The greedy inhabitants of Nazareth who had run to the battlefield were taken into captivity. All the Templars and Hospitallers died, except for three who, though wounded, managed to escape death. One of them was Gerard, and Balian tried to convince him to go on with him to Tiberias on the same day, all to no avail as Gerard described his wounds as too severe for him to ride. Yet only two months later he was in full form to participate in a new battle. In fact, the wounds were a perfect excuse so that he wouldn't have to face a hated man. Balian and

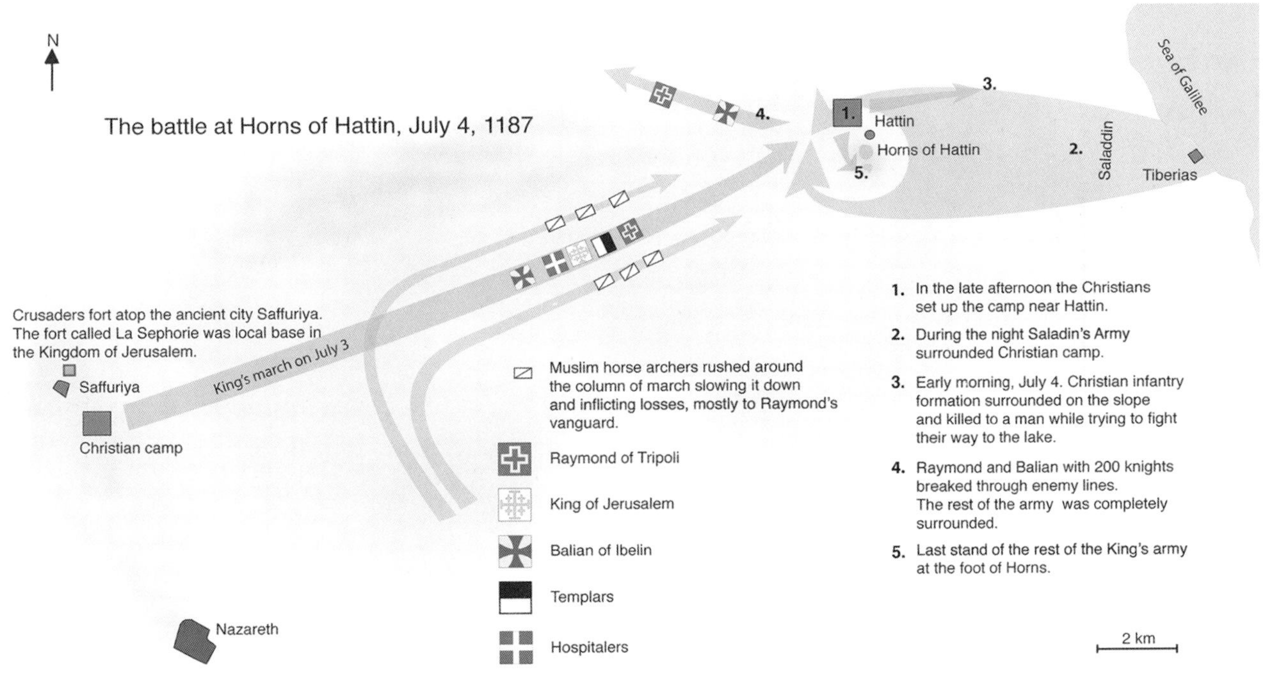

Map of the Horns of Hattin battle.

the archbishop went to Raymond who, deeply affected by the news of defeat and his own feeling of guilt, agreed to join the king of Jerusalem.

Over the following two months, both sides gathered warriors. By the end of July, Saladin had 18,000 men (12,000 regular army plus allies and volunteer units); he had never before led such a great force. He divided it into three files. He commanded the centre himself, his nephew Taqi ad-Din took over the left wing and Kukuburi the right. Having learned from his experience at Montgisard, he put the army into battle formation during the march itself. He crossed the Jordan on 1 July and, on the following day, encamped the majority of his army in the hills, 8 kilometres west of the Lake of Galilee, while the rest attacked the town and fortress of Tiberias, defended by the wife of Raymond of Tripoli. The king Guy was gathering his forces near Acre. He was only waiting for Antioch, whose unit was led by Baldwin of Ibelin, one of the greatest knights overseas. The Templars and Hospitallers brought all they could. The Templars had even spent the funds left with them by the English King Henry II for his future crusade. The unit they had fitted out with these funds carried a banner with the English king's coat of arms. When he heard that Saladin had crossed the Jordan, the king called a council of war. Careful Raymond advised the king to leave the army where it was, wait for reinforcements from Antioch and force Saladin to attack where it would be advantageous to the Christians, or else to return from whence he'd come since he would not be able to stay in the hills of Galilee for long, but there were opposing voices. Reynald de Châtillon and the grand master of the Temple Gerard demanded that the infidels be attacked. The king agreed with their opinion, so by the afternoon of 2 July, the army camped at le Saforie in a spot perfect for the purpose with plenty of water and grass for the horses.

Saladin was running out of time. He had to force the Franks to a decisive battle before the autumn when his vassals would take their men to their wintering bases. Because of that, he decided

Completely exhausted by the battle, thirst, heat and smoke, unhorsed and unable to hold their weapons, the Christians just awaited their destiny.

to lure the indecisive enemies into a trap. Having taken the town of Tiberias with no problem, he deliberately allowed a handful of the defenders to withdraw into the citadel. A messenger arrived at le Saforie, begging the king to hurry and help the wife of Raymond of Tripoli and her men. Yet another council was held and again, Raymond said the same thing. He reminded everyone that it was his wife defending his fortress, but that it would still be completely unreasonable to undertake a march of over 30km through desert lands with no water and in the middle of the day because that would play directly into Saladin's hands. The council sided with him this time, but later that night the Templars' grand master Gerard went to the king's tent to ask him to change his mind and not allow the chance of saving the fortress of Tiberias to slip away, together with the chance to avenge those killed at Cresson. In Gerard's opinion, Raymond was not to be trusted as he'd shown once before that he was prepared to turn his back on Christian interests. Guy yielded again, and issued the command to start towards Tiberias at dawn. This was a suicidal idea. His army had 1,200 knights (around 60 of which had been brought by the Count of Tripoli), up to 10,000 infantry and 4,000 turcopoles, and was almost equal in numbers to Saladin's force.

Any military leader knows that, unless his force is significantly stronger in number, there can be no victory over the enemy who had chosen his own terrain and defence position, particularly not when the battle comes after a forced daily march in unfavourable conditions; a similar situation to the one four years earlier at the Goliath Fisheries near le Saforie. On that occasion, Guy followed Raymond's advice and kept the defensive position; after a week, as a reasonable commander, Saladin decided to withdraw his army. One of the Templar grand masters showed himself as a poor leader in 1179 in the Valley of the Spring, but Odo might perhaps be understood as he was immediately reacting to the appearance of the enemy. Only two months before this new event, Gerard had led one-fifth of the overall number of Templar Knights to their deaths. He had learned nothing and now intended, equally unreasonably, to lead the entire army of Jerusalem into almost certain defeat. He was a brave knight, but extremely unskilled as a military leader.

If we now remember Bernard de Tremelay at the Siege of Ashkelon, it seems that the Templars did not know how to choose a good war leader, or perhaps they simply had no one to choose, and yet they were a top-notch military organization by medieval standards. Be that as it may, these examples demonstrate the lack of educated, irreplaceable warriors in medieval Europe.

In the morning, Jerusalem started towards its destiny. Following the right of the owner of the lands they marched through, the vanguard was led by Raymond of Tripoli; behind him was the king with the majority of the army, while the rear was brought up by Reynald and Balian of Ibelin. The king wanted to reach the fresh waters of the River Jordan and the Sea of Galilee by early afternoon. In normal conditions, that would have been a four-hour walk. The day was hot and the air full of dust clouds. Enemy archers rushed around and attacked first the vanguard, then the rear, and then disappeared before any kind of successful counterattack could be mounted. Although Saladin's men only intended to slow the enemy down, according to Ernoul, page to Balian of Ibelin, the Christians suffered significant losses on the way. Only in the late afternoon did the army reach the plateau above the village of Hattin, 8 kilometres west of Tiberias. Both people and horses were practically dying of thirst. Before the crusaders, there rose a hill with two rocky peaks, some 30 metres high, beyond which a gentle slope led down towards the village and the Sea of Galilee.

This was the place that Raymond of Tripoli had chosen for camp, knowing that there was a spring there but, to the Christians' horror, they found it had run dry. Although Raymond wanted to attack immediately, to reach the lake and the necessary water, the Templars' demand that the army should rest because they couldn't go on was accepted. Thus the army set up camp around the dried well on the plateau under the horned rock.

Whoever tried to reach any kind of water during the night was killed. Furthermore, the Muslims unwittingly set dry bushes on the slope alight, so the air was stifling and full of smoke which Saladin used as protection to distribute his forces during the night. At dawn, the Christians realized they were completely surrounded. Immediately after daybreak on Saturday, 4 July 1187, all the Frank infantry tried to fight their way to the lake in a firm fighting formation. The king's command to return couldn't prevent them from leaving. According to one written source, they were stopped on the slope and killed to a man. Many burned in the bushfire dying down. According to another source, the infantry surrendered but was followed by five of Raymond's knights who asked Saladin to kill them all. Later, the Hospitallers called it an act of treason, but it is possible that it was merely pity in order to shorten the death throes of dehydrated people.

Before Saladin's attack on the remainder of the Christian army, following the custom usual for both armies a duel between two hotheads took place. The Christian knight killed a Mamluk erroneously believed to be Saladin's son. Guy commanded Raymond to lead the breach with his knights. The honour was Raymond's because he was lord of the land on which they were fighting. As soon as he started the assault, Taqi ad-Din's men who he attacked moved aside and simply let him pass before the rest of the king's army could follow. He could no longer help those who remained surrounded, so he rode on towards Tripoli with his men. This was later described as a cowardly, traitorous act, even though Imad ad-Din of Isfahan, who was in Saladin's escort, wrote that Raymond's men had suffered serious losses. Immediately after Raymond, Balian of Ibelin and Reginald of Sidon[25] successfully did the same. Several knights of the Temple also escaped with them, as did the grand master of the Hospital, but he died of wounds the day after his arrival in Ashkelon. These two groups saved 200 knights.

Completely surrounded, the rest of the army fought bravely and tenaciously. Thirst and smoke quickly sapped the strength of the king's knights and their horses, so the king and the warriors around him started retreating uphill under the rocks. Almost all the Frank horses were killed and the remaining battle horses were left behind, thirsty, exhausted and wounded. They were no longer of any use. Close to the top of the hill the Franks had intended to set up camp. A red tent for the king was erected. The Muslims continuously attacked and retreated, but the number of surrounded grew smaller and the circle around the king and the Holy Cross, brought to the battle, became narrower and narrower. Finally, the Christian fighters found themselves completely exhausted, unable to hold their weapons and fight. Most knights just lay on the ground. Around noon, Taqi knocked down the red tent and took both the king and the Cross.

The king and his peers were taken before Saladin, who greeted them gracefully, seated the king next to him and offered him cold water. Reynald was immediately next to the king. Saladin would not forgive Reynald's predatory behaviour, so he turned to the knight and cut off his head with a sabre. He ordered that the king, his noblemen and other knights were to be treated with respect for as long as they remained prisoners. The Templars and the Hospitallers were killed, apart from the grand master of the Temple. Terence, one of the Templars who had got out with Balian's group, said that 260 brothers were killed. The following day, the Countess of Tripoli surrendered the fortress of Tiberias. Saladin let her leave for Tripoli in peace. Akko surrendered on 10 July; Balian was forced to surrender Nablus after a short siege, but managed to defend Tyre. Toron and Jaffa also fell. Sidon fell too, and Reynald, who had survived in Hittin, saved himself and now entrenched himself in the strong fortress of Beaufort. Beirut surrendered and by the end of August, south of Tripoli, the only Christian holdings were Tyre, Ashkelon, Gaza and Jerusalem. Saladin first went to Ashkelon and brought Guy and Gerard along. He promised the king freedom if he could persuade the defenders of Ashkelon to surrender. Both the king and the grand master obeyed and tried to talk the defenders into letting Saladin into the city, but the city refused in disgust. After a short siege during which Saladin lost two of his emirs, Ashkelon fell on 4 September. Gaza surrendered immediately, since the Templar garrison obeyed the command from their grand master Gerard. He was freed in return, which brought additional shame on the Christians. Jerusalem fell on 2 October after twelve days of heroic defence led by Balian of Ibelin. The last remaining city on the coast was Tyre, which Saladin failed to take thanks to the accidental arrival of Conrad of Montferrat,[26] who sailed into the city port on 14 July 1187 and immediately successfully organized the defence of the city. Saladin tried to take Tyre in October 1188, but with no success.

Count Raymond died in 1187 with no heir, so the city of Tripoli passed into the hands of Raymond, son of the former count's cousin, Bohemond of Antioch. Tripoli got protection from the Sicilian King William, who sent them a fleet of 50 galleons and 200 knights. Saladin dismissed half his army on the first day of 1188 and set about taking fortresses in the inner part of the Holy Land with the rest. Two strong fortresses, Kerak and Krak de Montreal, surrendered only after sieges of more than a year at the end of 1188 when the defenders ran out of food. Trapessac was lost after a heroic garrison defence. One eyewitness wrote that Templars used their own bodies to stop the holes in the bulwarks. Warriors with red crosses on their chests and shields stood next to one another like a wall. When one fell, the next brother took his place. The formidable Templar fortress Saphet fell after several weeks of bombing on 6 December 1188. Almost all the fortresses fell. The Hospitallers held Krak and the Templars had Tortosa.

The loss of Jerusalem was a heavy blow, primarily for the Temple. The Order dedicated its forces to the defence of the Holy Land, and the possible loss of all Christian lands on the coast of Asia Minor would throw the very need for their existence into question. It was by now vital to quickly increase the Order's military prowess, but it was only Pope Innocent III,[27] as supreme commander of the Temple, who allowed excommunicated knights, previously banned from entering the Order, to take the vow. The Pope thus gave them an opportunity to make up for their violent transgressions in the monks' robes of the Temple. This decision irrevocably undermined the strict discipline that had previously been typical of the brothers, which led to a gradual decline in their military prowess in the thirteenth century, but the Pope had no choice. After the great Christian defeats overseas, interest in joining knightly orders fell significantly.

King Guy was released in mid-1188. He organized a small army from the knights who were ransomed or, like him, released from Saladin's incarceration. He tried to enter Tyre, but Conrad would not let him in, explaining that he had promised to hold the city until the arrival of a new Christian army that would save the Holy Land. Only then King Frederick, the English King Richard[28] and French King Philip II,[29] all of whom had promised to come, would decide who would rule the city. Guy could not oppose this argument. With the reinforcements that had arrived in the meantime from Pisa and Sicily, as well as a unit of Templars, he besieged Acre in September 1189. That was a rather silly idea, given that the city had excellent walls and was defended by a garrison twice as numerous as Guy's force. As an additional problem, Saladin had forces nearby, so the besiegers were themselves besieged throughout the siege. Grand Master de Ridefort, who had vowed to defend the earthly kingdom of Jesus Christ with a sword in his hand and yet did all he could to destroy it now got a chance to make up for at least part of his blunders. On 4 October, Guy attacked Saladin's units around Acre.

On the left wing of the Christian forces, the Templars fought Saladin's nephew Taqi. Saladin was forced to weaken his centre to save Taqi and his men. In vain, his forces were crushed both on the wing and in the centre and he was forced to flee. Spurred on by success, Christian warriors started in pursuit of the dispersed enemy, destroying their own fighting line, which allowed Saladin's preserved left wing to strike. The Christians had to retreat to their camp in disarray. This complete annihilation prevented the Templars, who for an hour formed an unbroken and firm front, from giving relief to the rest of the army. More than half the Knights Templar were killed, including the notorious master Gerard de Ridefort and seneschal of the Order.

Guy constantly received reinforcements. Already in 1189, he was also joined by Conrad de Montserrat, who went to Antioch in the spring of 1190 and brought his cousin Frederick of Schwabia, together with the remains of Barbarossa's army. Conrad was wounded at Acre on 15 November. After his recovery, in early 1191 he tried unsuccessfully to take the Tower of Flies, protecting the entrance to the port of Acre. When, after a year and a half of siege and in spring 1191 it seemed that all the effort had been in vain, Leopold,[30] Duke of Austria, sailed in from Zadar. He immediately put all the remains of Barbarossa's army under his command. Then on 20 April the French King Philip arrived with 650 knights, 1,300 horses and 1,300 pages, and 8 July saw the arrival of 25 ships led by the English King Richard the Lionheart. The Templar Robert de Sable, as Richard's treasurer and messenger, also arrived and was elected grand master instead of Gerard de Ridefort. The newly-elected grand master was immediately drawn into business with the king. Travelling into the crusades, Richard landed in Cyprus, plundered and conquered the island that actually was an unnecessary hassle for him, so he offered it for little money (100,000 bezants) to the Temple. The Templars did not have that much money, so a deal was agreed for less than half the amount requested. Twenty brothers were sent to take over the island, but encountered fierce resistance from angry islanders who still saw the wounds of Richard's recent devastation. They managed to return to Acre and the leaders of the Order decided that there was no point in spending manpower and resources on the conquest of Cyprus. The island was returned to Richard, but the deposit was never returned to the Temple. The king resold the island to Guy de Lusignan for the same amount of 40,000 bezants. The king almost earned the required 100,000.

In order to tell each other apart, the newly-arrived crusaders had arranged in advance that the English would wear red crosses, the French white ones and the Flemish green ones.

Although Saladin and his army surrounded the crusaders' camp, he could not help the city because the Christians had fortified their encampment as early as October 1189 and in the winter of 1190/91 they strengthened the fortifications by adding a ditch and a bulwark. As the siege dragged on, a sort of coexistence had sprung up between the enemies. When they were not skirmishing, Christian and Muslim knights invited each other to feasts and games.

The French constructed numerous siege machines, among which the great catapults were of particular note. The Templars and the Hospitallers each had their own catapult. The city was showered with rocks and the walls started caving in; the attackers had several chances to take the city. However, they had to retreat every time because Saladin's army would attack them at the same time. The city received supplies rarely and in insufficient quantities because the port was blocked by English and French fleets so, after negotiations, the defenders surrendered on 11 July. Conrad raised the banners of the Kingdom of Jerusalem, Kings Richard and Philip and the Duke of Austria. Richard believed that the duke was unworthy and had his banner removed. This act made him a lifelong enemy. Frustrated by Richard's wilfulness, Philip (who also suffered from poor health) and Leopold left the Holy Land with their men in August. Richard, a merciless red-headed giant, was now left alone to command the crusaders' army.

The population of Acre was supposed to remain in Christian hands until the conclusion of the negotiations regarding their ransom and exchange of prisoners, but on 20 August Richard decided that negotiations were not going well and ordered all the prisoners killed. The English killed 2,700 imprisoned defenders and their families. Only a few of the most prominent Muslims were spared, and men physically capable of slave work. Although many authors justified this act as vengeance for the slaughter of Templars and Hospitallers after Hattin, there can hardly be any comparison. Saladin not only spared all the other imprisoned knights, but also released most of them with no ransom, letting them return to their headless families. He never touched women and children. Those of lower social standing ended up enslaved but alive. Richard showed himself as a cruel warrior who did not mind going back on his word.

At the end of August the English king took his army from Acre with the intention of recapturing Jerusalem. Before that, he decided to secure the port cities, which he needed as necessary logistics bases, so he swerved towards Jaffa. The crusaders marched along the coastline, followed by a fleet of ships and resting every other day. All along the way, Saladin's light cavalry attacked them. Richard constantly rode along the marching line, encouraging his men. The heat was murderous and many fell due to sunstroke or were killed by Muslim horsemen once they lagged behind the majority of the army. Saladin moved in parallel with Richard's army, carefully picking the terrain for the decisive battle. He chose a field near Arsuf (50 kilometres north of Jaffa), wide enough for him to spread his cavalry forces. The forest was a full 3 kilometres away from the coast here.

At dawn on Saturday, 7 September, Richard began moving his army out of the camp at the mouth of the River Rochetaillée. The king placed military orders at the front and rear of the column, the most exposed parts of the marching army. That was the only reasonable resolution because the soldiers of Christ were experienced and disciplined warriors who included light turcopole cavalrymen who were comparable to Saladin's light horse. Templars under Robert of Sable[31] were the vanguard (right wing of the army in the possible battle), followed by Richard's own troops, Bretons and Angevins, Poitevins who included Guy of Lusignan, and the Normans and English with the great army's standard on the wagon. The French, the Flemings, other crusaders and Outremer barons followed under Hugh of Burgundy.[32] The rearguard were the Hospitaller knights under Garnier de Nablus.[33] All the units were grouped into five formations disposed in parallel with the coast, along which Richard spread the carts protected by a portion of the infantry. The English archers were spread before the heavy cavalry line, facing the woodland. Hugh with the picked knights rode alongside the column to maintain the order of the marching army. The morning was well under way when Saladin started the attack, but only after the whole crusaders' army left the camping area. Combined Sudanese, Bedouin and Turkish light cavalry and infantry showered the crusaders with arrows and javelins. Behind the light troops three large columns of armoured heavy cavalry – Mamluks, Kurds and contingents of Egyptian, Syrian and Mesopotamian emirs – gradually appeared from within the woodlands. Saladin was surrounded by his bodyguard and escorted by a number of banners and kettle-drummers.

After the crusaders' army took up position, Richard and the Duke of Burgundy rode along the lines, raising the morale of their troops. The Muslims managed to force the retreat of first-row archers, who had no proper protection from the rain of projectiles, but the armoured horsemen were not discouraged. Then Saladin's infantry split their rows on the right wing and opened the way for Saracen horsemen to attack the Flemish, local knights and Hospitallers with the intent of ruining the left wing of Richard's fighting line. The Christians rebuffed several consecutive assaults with sabres and battleaxes and, after each rebuff, English archers returned to their position, attacking the enemies as they re-formed for the following attack. Several times, the grand master of the Hospitallers asked for Richard's permission to assault the Saracens, but the king waited until the whole of Saladin's army was close enough before he ordered a general charge. A Hospitaller marshal and one knight, Baldwin Carew, finally lost their patience and rushed towards the Muslims.

As was usual for knights, all the Hospitaller brothers spurred their horses to follow. Adrenaline kicked in, and the whole line of Richard's heavy cavalry was dragged into the charge. The king himself joined in, trying to maintain some semblance of order. The scene was described by Saladin's secretary, who watched the whole thing from a nearby hill: hundreds of horsemen under colourful banners, wire armour and helmets glistening in the sun; large shields with family arms or different-coloured crosses in a cloud of dust; the dull thunder of thousands of hooves; magnificent for Christians, but horrifying for Saladin's men. They did not wait for the enemy to reach them but started running. Saladin managed to get a portion of his men back in line, defending his camp and even starting a charge of his own, but without much success. He lost the battle, and Richard continued his march along the coast towards the south. The losses on either side were not great, which is not surprising given that a real clash never took place. Chroniclers only make particular mention of the death of the famous knight James of Avesnes,[34] whose body was found surrounded by fifteen dead enemies. This victory (the only defeat in pitched battle suffered by Saladin aside from Montgisard) significantly raised the morale of the Christians. After Hattin, this was the first time they had overcome the previously invincible Saladin. Richard showed himself as a great war leader. He took Jaffa without problems, which gave him control over the coast of the Holy Land and made him a serious threat to the sultan in Jerusalem.

However, no decisive event took place. Saladin gathered his dispersed forces, but he was no longer strong enough to attack again. In November 1191, as was his wont, the sultan dismissed half his army, expecting new units from Egypt, and went to spend the winter in Jerusalem. Richard intended to attack the holy city, but gave up at the insistence of the Templars, the Hospitallers and the local barons. The weather was unfavourable, Saladin's Egyptian army was spending the winter in the hills near Jerusalem, and the Christians didn't have the force to keep the Holy City, even if they had managed to conquer it. Richard dedicated himself to the reconstruction of Ashkelon, abandoned by Saladin; over the following four months Richard transformed it into the strongest fortress on the Palestinian coast.

The peace agreement between Richard and Saladin was signed on 2 September 1192. The peace was arranged for a period of five years, during which all cities on the coast north from Jaffa were left to the Christians, pilgrims were allowed to freely visit their holy places, and Christians and Muslims were allowed to cross into each other's countries with no obstacles. The condition was the dismantling of Ashkelon. Richard left the Holy Land on 9 October. On his return he was accompanied by ten knights and four sergeants of the Templars.

The Third Crusade was over. Exhausted by numerous battles and almost constant travelling, Saladin died on 4 March 1193. He had been a merciful, generous and tolerant conqueror and ruler who never went back on his word, unlike the Christian rulers.

Although brothers of the Temple were dedicated to fighting infidels overseas, they occasionally took part in military events in Europe, but those were exceptions rather than the rule. Starting with the battle at Covadonga in 722 when Visigoth leader Pelagius defeated the army of the Umayyad caliphate, the Iberian Peninsula was the stage for the Reconquista, the recapturing of territory taken by Muslims after 711. Immediately after its foundation, the Temple attracted the attention of Spanish and Portuguese rulers who tried to incite the Order to take part in their local wars through gifts such as strategically important fortresses. As in the Holy Land, the Templars undertook the protection of pilgrims on the way to Santiago de Compostela.

Along the pilgrims' road through Navarre, Castile and León they constructed numerous buildings, among which one stands out: the great fortress of Ponferrada in León, standing guard over the iron bridge over the River Sil, which gave the fortress its name. Among other castles held and strengthened in Castile and Aragon they built the magnificent monastery castles of Gardeney, Miravet and Peniscola. The Templars sent almost all warriors from Portugal and Spanish kingdoms, as well as horses, to the Middle East; however, smaller units participated in local battles, albeit reluctantly.

In the Battle of Las Navas de Tolosa in Andalusia on 16 June 1212, which marked a turning-point in the Reconquista, the Templars were part of the army of Pedro II, King of Aragon, who, together with the forces of Castile, Portugal and Navarre heavily defeated Caliph Mohammed al-Nasir. Master of Portuguese Templars, Gomes Ramires, was killed in this battle. Aragon King Jacob I the Conqueror (*Chaime lo Conqueridor*) undertook a campaign on Majorca in 1229 with an army of 1,500 knights and around 15,000 infantrymen. The Templars only represented around 4 per cent of this force.

The Templars were bound by oath to obey the Pope and the grand master, but there were some cases when knights of the Temple accepted service with secular rulers, even at the cost of working for a nobleman whose interests diverged from those of the church. John, Richard the Lionheart's successor and brother, was excommunicated by the Pope, and yet his only trusted counsellor was the Master of English Templars Aimery de Saint-Maur. Serving a secular nobleman compelled any knight to defend his master's interests with arms, so some Knights Templar, despite the ban on drawing arms against Christians, took part in feudal conflicts. The King of Aragon used the Templars in fights against Castile and the French.

In Greece, on Cyprus and in Cilicia, the Temple raised arms against the local Christian population due to their own interests. Together with the Hospitallers and Teutonic knights, Templars took part in the campaign against Greece (1205–10) and thus gained properties on the Peloponnese Peninsula. On Cyprus, the population of Nicosia protested the Templar presence in 1192, but the uprising was smothered in blood by the Temple, while in Cilicia they waged war against the Armenians regarding the fortress of Gaston over Antioch.

Under King of Jerusalem John of Brienne,[35] an army of crusaders that included the Templars, the Hospitallers and Teutonic knights captured the fortress of Damietta in the Nile delta on 24 August 1218. This was the beginning of the Fifth Crusade. In return, Al-Mu'azzam, Saladin's son and governor of Damascus, attacked the great Templar fortress of Atlit, 13 miles south of Haifa, in 1220. The Order began erection of the fortress known as Pilgrim's Castle in 1218. Atlit was the very best of Templar military architecture, built on the cape with two main walls – the outer 15 metres high and 6 metres thick – with three square towers and inner walls 30 metres high by 12 metres with two towers 34 metres tall. The Templars quickly withdrew their unit from Damietta to help defend their properties and the garrison numbered about 4,000 men. The failed siege ended in November. Knightly orders attacked and pillaged the town of Burlos, some 30 kilometres from Damietta. On return, they ran into an ambush and several Hospitallers were taken prisoner, including their marshal. The campaign against Egypt ended poorly and the crusaders' army left the Nile delta on 8 September 1221 after signing an eight-year peace agreement with the fourth Ayyubid sultan, al-Kamil.

Over the following few years, al-Kamil was preoccupied by fighting for power with his own brother, al-Mu'azzam, who represented a serious threat to Christian countries in the Holy Land.

Frederick II,[36] one of the strongest emperors of the Holy Roman Empire, King of Germany, Italy and Sicily, planned the campaign of the Sixth Crusade and left the port of Brindisi in August 1227 but returned immediately due to illness. Since he had failed to fulfil his vow to go on a crusade, Pope Gregory IX excommunicated him. Frederick II sailed from Brindisi again in June 1228, which the Pope took as provocation since an excommunicated person should not lead Christians into war. In the meantime al-Mu'azzam had died so the reason for the campaign effectively disappeared, but the emperor had already arrived overseas. In February 1229, al-Kamil and Frederick II signed a ten-year peace agreement that returned Jerusalem and Bethlehem to the Christians without any fighting, as well as providing them with a corridor to the coast. Muslims in Jerusalem could keep their property and have their own administration, but the city walls were not to be reconstructed.

This contract mostly damaged the Templars because they did not regain their monastery at the Temple hill. Now the Mosque of Al-Aqsa stood there.

In the 1230s, Bohemond IV and then his son, Bohemond V, lords of the duchy and county of Tripoli, kept peace with their Muslim neighbours. The Hospitallers and the Templars, whose behaviour Bohemond IV could not control, did not honour the neighbourly relations between Christians and Muslims. When al-Kamil attacked Damascus in 1228, the Hospitallers provoked him to try to conquer their strongest fortress of Krak. The following year they attacked Varin, and in 1230, together with the Templars from Tortosa, organized a campaign against Hama, which ended badly. They ran into an ambush and suffered a hard defeat. The Hospitallers held Jabla for a few weeks in 1231. That same year, a two-year peace agreement was signed.

Grand Master Armand de Périgord (1232–39) led the Templars in a series of unsuccessful campaigns against the Muslims around the Sea of Galilee, on Cana of Galilee, Sephora and Sapphita, which significantly weakened the Temple militarily. In order to regain Trapessac, one of the four northernmost fortifications held by the Templars in the Outremer, he suffered a heavy defeat in 1237. Armand led a rather strong Templar detachment from Gaston; as many as 120 knights, turcopoles and archers. Although he was ambushed under Trapessac, it looked like the Templars would prevail until the enemy received reinforcements from Aleppo. The Templars were massacred and only twenty, including Armand, managed to seize the 14 kilometre-distant Gaston.

Templars from the Bagras fortress suddenly attacked Turcoman tribes by Lake Antioch in 1237. An army from Aleppo started towards Bagras in order to punish this completely unprovoked Templar violence. Bohemond personally rode out towards the Muslims and negotiated a renewal of the peace. The offended preceptor of the Temple in Antioch, William of Montferrat, broke the arranged peace almost immediately. He gathered his knights and several local noblemen and attacked the fortress of Trapessac near Bagras. During the siege, a messenger informed the governor of Aleppo of the attack. A strong cavalry unit was immediately sent to help the garrison. Although he was informed that help for the defenders was on the way, William stubbornly continued his siege and was soon under attack. The few Christians were quickly scattered, most knights imprisoned and the belligerent preceptor killed. The prisoners paid a ransom and were released, and Templars and Hospitallers were forced, with the Pope's approval, to sign a ten-year peace agreement.

This tempting of fate passed with no consequences for the Christian lands overseas only thanks to Sultan al-Kamil, who was an honourable, peace-loving ruler, prepared to leave the Franks alone as long as they caused no problems. After al-Kamil's death in 1239, civil war broke out among his heirs. Crusader groups arriving overseas were not strong enough to use the weakness of the Ayyubids. None of the warring Muslim leaders and Christian princes was capable of achieving the final victory, so odd and previously unimaginable alliances were made.

In 1240 the governor of Damascus, Ismail, made an alliance with local barons and Templars against Ajub, who'd proclaimed himself sultan in Egypt. In return, the Templars were given the fortress of Safed. The Hospitallers, supported by Western barons, arranged with Ajub that they would have the right to reconstruct the fortress of Ashkelon if they remained neutral in his conflict with Ismail. By this act, the knights of St John shamed both the local Christian noblemen and the Templars, but also Ismail, who had previously debased himself to get Christians on his side.

The Templars and the Hospitallers were on the verge of war with each other. The Teutonic order kept away from the conflict. Only in 1243 did local noblemen and the Templars gain the upper hand and the alliance with Damascus was renewed. In the new agreement, Ismail allowed the reconstruction of the walls of Jerusalem and let the Templars return into the zone of the Temple, which was a great diplomatic success of the crusaders in the Holy Land, but also their last.

Satisfaction with the achievement was short-lived. Horezm Turks had been robbing the north of Syria for three years by then, and Ajub asked them to attack Damascus and Palestine. Thousands of Turkish horsemen started devastating the environments of Damascus in June 1244 but, as the city was too big for them, they went around it, continued to pillage Galilee, passed through Tiberias and Nazareth, and started against Jerusalem. They entered the city on 11 July with street-fighting. The Templar-reconstructed fortress held fast, but no help was forthcoming. After negotiating terms of surrender, the garrison left Jerusalem on 23 August and the Holy City was never again in Christian hands.

After pillaging, destroying and burning all they could, the Turks also left the city to join Ajub's army by Gaza. At the same time, near Acre, an army of allies gathered. The lord of Tyre and Toron, Philip of Montfort[37] and the Count of Jaffa, Gauthier de Brienne, led 600 of their vassal knights. Templar Grand Master Armand de Périgord and Hospitaller Grand Master William de Châteauneuf gathered 300 brothers each. The Teutonic order brought a smaller contingent of unknown size, as did the Order of St Lazarus. Bohemond of Antioch sent a unit of his own. The knights were accompanied by sergeants and around 6,000 infantrymen.

It was the largest army gathered by Christians overseas since Hattin. The army was led by the Count de Brienne.[38] The Emir of Homs al-Mansur Ibrahim brought 2,000 of his horsemen and a contingent from Damascus. An-Nasir of Kerak, nephew to the late sultan al-Kamil, king of Transjordania, arrived with 2,000 Bedouin horsemen. On 4 October the army started south. Christian and al-Mansur's warriors marched together, like true brothers in arms, while an-Nasir's Bedouins rode separately. They were greeted at Gaza by Mamluk Emir Baibars with 5,000 chosen Egyptian Mamluks and a horde of Horezm Turks, a total of around 11,000 people; i.e. similar in force to the Christian alliance. The two armies met at a sandy plain several kilometres north-east of Gaza at the village of La Forbie. The alliance held a council of war. Emir al-Mansur proposed that they make camp and fortify it, which would bother the Turks who, as horsemen, did not like attacking fortified positions. The emir countered that it could make them abandon the Egyptians, who would then become weaker. This seemed like a good idea. After all, Damascus already had years of experience in fighting the Horezm Turks and even defeated them at Edessa in 1241. Thus many of the barons agreed with the idea, but not the Count of Jaffa. He believed that they had to attack immediately since they had the advantage in numbers and this was an opportunity to destroy the Turks so that they wouldn't threaten Syria and northern Christian borders any more, while Ajub could be sent back to Egypt with his tail between his legs. Since the count was the commander of the Christian army, his inspired speech prevailed.

The armies took up battle positions on the morning of 17 October. The Franks were on the allies' right wing and Damascus held the centre, while al-Nasir and the Bedouins were on the left. The battle began with consecutive charges of knights against Baibars' line, but they didn't manage to crush the Egyptians and the day ended with no palpable result. The Count of Jaffa's predictions did not come true. The following morning, Baibars took the initiative and sent the Turks to attack the allies' centre. Al-Mansur's horsemen from Homs held fast before the charge of wild nomadic warriors, but the Damascus contingent scattered, dragging the Bedouins along. At the same time, in a cloud of dust, a cavalry battle raged between the Homs and the Turks until the persistent emir was forced to retreat with his remaining 280 horsemen. Now Turkish riders struck the unprotected flank of the Christian army. The strike pushed the Franks against Baibars' Egyptians. The battle lasted for several more hours. The Christians fought bravely but, pushed to a pile, they had no room to develop a front and it was only a matter of time until they would die or be captured. While some fought, others could only stand within the surrounded mass and await their turn. The knights said their last prayers and goodbyes. The grand master and marshal of the Templars were killed, while army commander de Brienne and the Hospitaller master were taken captive with 800 others. At least 5,000 allied warriors died.

Montfort managed to escape and, in Ashkelon, gather the remaining secular knights as well as thirty-three Templars, twenty-six Hospitallers and three Teutonic knights. He sailed for Jaffa. Baibars immediately started for Ashkelon, fortified and now held by the Hospitallers. It turned out that the reconstruction of the city walls had been successful, so any attempt to charge the city was senseless, so the Egyptians' only option was to block the city from both land and sea. Leading the captured Walter, Count of Brienne, Horezm Turks rode to Jaffa, asking the defenders to surrender or else they would kill the count. Gauthier bravely yelled that they should not surrender and in the end the Turks, unused to sieges, left and took the count with them; he later died in captivity. Ajub still had to settle his accounts with Ismail, and that saved the Christians. The Horezm Turks went inland and joined Ajub's army in the siege of Damascus. Al-Nasir lost Kerak and Transjordan. Damascus fell in 1245, and Ismail had to go and serve as emir in Ajub's vassal duchy of Baalbek. Ajub did not reward the Turks for their help so, dissatisfied with Ajub's ungrateful behaviour, they changed sides and decided to help Ismail return to Damascus. Ismail was defeated somewhere on the way from Homs to Baalbek, the Horezm Turks almost exterminated, and those who survived returned east and joined the Mongols. Then Ajub decided to settle the score with the Franks as well. In the summer of 1247 he took Tiberias, Mount Tabor and Belvoir, and finished the sequence by taking Ashkelon on 15 October. After that, he reconstructed the walls of Jerusalem and moved his court to Damascus, where all the Syrian princes bowed to him in 1249. The Ayyubid Dynasty had put internal matters in order again.

Far to the east, an army incomparable by its speed and number of warriors whose discipline was unquestionable began its unstoppable march. In 1212, the Mongolian army completed its first conquest, capturing the kingdom of Hsi Hsia around the upper part of the Yellow River. By 1240, the Mongols had taken China, Korea, Transoxania, Afghanistan, Iran, Russia and the Ukraine. They defeated the Cumans, a people of Turkish origin, and Russian dukes Mstislav the Bold and Mstislav III of Kiev in 1223 on the River Kalka, after which some 40,000 Cumani under Khan Köten moved to Hungary. Mongolian leader Batu Khan asked the Hungarian King Béla IV to give him the Cumans. The king's refusal was the pretext for the Mongolian campaign against Hungary. To prevent the Polish king from possibly jumping in to help his neighbour, Batu sent a division of the Mongolian army to Poland. It was part of Subutai's[39] army, the size of two *tumen*, under Genghis Khan's grandson Baidar. Baidar burned and pillaged Sandomierz and Kraków, and then started towards Wrocław. Informed that the combined forces of the Polish king and the Teutonic knightly Order were approaching, he went to meet them and, not far from Legnica, on 9 April 1241 he clashed with the forces of the Silesian Duke Henry II, religious men whose ranks included a small number of Templars and Hospitallers. The Mongols won, the duke was killed and the fallen included six Templars.

The main Mongolian army, under Batu Khan and Subutai, started towards Hungary through the Verecke Pass in the Carpathian Mountains. King Béla IV gathered his army by Pest, on the left bank of the Danube. The Mongolian vanguard arrived in the environment of Pest on 15 March and started pillaging. Since Béla's army had not yet gathered completely, he forbade attacking the Mongols, which disgusted the Hungarian noblemen who thought that this was cowardly. After a few skirmishes, Béla decided to go to battle after all, but the Mongols retreated, so the noblemen concluded that they had been right when they saw them as an unworthy enemy. Béla started in pursuit and, after a week's forced march during which Mongolian light cavalry often attacked his forces, he arrived at the River Sajó which had spilled from its bed. He decided to stop there and wait for supplies. He had a palisade camp erected since he didn't know where the enemy was, visibility being limited by the forest-covered opposite bank.

The Croatian Herzog (duke) and the king's brother Coloman, Archbishop of Kalocsa Ugrin Csák and Templar Master Remblad of Voczon took their men from the camp and went to defend the bridge over the River Sajó, situated some 10 kilometres further on. They arrived around midnight and found Mongols crossing the river with the intention of attacking the king's camp at dawn. Only a small number of Mongolian warriors had managed to cross so they were easily pushed away, and many fell from crossbow arrows on the 200m bridge. Celebrating his victory, Coloman returned to the camp at around 2.00 am, leaving only a few of his warriors to guard the bridge. He wasn't even aware that most Mongolian forces were still on the opposite bank.

A Mongolian answer was not long in coming. Shiban took a smaller contingent north to cross the river at a ford and get behind the crossbowmen guarding the bridge. Subutai and another portion of their forces went south and started building a pontoon bridge while Hungarian forces were occupied in guarding the existing one. Batu remained by the bridge with the majority of their forces, preparing seven catapults to attack the guards on the opposite bank. At dawn on 1 April 1241, the attack began with stones and was finished by the arrival of Shiban's men, after which the guards left the bridge and returned to the king's camp. By 8.00 am most Mongolian forces had crossed the River Sajó. The arrival of those fleeing the bridge alerted the Hungarian camp. Coloman was again the first to leave the camp with his Croatian warriors, the Templars and Ugrin. Béla still believed that this was only a minor portion of the Mongolian army and that Coloman would handle them on his own again, so he never ordered his forces to prepare for battle. He was completely stunned when the Herzog and his men were forced to retreat to camp under pressure of the numerous Mongol forces. Realizing his mistake, Béla finally ordered his men to move, but by then all the Mongolian units led by Batu and Shiban had crossed the Sajó.

The participation of all Béla IV's forces in the battle did tilt the advantage of numbers to the Hungarians' side. Subutai had not yet arrived because the construction of the pontoon was running late. The flooded plain behind the Mongols' backs limited the manoeuvring possibilities for the steppe warriors and prevented the khan from completely deploying his men. Some thirty armoured horsemen from the guard died while Batu personally led the attack. At the key moment, Subutai arrived on the battlefield and attacked the Hungarians from the back, which forced Béla's forces to flee into the cart camp in panic. In the afternoon, the battle went on around the camp, but the defence did not last long. Christian breaches from the camp were successfully stopped and numerous flaming arrows caused horror among the defenders. Mongols probably used Chinese firearms and powder in this battle as well. Many Hungarians lost their lives, stampeded over by their comrades' panicked flight. As usual, the Mongols left a passage to induce the enemy to try to run from the surroundings instead of fighting to the death. Batu did not pursue the fleeing enemies because Mongolian losses were too great. Béla and Coloman escaped, but the Croatian Herzog eventually died of his numerous wounds. Ugrin was killed in battle, as was de Voczon and his Templars, the last to defend the camp. If Béla had dragged all his army from the camp first thing in the morning, Subutai probably wouldn't have arrived on time to help the majority of the Mongolian forces and the battle could have ended differently.

In 1244 the French King Louis IX[40] had a severe attack of malaria and, fearing for his life, he vowed that he would start a crusade if he lived and Louis had never gone back on his word. Few could measure up to him in the honourable meeting of his duties, caring for the well-being of his subjects; a just rule, but also merciless punishing of those who failed to fulfil their obligations or heretics or infidels. In July 1245, Pope Innocent IV held a council in Lyon at which he confirmed the 30-year-old king's vow and sent Cardinal Odo to preach the crusade throughout France. Preparations took three years. Peace with the English king had to be ensured, and good relations with Emperor Frederick had to be retained as his son was the legitimate king of the Kingdom of Jerusalem, without whose approval Louis couldn't disembark overseas. Ships also had to be provided. Genoa and Marseilles agreed but Venice, which had very good relations with the Egyptian sultanate, refused.

The king disembarked at Cyprus on 17 September 1248. He was then joined by overseas barons, Templars and Hospitallers. English crusaders, led by William Longsword, Count of Salisbury, started separately. It was agreed to start on Egypt but, persuaded by the Templar and Hospitaller masters and overseas noblemen, the king gave up his intention to sail for Egypt immediately. Conditions on the Nile delta would have been very unfavourable for war in the coming winter months. During his sojourn on the island, Louis tried and failed to create an alliance with the Mongols. Additionally food supplies were a problem. By May 1249, most of the reserves for the Egyptian campaign were spent and William Duke of Greece arrived with twenty-four ships and numerous warriors.

Boarding the army onto 120 large and many smaller transport vessels started on 13 May, but dragged on due to a storm. Still, the king and a quarter of the army embarked on 30 May and disembarked on the Egyptian coast on 4 July. The rest arrived in a disorganized manner, individually or in smaller groups. Sultan Ayyub saw the beginning of 1249 while besieging Homs, which the

Duke of Aleppo, al-Nasir Yusuf, had taken from Ayyub's cousin al-Ashraf Musa. He was in no hurry to return to Egypt because he had expected the crusaders to disembark in Palestine. Once he realized Louis's true intentions, he rushed to Cairo personally, with the army to follow him as quickly as possible. He ordered that Damietta be supplied with the necessary ammunition, and that the defence be taken over by warrior Bedouins from the tribe of Banu Kinanah. The sultan took up position east of the main course of the Nile. He had long struggled with tuberculosis and was unable to lead the army himself, so he appointed his vizier Fakr al-Din commander. Contrary to advice to wait for the rest of the army, Louis started disembarking on the delta's sandy shores only a day after his arrival, at dawn on 5 July. The Egyptians attacked, trying to stop the Franks with their feet still in the water. A battle started and was decided by the courage of overseas knights led by the Count of Jaffa, John of Ibelin, who managed to force the Muslims to retreat with many losses. French warriors also fought well and in a disciplined manner, following their king. In the evening, the vizier decided to entrench himself in Damietta, but gave up on the idea when he saw how much the situation scared the citizens and the Bedouins. He evacuated the city and had its warehouses burned, but forgot to destroy the pontoon bridge leading to the city over the canal. The following day, crusaders entered Damietta. The king decided to stay there until the summer flooding of the Nile passed and his brother Alfonso arrived with reinforcements from France. A long sojourn in hot and humid conditions led to the start of epidemics in the crusaders' army, while lack of activity deflated their morale.

The sultan punished the vizier by dishonourable dismissal from command, while Bedouin Emir Banu Kinanah and the leading Mamluk commanders lost their heads. The killing of their officers led to revolt among the Mamluks. Although dishonourably discharged, Fakr al-Din proved himself loyal and saved the sultan from the revolting Mamluks, so Ayyub returned the command to him as a sign of his gratitude.

The sultan offered Louis an exchange of Damietta for Jerusalem, which the king refused. He would not negotiate with an infidel. Ayyub immediately sent his units to Mansoura (al-Mansoura means 'Victorious' in Arabic), a city erected in the spot where the crusaders were stopped in the Fifth Crusade. Ayyub himself asked to be taken there so he could organize defence. The idea was to make the Franks' life difficult and their movement limited, so Bedouin warriors were left to wander the environs freely and kill any crusader who dared go further than the camp. Louis was forced to dig a trench and build a bulwark to prevent the Bedouins from attacking even the edges of the crusaders' camp by Damietta.

Alfonso de Poitou and his reinforcements only arrived in October when the Nile's waters finally dropped. Now was the time to continue the conquest and it was proposed to attack Alexandria. The crusaders had enough ships to cross to the western bank of the delta, and it would be a move that would completely surprise the Egyptians. If the Christians could take Alexandria, they would rule the entire Egyptian coast and would be in a good position to negotiate. The king's brother Robert of Artois was against it though, and the king agreed with him and decided to go against Cairo. On 20 November, the crusaders' army started from the camp at Damietta where a strong garrison was left.

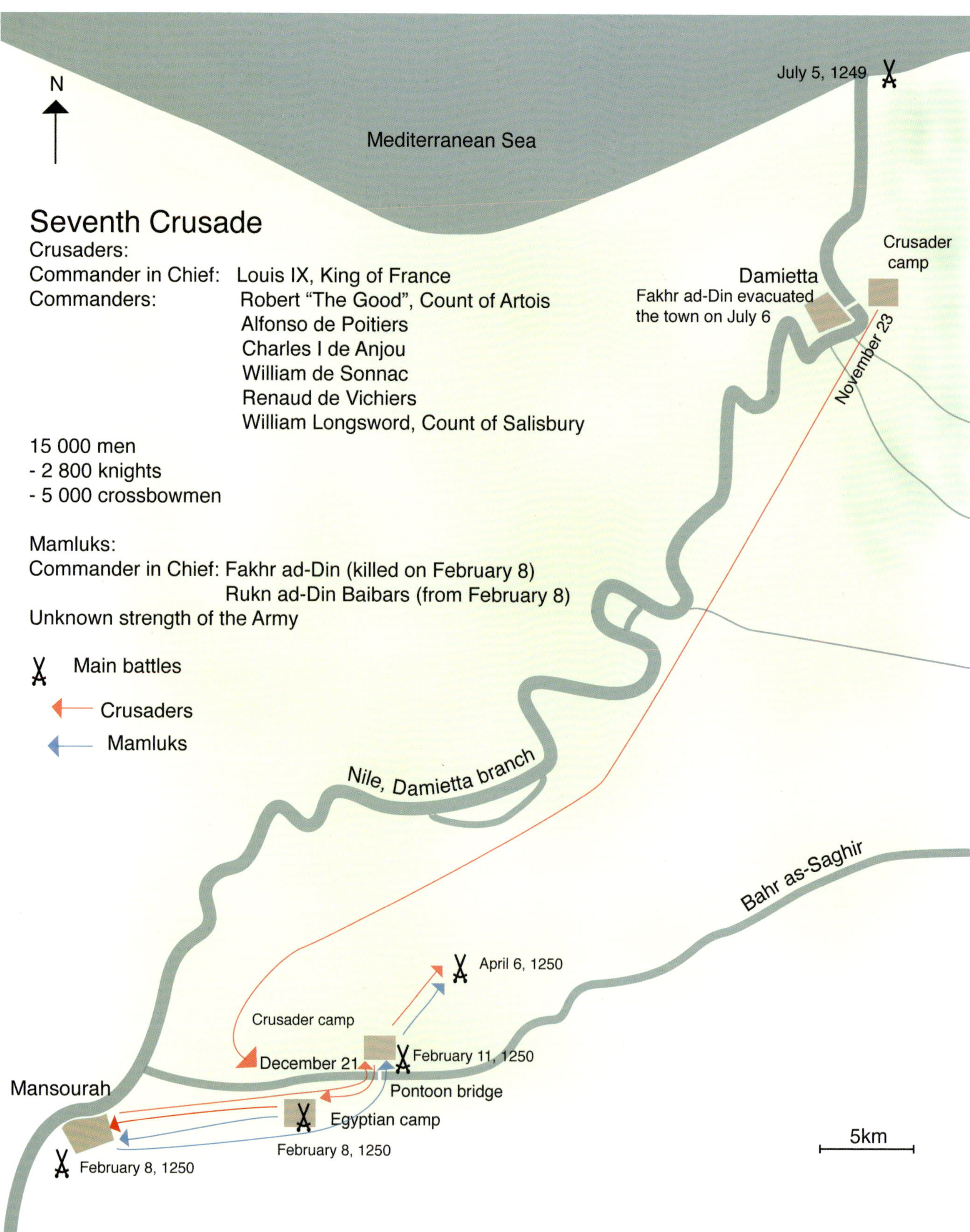

Map of the Mansoura operation.

Templars died almost to a man on the streets of Mansoura.

In the meantime, in Mansoura true drama unfolded. Capable ruler and the last of the great Ayyubids, Sultan Ayyub died on 23 November. The governance was taken over by his widow Shajar al-Dur, with the help of Fakr al-Din and eunuch Jamal al-Din Mohsen, who ran the court. They were waiting for Ayyub's only son Turan-Shah to arrive from the far away Mesopotamia.

Encouraged by the news of Ajub's death and expecting that the Mamluks would fight over the empty throne, Louis carefully made his way towards Mansoura. His way was criss-crossed by numerous smaller or larger channels. The ground was swampy and many horses had trouble moving through the muddy terrain. At every crossing, Muslim horsemen waited and made the passage difficult. In one such crossing, despite the king's orders, the Templars followed the retreating enemy too far and barely managed to return to the main force. On 21 December the king reached Bahr as-Saghir, the largest of the channels, which separated from the main course of the Nile just before Mansoura and flowed around the island on which Damietta is situated.

Neither army could make any significant move over the following six weeks. Egyptian cavalry's attempt to cross the channel and attack the crusaders from the back failed. The king's intention to construct a bulwark over the channel also failed, as the Egyptians stopped the construction with Greek fire. In early February, a Copt discovered a ford over the channel and, at dawn on 8 February, the king's army started to cross Bahr al Saghir. The Duke of Burgundy remained guarding the camp with a strong garrison. Crossing the wide channel through a dangerous ford could not be done quickly. The water was deep and fast, so only horsemen could cross. The vanguard was led by Robert de Artois. He was accompanied by the Templars and the English. Robert was uneasy, fearing that the Egyptians might discover their crossing of the channel. Impatient, he decided to go into action, although the king had explicitly ordered no attacks until all the army had crossed. Not even the Templars' warnings to stick to the initial plan had any effect, so they decided to join the attack simply so as not to leave the count and the English on their own. Some 3 kilometres further on, they rushed into an Egyptian camp where warriors were just then getting up. The heavy Western cavalry cut down those who were grabbing for their weapons in disbelief and, unarmoured, trying to organize some sort of resistance. Others rushed to Mansoura half-naked. Chronicler and diplomat Jamaleddin Ibn Wasse wrote that the vizier was caught in his bath, grabbed his weapon and rushed out with no armour, mounting and hurrying to see what was going on. He and his escort ran to the Templars and were immediately killed.

Everything worked for the crusaders. King Louis proved himself a good war leader. He correctly chose to disembark before all his forces had gathered, then waited for the summer floods to pass and reinforcements to arrive. He advanced carefully towards Mansoura, and then waited for the right opportunity to cross the Bahr al Saghir channel. Sultan Ayyub had died. Robert had scattered the Mamluks with surprise, and the commander of the Egyptian army was killed. The only thing left was to wrap up the campaign prudently. Everything was in the hands of the crusaders and only an unreasonable, rash commander could have ruined what had been achieved. Yet the Franks had one just like that.

After the enemy was forced to flee, the Templar master advised again to wait for the king, this time with the support of the leader of the English crusaders, Count William Longsword. However, in a victory-induced euphoria, the adrenaline-pumped Robert called both the count and the master cowards. He gathered all his men and took them to take Mansoura. The king's brother left the two knights no choice. If they didn't help him, it was obvious he would be killed or captured and they could not allow that. They started after him. Robert almost certainly knew they would do that.

If Robert had expected to find a panicked mob ready for slaughter in Mansoura, he couldn't have been more wrong. Mamluk commanders were capable officers and quickly put their warriors to order. The leadership was taken by Rukn ad-Din Baibars (not the one from the battle at Gaza), who disposed the Mamluks to important points in the city while leaving the city gates deliberately open and undefended. Robert simply rushed headlong into the trap and took French knights to the city, driving the distraught population before him. The Templars and the English followed. Frank warriors had, scattered through narrow city streets, almost reached the sultan's court when Egyptian warriors struck at them from side alleys. Arrows and javelins started flying from roofs and windows, and the Franks had no room to turn their horses towards the attackers. Those who were the deepest in the city tried to save themselves by swimming, but drowned in deep Nile waters under the weight of their equipment. The knights who had entered last had more luck. They managed to get away through the city gates. Among them was the king's nephew Peter de Brittany, who suffered a severe wound to his head but managed to escape and inform the king of the battle in Mansoura. The others were left with no alternative but to fight to the bitter end.

Robert and his escort tried to defend themselves from one of the houses they forced, but they were overpowered and cut down. The Templars, 280 of them, died almost to a man. Only nine brothers managed to fight their way from the city, among them Guillaume de Sonnac, the grand master, who lost an eye. It was a terrible loss considering that the number of Templar combat-ready knights in the Outremer was around 300 even in the best of times. English knights also suffered heavy losses. Their leader, the Count of Salisbury, died a recorded death. His left foot had been cut off, so he fought leaning on the shoulder of the knight Richard of Ashkelon. The Egyptians offered to spare his life if he surrendered, but he refused in disgust. He lost his right hand in the fight, but he grabbed his sword with his left hand and then lost it too. He fell to his knees, losing a lot of blood, and was finally cut down. Next to him, Richard also lost his life, as did Longsword's ensign de Guise, who fought while holding the banner with the bloodied stump of his left hand.

The majority of the army had by now crossed the canal almost in its entirety. Crossbowmen were still on the other bank with the task of protecting the ford in case of need. When he heard what was going on in Mansoura, Louis immediately commanded to set up a fighting line, expecting that Egyptians would attack as soon as the Franks' vanguard was finished. Soon light Mamluk cavalry attacked, rushing around and showering the crusaders with arrows. Once they'd spent their reserves, the king ordered a charge and scattered the enemy. In the meantime, a pontoon bridge was being constructed so that the king's crossbowmen could cross the channel as well. The enemy regrouped and attacked again using the same tactics, and it looked as if the crusaders would be pushed to the channel. Again, the knights managed to repel the enemy; the pontoon bridge was completed in the meantime, and the very much needed crossbowmen crossed the Bahr al Saghir. Under the combined attack of heavy cavalry and murderous heavy crossbow arrows, the Egyptians were forced to retreat to Mansoura. The king returned to the camp where he'd spent the night before the crossing of the channel. His forces were no longer sufficient to attack Mansoura, a questionable idea in the first place since Egyptian catapults in the city were bigger and stronger than those of the Franks. So Louis commanded to reinforce the camp on the opposite side of the channel and the pontoon bridge, which he expected to need later so he did not have it destroyed.

Reinforcements arrived for the Egyptians and, three days later, they attacked the crusaders again while they defended the pontoon. This was one of the largest battles of all overseas. Under a rain of arrows, the Franks stubbornly resisted continuous charges and, in appropriate moments, conducted counterattacks. The left wing, commanded by Charles de Anjou, and the left centre of the crusaders' line, held by the barons from Syria and Cyprus, held well but the right centre, held by the remains of the Templars and the French, was failing. The wooden palisade was set on fire and crumbled, and the enemy burst into the camp. The grand master of the Temple, William, lost his other eye and died. Lord de Joinville, the king's friend and one of the best of French captains, writes:

And know that immediately behind the place where the battalion of the Templars stood, there was a good acre of ground, so covered with darts, arrows and missiles, that you could not see the earth beneath them, such showers of these had been discharged against Templars by the Saracens!

The king's brother Alfonso, who commanded the right wing of the camp, was surrounded and almost destroyed but got help from the cooks and women from the camp. The Muslims finally decided that they could not overpower the Franks, so they retreated to Mansoura again.

For the following eight weeks Louis waited in the camp, expecting upheaval in Egypt due to the empty throne. What he did not know was that on 28 February 1250, Ajub's son Turan-Shah had arrived and his command increased the pressure against the crusaders. Louis was finally forced to return to Damietta. The retreat started on 5 April, but the crusaders did not destroy the pontoon bridge, so the enemy followed them immediately. The king would not go forward and leave his army. On the following day, the Franks were surrounded and, after a short battle, surrendered. The prisoners included the king and his brothers Charles de Anjou and Alfonso de Poitou. Ransom was arranged, and the surrender of Damietta. In the meantime, Turan-Shah fell into the bad graces of his stepmother, Sultana Shajar al-Durr, who was the reason he'd managed to succeed his father in the first place. She asked for Mamluk help and the sultan was killed. The highest Mamluk commander al-Din Aybak was appointed regent (he married the sultana to get legitimacy) for the sultan's juvenile nephew al-Ashraf Musa. The regent continued the process of ransoming and freeing the prisoners. As ransom arrived, the king, his brothers and noblemen as well as 3,000 warriors were gradually released. By the end of March 1252, everybody was released, including those captured in 1244 by Gaza, so the grand master of the Hospitallers also saw freedom. The king went to Acre. Damietta was surrendered on 6 May 1250. Many wounded soldiers left in the city were killed, despite promises that they would be spared. The Seventh Crusade ended in tragedy.

In January 1256, the great Mongolian army crossed the River Ama Darya in Central Asia. The army was led by Hulagu,[41] brother of the great Mongke Khan. His goal was to depose the Abbasid caliph in Baghdad. Hulagu entered Baghdad on 15 February 1257. Over the following forty days some 80,000 inhabitants were slaughtered. The only ones to be spared were those taken as slaves, and the Christian community, at the explicit request of Hulagu's first wife Dokuz Khatun, who belonged to the Nestorian Christian Church. In September 1259, the Mongolian army started towards Syria. The vanguard was led by Nestorian Christians from the tribe of Naiman, Kitbuqa Noyan. The lord of Damascus, Sultan An-Nasir Yusuf, ran to Egypt and the Mongols took Damascus on 1 March 1260.

For the first time after six centuries, three Christian noblemen entered the former capital of the caliphate: Kitbuqa, the king of Armenia and the duke of Antioch. In the spring the Mongols also conquered Nablus and Gaza. They did not enter Jerusalem. Frank lands overseas were completely surrounded by Mongols, who had no intention of attacking Christians. The great Mongke Khan died in August 1290, so Hulagu was forced to withdraw most of his units from Syria in order to protect his interests until the election of the new great khan. Khan's friend and loyal military leader Kitbuqa was left to govern Syria.

Mamluk Sultan Qutuz took the army from Egypt to gain back Syria, while the majority of Mongolian forces were away. The battle took place on 3 September by the Goliath Fisheries, where Christians had defeated Saladin in 1183. The Mongols were defeated for the first time in history. Kitbuqa was taken prisoner and then killed.

This battle marked a historical turning-point for the Middle East. If Hulagu had managed to enter Egypt and overthrow the Mamluk sultanate, Muslim states east of Morocco would have disappeared and Christians would have been in a position to rule over Asia Minor. Qutuz returned to Egypt as the victor. The best Mamluk commander, Baibars, asked to be appointed governor of Damascus but the sultan refused, fearing that would make Baibars too strong. With the help of his followers, Baibars killed the sultan during a hunt at the Nile delta on 23 October 1260, after which he was made sultan of the Mamluk Empire.

Rukn al-Din Baibars was a Kipchak Turk, blue-eyed, tall and dark-skinned. As a young slave, he was sold to the Mamluk emir and taken to Egypt to become a warrior in the sultan's Mamluk guard. Prone to dishonourable and ruthless behaviour, he soon showed himself to be a capable warrior and commander, and later even a clever statesman.

In early 1265 he started with a strong army from Egypt with the intention of attacking the Mongols in the north of Syria, but he was informed that his Syrian forces were handling the enemy well so he stayed in Palestine. He took Caesarea on 5 March, and then unsuccessfully attacked the strong Templar fortress of Atlit. Then he besieged the well-supplied Hospitaller fortress of Arsuf, defended tenaciously by 270 Hospitaller knights. The city fell after five days, while the Hospitallers retreated to the citadel and resisted for another three days. One-third of the knights died, and the Hospitaller commander was forced to negotiate a surrender. After he was promised that the garrison would be allowed to leave freely, he surrendered the citadel on 29 April. The sultan then changed his mind and took the survivors as prisoners. He left guards before Acre and returned to Egypt. He returned in the summer of 1266 with two armies. He took one to Galilee himself, but again kept away from Acre, where the garrison was reinforced by French warriors sent by King Louis; instead, the sultan passed by the Teutonic knights' fortress of Montfort to attack the Templars in Saphet.

The Templars had reinforced the fortress: 850 workmen and 400 slaves reinforced the walls with seven round towers, each 18 metres in diameter. The garrison was numerous, with some 2,200 men. The first charge on 7 July was repulsed, and the same happened with the following ones on 13 and 19 July. Then the sultan announced that he would spare any defender who surrendered and was of Syrian origin. Baibars was known as a liar who could not be trusted, but Templar suspicions became unbearable so many men deserted, after which the Templars' garrison was not numerous enough to defend the fortress. A negotiator was sent and it was agreed that the Templars would be allowed to go to Acre without hindrance, but when they left the fortress they were caught and killed. Toron then fell without a fight and Baibars was in control of Galilee.

When the sultan returned to Egypt, the Duke of Antioch, Hugues,[42] Regent of Cyprus, started on a campaign of vengeance throughout Galilee. He was ambushed on 2 October by the garrison of Saphet and local Arabs and forced to return to Akko after serious losses. The second Mamluk army attacked the Armenian King Hethum I.[43] The decisive battle took place on 24 August; the Armenians were dispersed and no longer played a significant role in local circumstances.

The following year, 1267, Baibars was under Acre again. His units carried captured Templar and Hospitaller banners and thus arrived under the very city walls before the trick was discovered. They could not attack the city, so they settled for pillaging and robbing the environments. Baibars arrived the following year too. After a half-day battle, he took Jaffa on 7 March, killed the inhabitants and allowed the garrison to go to Acre. The fortress itself was demolished. Immediately after, the Templar fortress of Beaufort was also attacked and surrendered on 15 April after ten days of bombing. The sultan avoided Tripoli with its strong garrison, as well as the Templar fortresses of Tortosa and Safita, and arrived under Antioch on 14 May. The following day, the first charge against the city was repulsed, but the defenders were few and could barely cover all the sectors of the long city walls.

The following attack took place on 18 May 1268. Now the Mamluks attacked from all sides. After a bloody battle, the wall was breached in one spot and the attackers entered the city. The sultan had the city gates closed so that nobody could get out. Whoever was found in the streets was killed, while those in houses resisted for a short while. Several thousand inhabitants tried to save themselves by fleeing to the great citadel on top of the hill. Their lives were spared, but they were enslaved and distributed to the victors. Every one of Baibars' warriors received at least one slave. Antioch had been famed as the richest Frank city overseas, and the spoils that Baibars had won were enormous. The city never recovered, remaining only a fortress of local importance, completely irrelevant to Muslim authorities. The Duchy of Antioch, the first Christian state to be founded overseas, ceased to exist. The Templars abandoned the fortresses of Bagras and La Roche de Roussel without fighting as there was simply no point in keeping them further.

In February 1271 the sultan attacked the White Fortress near Safita; obeying their grand master, the Templars surrendered and retreated to Tortosa. The next in line was the majestic Hospitaller fortress Krak des Chevaliers. Heavy rain had been falling for almost two weeks, so the Muslims could not set up their catapults. Once the weather calmed down, on 15 March the bombing of Krak began. It took a month and a half before the outer wall was breached. The sultan concentrated the attacks on the south and east walls. The first to suffer serious damage was the tower on the junction of the south and east walls; then the other eastern tower and, finally, the tower on the junction of the north and east walls. Over crumbling bulwarks, the attackers reached the outer courtyard. Many defenders died or were captured there. The others retreated to the inner courtyard and defended it for another ten days. The Muslims were unable to take the strong inner fortress by direct assault, so Baibars dragged the siege machines to the outer walls. The Hospitallers had no answer to this new threat and agreed to surrender Krak. They left it on 8 April 1271.

Another Hospitaller fortress, Akkar in Lebanon, fell on 1 May after four days of siege. The sultan's way to Tripoli was now free. Still, he offered a ten-year peace to Bohemond VI,[44] Count of Tripoli and Duke of Antioch (Latakia being all that remained of the duchy), since the crusading army of the English Prince Edward[45] had disembarked at Acre on 9 May. After peace was arranged, Baibars started for Egypt and, along the way, after a seven-day siege on 16 June they took the fortress of Montfort in Galilee. This Teutonic fortress was the last one that the crusaders held inside the Holy Land.

Then 30 years old, Edward was an enterprising and cold-blooded knight, but he only brought 1,000 warriors. He was joined by the Cyprian King Hugues and, several months later, Edward's brother Edmund of Lancaster arrived with reinforcements. The only thing that Edward achieved overseas was the peace of 22 May 1272, arranged to last for ten years and ten months, between the commune of Acre and the sultan, guaranteeing the safety of the narrow strip of land from Acre to Sidon.

The knightly Orders were in very different situations when the two peace agreements that ensured the survival of the remaining crusaders' properties overseas were concluded. The Order of St John was seriously shaken. In a letter from 1268, the Hospitallers' Grand Master Hugues de Revel says he only had 300 knights overseas instead of 1,000 as used to be the case. They only had one fortress left: Margat in Syria, situated 2km from the Mediterranean coast and some 6km from Baniyas.

The Templars held Sidon, Atlit and Tortosa, the fortress in the city of Tartus, after Latakia the largest port of Syria. Tortosa was the see for the Temple's military headquarters. They had spread their banking business, providing them with a large secure income throughout the Levant.

Sultan Baibars, the greatest enemy of Christianity, a great warrior, capable governor and statesman, ill-mannered and shifty, died on 1 July 1277. Barakah, Baibars' son and heir, was deposed in the 1279 uprising of the Emir Kalavun, who had proclaimed himself the Sultan of Egypt several months earlier. In July 1283, Kalavun renewed the peace agreement with the commune of Acre and the Templars in Atlit and Sidon. His goal was to prevent a possible alliance between Franks and Mongols in Persia. The peace did not include Tyre and Beiruth, and Kalavun prepared to attack the Christian enclaves not yet protected by the agreement. His first goal was the Hospitaller fortress of Margat. The time had come for him to punish the monks from this fortress who had, in autumn 1281, joined the Armenian king's forces and on 20 October by Homs sided with Mongols in the battle against the Mamluk army.

The great sultan's army set up camp on 17 April 1285 under the hill that housed the powerful fortress. More mangonel catapults were dragged over than in any previous siege. The bombing of the fortress did not produce any particular results since the Hospitallers also had mangonels and, as their position up the hill gave them the advantage, they destroyed many of the Muslim machines.

When, after a month of siege there was no progress, the sultan ordered a tunnel to be dug under the fortress wall. It was decided to do it under the Tower of Hope at the end of the north wall. The tunnel was filled with wood and set on fire. The stone above cracked from the heat and the tower crumbled on 23 May. Although the debris momentarily prevented the attack, the defenders realized that they would not be able to resist for long and the fortress surrendered. Twenty-five Hospitaller knights were allowed to leave Margat on horseback and with full equipment, while the others left weaponless and on foot.

Great rivals Venice and Genoa were constantly on the verge of war regarding maritime ways and trade with Egypt and Levant. When Bohemond VII,[46] Count of Tripoli, died, his sister Lucia succeeded him and in 1288 approved the privileges giving Genoa certain streets in Tripoli and allowing a separate governor for the Genoan colony. Venice interpreted this as a serious threat to its interests and sent emissaries to the sultan in Egypt, warning him that Genoa could rule the trade on the Levant from Tripoli, pushing out Muslim traders from Alexandria. This was reason enough for Kalavun to intervene. In early 1289 his army attacked the city. Most of the non-fighting population had already fled to Cyprus. Tripoli was aided by the Templars under Marshal Geoffrey de Vendac, the Hospitallers under Marshal Matthew de Clermont, the French from Acre under Jean de Grailly[47] and Amalric,[48] the Cypriot king's younger brother, with a contingent of knights and four galleons. Mamluk siege machines again did their job: they destroyed the towers and the wall that divided the city, situated on a peninsula, from the mainland. Warriors from Venice and Genoa decided that further fighting made no sense, and two Venetian galleons as well as four Genoans left the city port, which confused the defenders. On the morning of 26 April, the sultan ordered a general assault. A torrent of attackers rushed over the ruins of the city walls. Part of the defenders saved themselves by fleeing on the remaining vessels; this included the marshals of the Templars and the Hospitallers. The commander of Templars in Tripoli, Peter de Moncada, was killed. The surviving men were all killed, women and children taken as slaves and the city pillaged and then thoroughly destroyed, so that it would not get into the hands of the Franks overseas.

After the fall of Tripoli, the Cypriot King Henry[49] came to Acre, where he was found by the sultan's emissaries. The sultan held the defence of Tripoli against the king and the knightly Orders, but he was told that the peace agreement from 1283 did not include Tripoli because, if it did, the sultan would have been in the wrong to attack the city in the first place. Satisfied with this response, the sultan prolonged the peace with Acre for a further ten years, ten months and ten days. Thanks to this peace agreement, trade started growing in Acre, caravans arrived from Damascus and the peasants sent their grain to be sold after the rich harvest of 1290.

Amid the lively city swarming with merchants, in August Italian crusaders arrived. This was a dissipated warrior mob that their commanders could not control as they had nothing with which to pay them. Drunken and arrogant warriors created many problems for the city authorities, getting into fights with the population. They treated peaceful Muslim merchants and peasants as enemies to be dealt with because they saw themselves as heroes on the warpath with the infidels. By the end of August, the tense situation led to bloodshed. What was the first cause we do not know, but the consequences were horrifying. Italian crusaders rushed to the streets and started cutting every man with a beard, believing them to be Muslim, so numerous local Christians were also killed. Local knights and knightly Orders managed to save a few Muslims and send a few killers to prison.

The news of the massacre on the streets of Acre enraged the sultan, quite justifiably. He asked that all the rioters be given to him for punishment. Apologies and regrets from the Acre authorities did not help. The grand master of the Templars proposed that the sultan's request be approved, but the others believed no one should be delivered to the infidels as this would mean certain death and that opinion prevailed. It was implied to the sultan's emissaries that Muslims were the ones who had provoked the riots by their behaviour.

Map of the Siege of Acre.

The sultan saw no alternative but to order a campaign against Acre. While he was gathering Egyptian forces, the Syrian army gathered by Caesarea and started building siege machines. In order to confuse the enemy, the sultan spread word that he was going on a campaign in Africa. The grand master of the Templars, Guillaume de Beaujeu, found out the sultan's true intentions through his spy network and sent negotiators to Cairo without consulting anyone. The sultan promised to spare Acre if they paid repairs in the amount of one Venetian gold piece per head. Guillaume communicated the offer to the city authorities. There was much hullabaloo, the offer was refused, and the grand master was accused of treason and exposed to insults.

Nothing could now stop the war. The sultan swore he would spare no one in Acre, but as soon as he started from Cairo leading his army, on 4 November 1290 the sultan fell ill and died six days later, only 12 kilometres away from his capital. Kalavun had been a great sultan, a ruthless warrior with a sense of honour. He kept every one of his agreements. His son, Al-Ashraf Khalil, was prepared to succeed his great father and to continue his way. He did not give up on the conquest of Akko, but he had to postpone the campaign until spring. The authorities in Acre thought they might be able to negotiate with the new sultan, but Al-Ashraf wouldn't even receive the delegation. He had the four emissaries killed in prison.

Until spring, throughout the sultanate, siege machines were being prepared. There were around 100 of them. The largest waited by Krak. It was called 'Victorious'. The care of this huge military apparatus was entrusted to the sultan's 18-year-old son Abdul-Fida. Another catapult that was particularly large was known as 'Furious'. Al-Ashraf arrived in Damascus on 6 March 1291. The army, burdened with the weight of siege machines and equipment, dragged itself from Hama to Acre through mud in torrents of rain. The sultan joined them on the way with the units from Egypt and on 5 April arrived under Acre with an army significantly larger than that of the defenders. There is mention of 60,000 horsemen and more than 100,000 infantry, which is almost certainly an overestimate.

During the winter the Franks sent a call for help to the West, but met with no success. Some knights dropped in now and then in a haphazard manner. The Templars and the Hospitallers gathered all their available warriors and numerous Teutonic knights also joined them. The Cypriot King Henry again sent his units under the command of his brother Amalric, who was supposed to command the defence of the city; Henry promised to come and bring reinforcements. All able-bodied citizens were included in the defence. The city was defended by around 1,000 heavy cavalry, knights and sergeants; there were no more than 30,000 citizens and up to 14,000 infantrymen. The city on the peninsula and its northern suburb of Montmusart were defended by a double bulwark. Each of the walls was reinforced with twelve irregularly disposed towers. The suburb was divided from the city by another wall with four towers. Near the place where the wall met the city bulwarks there was a citadel. At the most exposed spot on the city walls, where the wall going northward from the bay swerved towards the west, the great tower of King Henry II was situated and directly before it King Hugues' barbican. As commander of the defence, Amalric and his royal troops took this most exposed position, the barbican and the surrounding walls. To his right were the French knights under Jean de Grailly and English knights under his friend, the Swiss knight Otto de Grandson,[50] then the units from Venice, Pisa and Acre. Craftsmen from Pisa had built the largest catapult at the disposal of the defence. To Amalric's left the wall was defended by the Hospitallers and the far left wing by the Templars. Teutonic knights were added to the king's men. The defenders had too few fighters to effectively cover all the parts of the wall. Some of the elderly and children were transferred to Cyprus, and some who could have helped in the defence certainly fled along with them. The garrison had support from the sea and food was in regular supply from Cyprus. They also had a galleon with a catapult, which was a big problem for the Muslims.

The army from Hama took up position opposite the Templars, Damascus opposite the Hospitallers and the largest army, the one from Egypt, besieged the city walls from the inner wall between the city and its suburbs to the bay. The sultan had his tent erected near the bay, opposite the Legate's Tower. The siege began on 6 April, with the usual bombing of the walls and the city with rocks and clay vessels filled with an inflammable explosive mixture. The archers tried to hit the defenders in galleries on top of the bulwark, while the engineers started digging underground tunnels beneath the most important parts of the wall. Mutual showering with projectiles lasted for days. The galleon with the catapult threw stone blocks towards the encampment of the Hama contingent. On the ships following this one, siege towers covered in oxen skins were erected, so Frank archers used them to shoot at Saracen warriors. Under the crossfire from the city walls and the sea, the Hama army suffered many losses. They were saved by nature. One night a strong wind arose and the ship rocked so much that the construction of the catapult broke.

The night of 15 April was moonless and the Templars used it for a sudden assault on the Hama army camp together with the English. Although they'd managed to surprise the Muslims, the Templars found themselves in trouble. Once they were among enemy tents they could not see their way well, so many of them fell over the ropes holding the tents to the ground. Confusion ensued and many were captured without even getting off the ground, while the others were pressed back to the city with many losses. Al-Muzaffar, the commander of Hama, had the heads of the dead enemies tied to the tails of horses which he then presented to the sultan.

The following assault was attempted by the Hospitallers on a dark night, but the Muslims were now ready for them and quickly lit numerous torches and fires. This attempt also ended poorly, so it was decided to stop the practice. This decision had a deteriorating effect on the morale of the defenders, since the initiative was now completely in the hands of the Muslims. On 5 May, King Henry arrived as he had promised with reinforcements of 100 horsemen and 2,000 infantrymen on 40 ships, but this was insufficient to change anything in the defence of the city.

After a month, mining and engineering work bore fruit. The barbican could not be saved, so its garrison abandoned it and set it on fire on 8 May, after which it crumbled. In the following week, the English Tower and the Tower of Countess Blois were also mined, and the wall around St Anthony's Gate and St Nicholas's Tower started crumbling from the bombing. Under the torrent of stones, the outer wall of King Henry II's Tower also crumbled on 15 May, so on the following morning the Mamluks penetrated the grand tower's ruins and the defenders were forced to retreat to the inner wall. The following day, the Muslims aimed a strong attack at the crumbling wall by St Anthony's Gate, jointly defended by the Hospitallers and the Templars. Hospitaller Marshal Matthew de Clermont stood out by his courage. On 17 May the Mamluks merely strengthened their position at the outer wall.

Knights of the Temple and St John fought side by side at the Cursed Tower.

On the morning of 18 May, the decisive attack on the city began. The sultan decided to attack the part of the wall from St Anthony's Gate to the Patriarch's Tower by the bay. He sent his strongest forces to the Cursed Tower. Mangonels and catapults constantly showered the city and the walls, archers prevented the defenders from even peeking behind the crenellations of the wall, trumpets and cymbals mixed with the attackers' war cries and 300 drummers on camels gave rhythm to the attackers. The number of attackers was such that there was no question of whether they could take the inner wall, merely when. Cypriot knights who were defending the Cursed Tower were starting to fail, and the help of Syrian knights was not sufficient either. The Hospitaller master led his warriors and the Templars over the wall in an unsuccessful attempt to repulse the enemy. The Templars' grand master received a fatal wound and was taken to the Temple building, where he died. He was accompanied on that final path by de Clermont, who then returned to the battle and was killed.

On the east wall, the French and the English held for hours more but the enemy, attacking from the conquered Cursed Tower, pushed them towards the bay. They were pushed all the way to St Nicholas' Gate, through which a mass of Muslim warriors now poured. Street-fighting began. The grand master of the Hospitallers, John of Villiers, was wounded and taken to a ship in the harbour despite his protests. King Henry II and his brother Amalric had embarked and sailed away even before that. This could have seemed cowardly, but nothing more could be done and the brothers had to think about the future of the Cypriot kingdom.

De Grailly, the commander of the French knights was wounded and his friend Otto was now in command of the east sector of the wall. He filled all the ships he could find with warriors, including de Grailly, and sailed away. Everyone was trying to get on board: warriors, women and children, but there were few ships. Many fell into the water and drowned. Some ship captains even asked for money to let people on board. Most people remained in the city. Muslim warriors cut down everyone they found in the streets, while those found later in houses were taken as slaves. Later, travellers met former Templars working as woodcutters on the Dead Sea. After some ten years, some were allowed to return to the West.

The whole city was under Muslim control by nightfall on 18 May apart from the large Templar castle by the sea in the south-west corner of the city. The remaining Templars sought refuge there, together with many civilians. They lasted for a few days, since the Muslims couldn't break through the building's thick walls. Even some ships from Cyprus returned to help the surrounded Templars. At last, the sultan proposed to the marshal of the Temple Peter de Severy to freely embark on the ships with all the people who had sheltered there and their property on condition that the building be surrendered peacefully. The marshal agreed and one emir entered the fortress together with around 100 Mamluks, while the sultan's banner was raised on the roof. Undisciplined Muslim warriors started assaulting the imprisoned girls and boys. The knights could not accept this: they cut down the Mamluks, pulled down the banner and boarded up the castle, prepared to fight to the death. During the night, the marshal put Templar treasure on one of the ships and, under the command of Thibaud Gaudin, sent it to Sidon. The sultan was aware that he would hardly be able to take the castle without many losses, so he offered the same conditions of surrender again. The marshal and a few of his men went to negotiate the conditions, but they were captured and killed immediately before the sultan's tent. This did not discourage the defenders. They boarded themselves up again and continued fighting. On 28 May the sultan sent 2,000 Mamluks against the castle. The building could not hold so many people and it fell apart, burying both the attackers and those inside. The city was then pillaged and set on fire, the fortifications demolished and, in the following years, only a few remained to live on the remains of a once powerful city.

On 19 May, before Acre had fallen completely, the sultan had sent his army to Tyre, which was abandoned and surrendered without a fight. In Sidon, the Templars decided to fight. They chose Thibaud Gaudin as their grand master. A month passed before the Muslim army appeared under the city walls. As Templars were not numerous enough to defend the city, they retreated to a fortress on a small island some 80 metres from the coast. The grand master sailed to Cyprus to get help, or so he said, but in fact he did nothing; he simply remained on Cyprus. The Templars in the sea fortress held fast until Muslims started building an embankment from the coast towards the islet holding the fortress. Then they sailed to Tortosa. On 14 July, Emir Shujai took the fortress and had it demolished. Beiruth surrendered to the same emir on 31 July. The sultan conquered Haifa on 30 July. The Templar fortress of Tortosa was evacuated on 3 August and Atlit on 14 August. The only Templar fortress remained on the island of Ruad, some 3 kilometres from Tortosa, which lasted for another twelve years until 1303, but by then the Temple's fate was already sealed.

Chapter Ten

Epilogue

Unique among the knightly orders due to their exclusively military mission, warriors under the white and black banner were led by the belief that God had chosen them to defend all of Christianity with swords in their hands and that doing so would grant them eternal glory and the Kingdom of Heaven. Their faith produced high morale and a feeling of community. Through their monastic vows the Templars gave up profane values, material goods and the dissipated lifestyle characteristic of the knightly caste of their times. They learned to live with military modesty and without unnecessary flashiness. They followed orders unquestioningly and in silence. Their chain of command was experienced and well-established and the warriors and their supplies highly mobile. All this describes a top-notch fighting unit, something with which the secular feudal army could not even begin to compare.

At the pinnacle of its power, the Temple had around 7,000 members, of which 1,500 were knights, mostly overseas. Unordained assistants and outside members numbered seven times more. The Order always had thousands of war, riding and pack horses in the East, although they died all too easily in the difficult terrain. The warriors themselves were exposed to exhaustion, illness and death in battle. At the time, even a small wound was often fatal due to infection. All of this required enormous funds. It is unknown how many people exactly passed through the Temple, but it is certain that we are talking about tens of thousands, if not even more than 100,000 monks and associate members. Many lost their lives bravely fighting the infidels, sometimes without intending to win the battle. Heroic fighting was more important than victory. They believed that God would know how to value their knightly actions.

Military understanding of the Knights Templar, achieved in the dust of the Holy Land, was highly esteemed. Pope Urban IV appointed three Knights Templar as chaplains in his state's fortresses. During his sojourn overseas, Richard the Lionheart trusted only the military prowess of the Templars and the Hospitallers.

At the time, many complained that the Templars were not spending the riches gathered through gifts of devoted Christians for the fulfilment of their vows but rather on acquiring and maintaining properties. As Cistercians, the Templars did work on the maintenance of their properties, contributing to the spreading of farming and craft knowledge. It is possible and even probable that in such a large organization as the Temple, with thousands of houses throughout Europe and overseas, there was some corruption but the Order's military service was primary and required large investments.

According to contemporary sources, in the year 1180 in Burgundy a knight needed a property of 3 square kilometres for his own upkeep, while eighty years later he needed 15.6 square kilometres. The cost of a knight, his sergeants and servants plus battle, riding and pack horses, armour, weapons and other equipment can be compared to the cost of a tank today, and Templars had more than 1,000 such knights at one time. Not all the expenses were covered by the Temple; each new monk had to join the order with full knightly equipment and a horse. However, all other expenses were the Temple's obligation: buying and producing additional and replacement weaponry and armour, equipment repair, horse-raising, buying and producing food for the monks and other members of the order, masonry work on fortresses, ship-building, etc.

At the pinnacle of their power, overseas alone the Templars held fifty-three fortresses from the largest, the Pilgrims' Fortress in Atlit, to lonely towers next to pilgrims' roads, and the Order cared for the garrisons, maintenance, supplies and equipment for all these fortresses. Templar buildings were characterized by their simplicity and functionality, so their fortifications could not compare in grandiosity with the famous Hospitallers' Krak and Margat.

Their own finances were an important advantage of the Temple. At the Lateran Council in 1179, lending money with interest was condemned and described as usury. Usurers were to be considered thieves deserving eternal punishment, except for the Templars because they had no personal property; everything belonged to the Order. The Order transferred alms, money from renting out their own property and profits from everything they made on European properties overseas to equip and maintain their own military power. Dealing with significant sums, the Temple, quite naturally, started dabbling in banking business, lending money at low interest rates as was then usual among church officials and orders. Although the church had condemned banking as usury, it was impossible to stop the transformation of feudal economy from a simple exchange of goods to the beginnings of monetary trade.

As a rule, the Templars treated Muslim populations on the territory of newly-created Christian states peacefully, constantly using the knowledge and service of the indigenous population for their own needs. Thanks to the long years of continuous sojourn in the Holy Land, Knights Templar gained rich insights into living with people of a completely different mentality and world views. They were used to avoiding issues of religion in communicating with Muslims. They even went so far that, for instance, they allowed Emir Usama[1] to prey on the Holy Rock, then situated within the Order's see. Yet even then, the Templars remained very far in religious terms from their friend Usama, who considered it serious blasphemy to believe that God had once been embodied in the Virgin Mary. Due to such adaptable attitudes in religious issues, the Templars were suspected of losing their faith, particularly by Western noblemen who did not understand the circumstances in the Middle East or deliberately misinterpreted them for their own reasons. Only Philip the Beautiful dared to publicly accuse them of heresy.

Excellent negotiators and diplomats, the Templars could achieve things around the negotiating table that they could never have achieved on the battlefield. They were so esteemed that popes and many courts used their services, and they were schooled in very complicated political relations overseas. Of course, some unreasonable acts were carried out by grand masters of the Temple, which directly influenced the fortunes of war and even the fate of Christian lands overseas. In this respect, no one could measure up to Gerard de Ridefort, a brave knight with a dishonourable secular past who used the Temple to gain personal vengeance. However, there were also very clever and brave masters, such as Guillaume de Beaujeu, the man who did all in his power to ensure the survival of Acre and then lay down his life in the defence of the city.

After the fall of Tortosa, the Templars moved their command to Cyprus. They still had significant properties and funding, but the very point of their existence came into question. They were going to constitute their own state, either on Cyprus or in Languedoc in the south-east of France, following the example of the Teutonic Order in Prussia. They could travel throughout Europe without paying taxes to anyone and they had their own army. They were a kind of a state within a state and completely out of control.

Additional problems were created by the fact that the French King Philip's treasury was empty and he was deeply in debt to the Templars. It was the custom of the French kings, including Philip, to employ the Templars as controllers of the state revenues in the royal treasury. Apparently he had unlimited confidence in them. The king borrowed 500,000 livres from the Temple in 1299, the amount he spent on the Flemish War and his sister's dowry. In the meantime, he imposed new taxes and forged coins, which provoked an uprising in Paris, during which the king took refuge with the Templars [location unknown]. Eight years later, in the spring of 1307, Pope Clement V[2] and Templar Grand Master Moley[3] met to rectify the situation in the Order. The Pope planned to meet again with the grand master in mid-November of the same year, but he received news of the arrests of Templars in France a week earlier. As early as September, bailiffs and seneschals in France received the king's secret order to prepare the imprisonment of all members of the Temple. On charges of heresy, idolatry and homosexual behaviour prepared by the king's seal-keeper and law adviser Guillaume de Nogaret, on Friday, 13 October 1307 Templars throughout France were arrested, including Grand Master Moley.

The accusation of heresy was not accidental. Pope Gregory IX founded the Papal inquisition in 1233 (mostly Dominican and Franciscan monks) to bring about the persecution of heretics. Inquisitors in the northern Apennine Peninsula were allowed to interrogate monks of exempt and protected Templars, Cistercians and Hospitallers only in case of heresy. Since the time of Louis IX (the Albigensian Crusade), French kings had had a free hand in exterminating heresy in France and Philip was given two legal bases as an opportunity to deal with the Templars. If not heretics, Templars were untouchable by the king of France!

Although the arrest of the Templars meant contemptuous trampling over papal authority (only the Pope had the right to try the Temple), the king succeeded in getting the Pope to support his actions and on 22 November a papal decree ordered all sovereigns of the Catholic faith to arrest the Templars and confiscate all their property in the name of the Pope and the church. The king's people attributed a total of 127 charges against the Templars. It looks as though the writers of the charges simply counted up all the contemporarily-known blasphemies. No one would have been able to think up and practise at the same time all these mostly unreasonable and stupid acts. Accusations against which Templars must defend themselves were altogether lucid, and in normal circumstances nobody would confess any such stupid activities.

Trials in France began in Paris at the end of 1307, in which 138 Templars were brought before the inquisitors, of whom only a few were knights, mostly brothers in the service of the Order. The average age of the detainees was 41, which is not strange because the able-bodied went straight to the war zones. Some were young and only just ordained. Many were tortured and 123 of them signed confessions. The following year a new trial was held at Poitiers before papal investigators, and after a hearing the Pope absolved seventy-two Templars. The Provencal Templars – twenty-one of them – were imprisoned in early 1308. There were no trials and their fate is completely unknown.

At a new trial in Paris in 1310, again before the papal investigators, there were about 600 Templars ready to defend the Order. Dissatisfied with the development of the trial, Philip ordered the Archbishop of Sens, Philippe de Marigny to take over the process. Although the Pope intervened and directed his commission to continue the trial, the Archbishop of Sens turned a deaf ear and, despite the Pope's instructions, decided to execute fifty-four stubborn Templars who pleaded not guilty. On 12 May 1310, outside Paris, fifty-four Templars were put to death by burning. According to some sources they were burned at the stake; others say that the carts in which they were loaded were set on fire after the horses were removed.

The papal commission ended on 5 June 1311 with no confirmed evidence of Templar heresy. In the same year the Council of Vienne voted for the right of the Temple to defend itself against Philip's accusations which were untenable without straining canon law. In 1312, without consulting the council, Pope Clement V issued the edict *Vox in excelso*, which suspended the Temple without having unequivocal proof of the Templars' heresy. The Pope, with his bull *Ad Providam*, distributed the Templar estates to the Hospitallers. With the same bull, the Pope separated the Templars who did not repent from those who were not found guilty and those who returned under the auspices of the church. In March 1314 Jacques de Molay and the Templar Commander of Normandy Geoffroi de Charny withdrew their confessions from 1307 and pleaded guilty only to treason to the Order, because under torture they had confessed to something they had never done. They were immediately declared heretics and burned at the stake on 22 March, which silenced the other detainees. Only the fate of those fifty-four Templars burned at the stake is known, but it is almost certain that many more in France died as a result of torture or were secretly killed. Nogaret and the Pope died in April and the king in November 1314.

In the British Isles the fate of the Templars was not so black. Ever since the time of Richard the Lionheart the English had seen the Templars as sincere and faithful comrades. At that time the Templar estates in England were large and the number of monks small, only 144 of them: only 20 knights, 108 sergeants and 16 Templar priests. Numerous tenants and servants took care of the Templar estates throughout England, Scotland and Ireland. According to records of inventory confiscated from the Temple in 1309, it is evident that the annual income from the Templar estates in England, Scotland and Ireland was about £5,000. By comparison, the revenues of the counties ranged from £500 to £3,000.

English King Edward II did not take the accusations against the Templars seriously and it was not until late 1307 when he received a direct papal order to imprison Templars that he gave the order for all to be arrested in England, Scotland and Ireland. Unlike in France, the monks of the Temple in England were kept in decent custody and received financial support. They had a bed, clothes and personal items. It was not until the autumn of 1309 that two papal inquisitors began the trial of the Templars. In England, the torture for the purpose of investigation was forbidden, so the Templars in turn confessed only some minor sins and their trial ended with a pardon in 1310. Master of Templars in England William de la More did not confess any guilt and died in the Tower of London. Two Templars in Scotland confessed minor sins, and in Ireland the trial of fourteen Templars yielded no results.

After reconciliation with the church many English Templars transferred to the Hospitallers, others joined the Cistercian Order and some lived on a pension. Numerous Templars in Germany were banned by a decision of King Henry VII, and repression of the Order varied by province. In Magdeburg, the archbishop Burchard III imprisoned the Templar Commander of Germany, Friedrich von Alvensleben, and several Templars. He appropriated the Templar estates which, according to records from 1318, he did not return to the Hospitallers. At the trials in Luxemburg and Trier the property of the Order was confiscated in 1310 and the Templars were released. Otto, the Templar commander of Brunswick and the duke's brother, joined the Hospitaller House of Supplingenburg.

In other countries, Templars were also imprisoned and questioned but not tortured, and were subsequently released. Some 500 brothers bravely gave themselves up to the Inquisition, proving their innocence and impregnable loyalty to the Order.

In Mainz, Templars decided to fight for the truth. About twenty fully-armoured Knights Templar under Count Hugo of Grumbach fell into the place of local council convened by the Archbishop of Mainz during 1310. Hugo clearly and loudly rejected accusations against the Temple, called Pope Clement V an unjust tyrant and demanded a petition to the Pope for fair investigation just to be able to prove the innocence of brother Templars. Fearing bloodshed, the archbishop granted the Templars' wishes and after one year of investigation he affirmed that Templars in his region were innocent. Hugo's brother, Frederick of Salm, Commander of the House of Rhineland, told the inquisitors that he knew de Molay personally and did not believe his guilt. He was not tortured and was found not guilty.

Public opinion in Germany was on the side of the Templars. All in all, few were imprisoned and no one was killed. Acquitted, the German Templars were given the opportunity to act according to their own discretion. Some joined the Hospitallers or the Teutonic knights, others sought peace in monastic life and retirement and still others, as the Order no longer existed, concluded that no vow bound them any more and continued to live a worldly life. The situation was similar in the Hungarian-Croatian kingdom.

In Cyprus the Temple owned the strongholds of Nicosia, Limassol and Gastria. The strong Templar garrison under command of the marshal of the Order of Cyprus, Ayme de Osilliers, consisted of forty-one knights, thirty sergeants and two Templar priests. Unlike the Templars tried in other Templar provinces, these monks were younger but were experienced warriors, many of high birth and ordained throughout Christian lands. It could be said that they were the elite of the Temple. The Temple in Cyprus was under the protection of Amalric de Lusignan; however, the Templars helped to expel his older brother and the King of Cyprus, Henry II de Lusignan, became governor of the island. Amalric disobeyed the papal decree and it was not until June 1308, after a minor revolt by local barons, that he was forced to imprison the Templars at Lefkara. They were imprisoned without trial for two years until Amalric was killed in 1310. King Henry II returned, understandably averse to the Templars, but even then they were not subjected to maltreatment like the brothers in France.

According to a poorly-preserved manuscript from the Vatican archives,[4] the trial started in May 1311. The hearing began unusually, with the examination of twenty-one non-Templar witnesses. None testified against the Templars. It was only after them that the Templars were questioned, and they resolutely rejected the accusations of idolatry and testified that they were accepted to the Temple through the Templar provinces strictly according to the Rule of the Order. Each member of the Order was asked one of 123 questions relating to one of 127 charges. Everyone rejected everything. Their testimonies were equal to those of the grand master and other high officials of the Temple in France. Thirty-one other non-Templar men then testified, among them the clergy and the Bishop of Beirut. Again, no charges were brought against the Temple. Only the very last witness, a Hospitaller, testified against the Templars, almost certainly with the intention of his Order gaining rival property. That concluded the trial. Hospitallers were given real estate but not money, and movable property was used to cover the trial costs. What happened to the Templars from Cyprus is not exactly known. According to some sources they were drowned and, according to the Chronicle from 1316, many died in prison.

The Apennine Peninsula, formerly largely part of the Holy Roman Empire, was split between the Lombard League (a military alliance of urban communes and one of the first examples of a confederate system) and numerous city-states, as well as the Papal State and the kingdom of Naples.

King Charles II of Naples was the uncle of Philip IV, so it was to be expected that the persecution of the Templars in his kingdom would be fiercer than elsewhere in the Apennines. Yet, according to the preserved documents from 1310, only six Templars were tried and tortured. Under torture, one of the monks said that he had been accepted into the Order in Catalonia and that all the Templars there denied Jesus. It turned out that he was ordained in Italy and that he was never in Catalonia. Of the thirteen Templars imprisoned in Tuscan cities, six were subjected to torture.

There were thirteen Templar Houses in the Papal State and only seven Templars were arrested – six monks and one Templar priest – none of whom ever left the Apennines. They all admitted to spitting and trampling on the Cross, four said they had to worship the idol and each described it differently. They were tortured and forgiveness was granted to all.

As warriors, builders and protectors, the Templars enjoyed a good reputation among the population in the Iberian Peninsula. King Denis I of Portugal refused to persecute the Templars on any chapter of the indictment and to dissolve the Order. After lengthy negotiations, in 1319 he succeeded in obtaining permission from the new Pope John XXII to establish a new Order, the successor of the Templars, the Order of the Knights of Our Lord Jesus Christ (*Ordem dos Cavaleiros de Nostro Senhor Jesus Cristo*). In silence, numerous Portuguese Templars and their vast estates entered the newly-formed Order.

Louis I,[5] ruler of Navarre, imprisoned some Templars from his kingdom and three Templars from Aragon who came to see what it was all about. The Order in Navarre was dissolved and the estates allotted to the Hospitallers. In Castile, Templar estates were annexed to the crown.

The King of Aragon, James II, refused to accuse the Templars. Pressed by letters from Philip IV demanding that the Templars must be imprisoned as a heretical and homosexual bunch, and with the knowledge of the confession of the grand master and other French Templars, James decided to bring the Temple under control. However, that was easier to decide than enforce because the Templars held strong fortifications and many were of high birth and had good connections throughout the kingdom. Few were found at all; the rest either escaped or took refuge in Templar castles. The brothers heard rumours of how their comrades had been treated in France and decided not to surrender to the mercy of the authorities. It was only after eighteen months of siege that the last Templar fortress surrendered. Miravet fell in December 1308. There is a legend that on the anniversary of the fall of the castle, the voice of a ghost Templar is heard encouraging fellow-fighters to resist. The Templars were not imprisoned but left under guard in their Houses, decently fed and settled down. Local and papal inquisitors at Tarragona did not launch an investigation until late 1309. After almost no confessions were extorted, eight Templars were unsuccessfully tortured in 1311. A council met and declared the Templars innocent in 1312. The brothers did not have to go to monasteries and remained living in the former Houses of the Temple, enjoying a regular pension.

On the former Templar estates the king founded a new knightly Order to fight Moors and pirates. The command was located in the fortress of St Georg in Montesa, so Pope John XXII recognized on 10 July 1317 the newly-founded Order of Montesa (*Ordre de Montesa*), based on Cistercian rule and dedicated to Our Lady. The order was annexed to the Order of Calatrava.

Some of the Templars were still very young warriors and continued to wage war either against Moors or against the Christians as mercenaries at the expense of local nobles. Bernardo de Fuentes fought at the head of the local militia in Tunisia. Jaime de Mas even made a decent career as a pirate. In 1350, Berenguer del Coll was mentioned as the last to whom Hospitallers paid a pension.

All in all, outside of France only a few Templars pleaded guilty and even fewer were convicted. Only exceptionally did local church authorities choose to use torture during the inquisitional investigations. There is no reliable information that any Templar was executed. It all came down to the seizure of land and movable property, which was basically the goal.

There is no information on what happened to the numerous Templars who were not incarcerated. Throughout Europe, there were 970 Templar Houses and still around 7,000 monks. In France alone, at the time there were 3,000 monks of the Temple. Many discarded their habits and disappeared among the local population. There is a story that claims some of the knights of the Temple hid in Swiss mountains. In 1314, Leopold of Austria took his army to Switzerland and was defeated by the small militia, even though the Swiss had no knights nor were they educated in the art of war. The legend mentions armoured white horsemen who helped the Swiss. Truly a pretty story, if it has anything to do with the Templars. Maybe some of them even embarked on the ship with the Holy Grail and treasure and sailed to waters unknown, like Bilbo and Frodo[6] on the elves' sail boat. Whatever did or did not happen, the Templars will always remain an inexhaustible well of inspiration for novelists, film-makers, historians and all those who merely like to fantasize about knightly times of long ago.

Notes

Prologue:

1. Gelasius, an ecclesiastical writer of the fifth century. He wrote *Syntagma*, a collection of writings from the First Nicene Council (325) divided into three books, the first of which deals with the life of the Emperor Constantine I.
2. Rufinus, born in 344/45 in Concordia Sagittaria in today's region of Veneto; monk, historian and theologian. In addition to his original works, he translated Eusebius' *Historia Ecclesiastica* from Greek to Latin, and added the era of Constantine I until the death of Theodosius I (395).
3. The Church of the Holy Sepulchre within the city walls of Jerusalem, today in the Christian quarter near Muristan, a complex of alleyways and markets. At the time of the crusades, the area housed the hospital of the order of St John. According to Christian belief, it is the spot where Christ was crucified and buried.
4. See the knightly order of St John.
5. Rulers of Persia (224–651). The founder of the dynasty Ardashir I (180–242) proclaimed himself *Shahanshah* ('King of Kings') in 224 after he defeated the Parthians near today's Bandar Abbas, the town controlling the Strait of Hormuz at the entrance to the Persian Gulf. The Sassanids, named after the House of Sasan, whose rule marked the pinnacle of the Persian Empire, got their name from Sasan, the grandfather of Ardashir I.
6. Flavius Heraclius Augustus (Byzantine Emperor 610–641) introduced Greek as the official language of the Byzantine Empire. He conducted military reforms, threw Persia out of Asia Minor and was the first Byzantine ruler to fight with the Muslims. He also conducted the Christianization of the Balkans.
7. Abu al-Qasim Muhammad ibn Abd Allah (570–632), born in Mecca; Muslim prophet and the founder of Islam.
8. Abrahamic monotheistic religion. God's words to the prophet Muhammad are written in the Quran, the holy book of Islam.
9. Abdullah ibn Abi Uthman (573–634), nicknamed Abu Bakr, a follower and father-in-law of the prophet Muhammad.
10. The person considered the political and religious heir of the prophet Muhammad.
11. King of the Ghassanid Dynasty. According to oral tradition, the Ghassanids (members of Azd Arabic tribes) moved from Yemen to the Syrian region of the Levant in the third century. Some of them had been Christians in their homeland, while others were Christianized upon arrival. They became military allies of Rome, a vassal state located at the Golan Plateau, and were leaders among the Azd tribes.
12. Abu Sulayman Khalid ibn al-Walid ibn al-Mughirah al-Makhzumi (592–642), also known as Sayf Allah al-Maslul ('Sword Drawn by God'), follower of the prophet Muhammad, fought in around 100 battles and remained undefeated, which puts him among the greatest military commanders in history.
13. Flavius Mauricius Tiberius Augustus (Byzantine Emperor, 582–602).
14. Flavius Claudius Constantius Augustus (Roman Emperor, 337–340).
15. Mahmud of Ghazni (971–1030), born in the town of Ghazni, Khorasan, the most important ruler of the Ghaznavid Dynasty. He was the first to have the title of sultan.
16. In Turkish, *ogur* means 'clan' or 'tribe'. The Ogurs were tribes of Turkish nomadic confederations of the early Middle Ages and included the Khazars, Avars, Bulgarians and Uyghurs.
17. Odo of Châtillon (1042–99), cardinal in Ostia, then Pope from 1088 to his death. In addition to starting the First Crusade, he organized the Roman Curia in its current form, like a royal court.
18. Alexis I Comnenus, emperor from 1081 to 1118. He abolished the previous division of the country, introduced the rule of feudal military aristocracy and started a mercenary army numbering around 70,000

people, mostly deployed in border garrisons. The Byzantine Emperor could appear on the battlefield with an army of 20,000 warriors with first-class equipment and training. It was, at the time, the best-organized and best-paid army in the world.

19. Raymond IV of St Gilles (1041–1105), Count of Toulouse, Duke of Narbonne, Margrave of Provence, son of Pons, Count of Toulouse. He lost an eye on a pilgrimage to Jerusalem prior to the First Crusade.

20. Charlemagne (747–814), Frank co-ruler (768–771), sole king (771–814) and Emperor of the Holy Roman Empire from 800.

21. Walter Sans Avoir, Lord of Boissy-sans-Avoir in the Île-de-France. He died on 21 October 1096 in a battle with the Turks, hit by seven arrows.

22. Peter the Hermit (c.1050–1115), a priest from Amiens. Some authors believe that the First Crusade was his idea, as is written in *Gesta Francorum*, a chronicle of the First Crusade from the year 1101.

23. Kilij Arslan, who ruled from 1092 to 1107, sultan of the Sunnite Seljuk state in Anatolia.

24. Godfrey of Bouillon (c.1060–1100). His father, Eustace II, participated in the Battle of Hastings, where he allegedly killed the Saxon leader Harold II. According to legend, during the battle Eustace gave his horse to William the Conqueror after William's horse was killed. William of Tyre describes him as 'a tall knight of wide chest, with light beard and hair'. Godfrey died in Jerusalem after a long illness. It was suspected that the cause of death was in fact a poisoned apple.

25. Baldwin I of Jerusalem (1058–1118). William of Tyre gave us a detailed description of the first king of the Kingdom of Jerusalem: a tall man, much stronger than his brother Godfrey, with dark brown hair and beard, an aquiline nose and pouting upper lip; a skilled warrior and rider, of noble mien, serious in speech and dress.

26. Bohemond I, Prince of Taranto, one of the leaders of the First Crusade. Born in San Marco Argentano in Calabria as the oldest son of the Norman nobleman Robert Guiscard, Duke of Apulia and Calabria.

27. Robert (1054–1134). At the time before the First Crusade, he was so poor that he would keep to his bed during the day because he had no clothes. He pawned his duchy to cover the cost of participating in the First Crusade.

28. Stephen Henry (c.1045–1102), son of Theobald III, Count of Blois. He returned from the First Crusade during the siege of Antioch. Adela persuaded him to participate in the meaningless crusade of 1101. He was killed at Ramla during the charge of Baldwin I leading 500 knights at several thousand Egyptian warriors.

29. Robert II (1065–1111), also known as Robert the Crusader or Robert of Jerusalem.

30. Publius Aelius Traianus Hadrianus (76–138), emperor from 117 to 138. The third of the Five Good Emperors (Nerva, Trajan, Hadrian, Antonius Pius and Marcus Aurelius) who marked the era of the Roman Empire's pinnacle of power. He constructed the wall between Britain and the then barbaric Scotland.

31. Shia (Arabic: *Shī'atu 'Alī*, the followers of Ali) comprise the second largest branch of Islam. They recognize Muhammad's cousin Ali and his descendants as the only proper successors to Muhammad's spiritual and secular power (caliphs and imams).

32. The Sunni are the largest denomination of Islam. Its followers recognize Abu Bakr as Muhammad's secular and spiritual successor.

33. Malik, Melik or Malka is a Semitic word meaning 'king', 'duke' or 'chieftain'.

34. The Turkmens, one of the tribes in the confederation of Ogurs. In the early Middle Ages, they inhabited today's Mongolia and the surroundings of Lake Baikal. In the eighth century, they migrated to the steppes between the Caspian and Aral lakes (the Ogur Steppes). In written sources, the name Turkmen appears in the tenth century and is used for the Ogurs who joined the Seljuks and accepted Islam as their religion.

35. A French word for Levant, meaning 'across the sea'.

Chapter One:

1. Hugh of Champagne (c.1075–1125), third son of Theobald III, Count of Blois. His son Odo I, who he renounced as he believed himself to be impotent, had two sons, Odo II and William I, both of whom played important roles in the Fourth Crusade.

2. In 528, Benedict of Norcia founded the oldest monastery order in Monte Cassino, with the motto *Ora et labora* ('Pray and work'). In addition to the three previous monks' vows, Benedict added the fourth, *Stabilitas loci* (Vow of Stability), so the monks vowed to spend their entire lives in one monastery. Benedictine monasteries are known as abbeys and are run by abbots. Every abbey is independent.

3. Bernard the saint (1091–1153), from one of the most powerful Burgundian families, at the time the spiritual leader of Europe.

4. According to legend, Payens and Saint-Omer were so poor that they only had one riding horse, which is the origin of the Templar seal showing two riders on a single horse.

5. Written around the year 400 and divided into eight chapters. It provides the main prescriptions for religious life in a commune. It is used to this day in many church orders.

6. Fulk of Anjou (1089–1143), Count of Anjou, king of the Kingdom of Jerusalem, grandfather of English King Henry I.

7. An associate, unordained member of the order.

8. Ramon Berenguer III (1082–1131), Count of Barcelona, Girona, Ausona and Provence; fought against Muslims in Spain.

Chapter Two:

1. The birthplace of St Andrew, between Caesarea and Château Pèlerin.

Chapter Three:

1. Thomas Becket (1118–70), Archbishop of Canterbury from 1162. The young King of England Henry II was crowned in York in 1170 by the Archbishop of York and the Bishops of London and Salisbury. As the coronation was in the jurisdiction of the archbishopric of Canterbury, Becket excommunicated his three colleagues for disregard of church rule, together with some other of his opponents in the clergy, which upset the young king. According to his indirectly expressed wish, Becket was killed by four knights on 29 December 1170.

Chapter Four:

1. In fact two anonymous chronicles written at the Benedictine Battle Abby near Hastings in the twelfth century.

2. Harald Sigurdsson (1015–66), king of Norway from 1046 to 1066.

3. All *Song of Roland* quotes are from the translation by C.K. (Charles Kenneth) Moncrieff [translators' note].

4. The 70-metre-long cloth is not, in fact, a tapestry. Embroidered with wool thread in colour, it represents, in around fifty images, the events leading to the Norman Conquest of England. It is believed that it was ordered by Bishop Odo, William the Conqueror's half-brother.

Chapter Five:

1. Shams al-Din Abu Al-Abbas Ahmad Ibn Muhammad Ibn Khallikan, Muslim scholar of Arabic or Kurdish origin from the thirteenth century.

2. A measure of height used for horses, equal to 10.16cm.

3. The Rule, clause 138.

Chapter Six:

1. Publius Flavius Vegetius Renatus, late Roman writer (fifth century), author of *Epitoma rei militaris*, a work on Roman warfare, methods and exercises used in Roman units of his time.

2. Leo VI the Wise (895–908), Byzantine Emperor, author of *Tactica*, a work detailing the cavalry and infantry formations, training, sieges, maritime warfare and ancient tactics.

3. Measure of length; 1 league = 4.8km.

Chapter Seven:

1. Raymond du Puy (1083–1160), son of Hugues du Puy, military commander under Godfrey de Bouillon and governor of Acre. Raymond was the first grand master of the Hospitallers (1120–60). The cross with eight points, today known as the Maltese cross, was his idea.

Chapter Nine:

1. William de Bures, French crusader who died in 1242. Together with his brother Geoffrey, he arrived in the Holy Land before 1115. Became prince of Galilee, then constable and regent of the Kingdom of Jerusalem during the time Baldwin II spent in Muslim captivity (1122–24).
2. Atabeg (or atabey) is a hereditary noble title of Turkish origin. The atabeg is the governor of a province, answering to the sovereign.
3. Nur ad-Din (1118–74), second son of Imad al-Din Zengi, Atabeg of Aleppo and Mosul.
4. Raymond de Poitiers (1115–49), son of the Duke of Aquitaine William IX, who had been one of the military leaders in the small crusade of 1101. He ruled the duchy of Antioch from 1136, when he married Constance, heiress of Bohemond II, Duke of Antioch.
5. Assassins or 'Hassassins' (Arabic: *Hashshāshīn*, users of hashish), a Muslim religious and political sect founded in the late ninth century.
6. Joscelin II was the son of Joscelin I, during whose reign the county of Edessa, the weakest of the Crusader States, reached its pinnacle. His grandchildren Baudouin IV and Sibylla ruled the Kingdom of Jerusalem, as did his great-grandson Baudouin V.
7. Baldwin III (1130–63), king of the Kingdom of Jerusalem from 1143 to 1163. Fulk and Melisende, daughter of Baldwin II, were his parents. Fulk died in a hunting accident when Baldwin was only 13 years old. The throne was taken by his mother, while Baldwin was proclaimed co-ruler and her heir. Seven years after he turned 15, which was considered mature enough to rule the country independently, Baldwin asked for his throne. With the support of his younger brother Amalric, Melisende refused to step down and an agreement was reached only after a short civil war in 1152. Melisende got to keep Nablus for life and held great sway at court, so she acted as regent every time her son went away to war.
8. An Arabic word meaning 'fight'. In classic Islamic belief, it marks the fight against those who do not believe in Allah. It does not necessarily refer to physical fighting, but to spiritual struggles against sin and passion. As Muslims were not allowed to wage wars of aggression, they were called to *jihad* (holy war) to defend themselves from attacks and protect their very existence.
9. A vizier is a high-ranking political advisor or minister to the caliph.
10. Reynald de Châtillon (1125–87), became Duke of Antioch by marriage (1153–60), and on his second marriage became the lord of Transjordan in 1177. Muslims proclaimed him the biggest enemy of Islam.
11. Toros II the Great was the sixth Lord of Armenian Cilicia (1144–69), known also as 'Master of the Mountains'. He also fought against Byzantium and against the Seljuk.
12. Amalric I (1136–74) was the Count of Jaffa and Ashkelon prior to his coronation. His children, Sibylla, Baldwin IV and Isabella I, were the future rulers of the Kingdom of Jerusalem. His very good friend William of Tyre wrote: 'He was a man of wisdom and discretion, fully competent to hold reins of government in the kingdom.'
13. Bohemond III the Stutterer (1144–1201) ruled the duchy of Antioch from 1163 until his death; cousin of Raymond III, Count of Tripoli, and king of the Kingdom of Jerusalem Baldwin IV. He was excommunicated by Pope Alexander III in 1180 when Bohemond cast aside his wife Theodora, niece of the Emperor Manuel, and married Sibylla who, according to William of Tyre, practised the devil's crafts. In Antioch, the Pope also proclaimed a ban on the performance of church rituals.
14. Baldwin IV the Leper (1161–85). He was a capable and courageous ruler. A pupil of William of Tyre, who first noticed the signs of the most dangerous form of leprosy in the boy.
15. Raymond III (1140–87), son of Raymond II and Hodierna of Jerusalem, sister of King Baldwin II, Count of Tripoli (1152–87) and Duke of Galilee and Tiberias.
16. Salah ad-Din Yusuf ibn Ayub (1137–93), founder of the Ayyubid Dynasty.

17. Kilij Arslan II, Sultan of the Sultanate of Rum (1156–92).
18. John of Ibelin (1179–1236), son of Balian of Ibelin and Maria Komnene. Known as 'The Old Lord of Beirut', a famous crusader from the family of Ibelin, which was named after the fortress of Ibelin, built in 1141. In the last year of his life, John joined the Templars so that he could die as a Knight of the Temple. The progenitor of the Ibelin family was Barisan, a knight serving the Count of Jaffa, originally from Northern Italy.
19. Baldwin of Ibelin (1130–c.1187), Barisan's middle son, lord of Ramla. With his brother Balian, he strongly supported Count Raymond III of Tripoli and Duke of Antioch Bohemond III in their conflict with Guy de Lusignan.
20. Balian of Ibelin (1143–93), Barisan's youngest son. He held the family fortress of Ibelin as vassal to his older brother Baldwin. He married Maria Komnene, widow of King Amalric, and became Lord of Nablus.
21. Joscelin III, Count of Edessa. He spent twelve years in Seljuk captivity after the Battle of Harim in 1164. Baldwin V, his nephew, appointed him the Seneschal of Jerusalem. At Hattin in 1187, together with Balian of Ibelin, he commanded the defensive forces of the crusaders' army.
22. Roger de Moulins, Grand Master of the Hospitallers from 1177 to 1187. He founded the Hospitallers' priories in England, France and Germany. Opponent of Guy de Lusignan and Reynald de Châtillon.
23. Manuel I Comnenus (1118–80), Byzantine emperor 1143–80.
24. Guy de Lusignan (1150–94), born in Poitou, France.
25. Reginald of Sidon (1130–1202), a prominent nobleman of the Kingdom of Jerusalem. He was one of the few noblemen who spoke Arabic. He was described as ugly and wise.
26. Conrad of Montferrat (mid-1140–92), originally from Northern Italy, count of Frederick Barbarossa, Louis VII and Leopold V of Austria. He was an attractive man, brave and smart, a diplomat and military commander. He married Isabella of Jerusalem who inherited the throne after the death of her half-sister Queen Sibylla. Although he was elected king in early 1192, he was never crowned. He was murdered by two assassins on 28 April 1192.
27. Lothar of Segni (1160–1216), Pope from 1198 to his death. One of the strongest and most influential popes, he called for the Fourth Crusade.
28. Richard I the Lionheart (1157–99), King of England, Duke of Normandy, Aquitaine, Gascoigne, Lord of Cyprus, Count of Anjou, Maine, Nantes and Brittany. He gained the nickname of the Lionheart due to his amazing courage and warrior skills.
29. Philip II Augustus (1165–1223), French king from the family of Capet; one of the greatest medieval rulers of France and Richard I's half-brother.
30. Leopold V (1157–94), Duke of Austria and from 1192 also Duke of Styria. Suspecting that Richard the Lionheart had participated in the murder of Leopold's cousin Conrad de Montferrat, the duke threw the Lionheart into the dungeon while he was returning to England through Austria in 1192. Leopold gained a large ransom but was excommunicated by Pope Celestine III for imprisoning a comrade from the crusades. At a tournament in Graz, he fell and a horse broke his foot so badly that it had to be amputated. As there was no surgeon on hand, Leopold instructed one of his servants to cut it off, but the servant only succeeded on the third stroke. Leopold died of gangrene.
31. The eleventh grand master of the Temple; member of a respected military family in Anjou. Supporter of Henry the Young King in revolt against his father Henry II, the king of England. Later he led King Richard's navy to the Mediterranean (Richard was instrumental in Robert's appointment to grand master).
32. Hugh III de Burgundy (1142–92), one of Richard the Lionheart's most loyal allies in the Third Crusade. He died during the Siege of Acre in 1192.
33. The tenth grand master of the Hospitallers.
34. James of Avesnes (1152–91) participated in the Third Crusade as the leader of French, Flemish and Frisian warriors who arrived in the Holy Land in 1189.
35. John de Brienne (1155–1237), born in Champagne. He gained fame in tournaments. In 1210, by marrying Maria, heiress to the throne, he became king of the Kingdom of Jerusalem. From 1235 he was also emperor-regent of the Latin Empire in Byzantium. He ended his life as a Franciscan monk.

36. Frederick II (1194–1250), one of the greatest rulers of the Holy Roman Empire from the house of Hohenstaufen.
37. Philip of Montfort (died in 1270). His uncle, John of Ibelin, helped him to become the constable of Jerusalem in 1244. Lord of Tyre and Toron. One of the few who managed to escape with their life at La Forbie.
38. Gauthier IV de Brienne (1205–44), one of the leading feudal lords in the Kingdom of Jerusalem. Lord of the county of Brienne in France and the county of Jaffa in the Holy Land. He arrived in the Holy Land while the throne in Jerusalem was held by his uncle John de Brienne.
39. Subutai (1175–1248), the greatest military strategist and leader for Genghis Khan and Ogotai Khan. During his career, he won sixty-five battles and conquered more territory than any other military commander in history.
40. Louis IX (1214–70), also known as St Louis, from the family of Capet, the only French king to be proclaimed a saint.
41. Hulagu Khan (1218–65), great-grandson of Genghis Khan, brother of Kublai, Mongke and Arik, conqueror of South-Western Asia.
42. Hugues de Poitiers (1235–84), king of Cyprus from 1267 and King of Jerusalem from 1268. Great-grandson of Bohemond IV of Antioch, through him connected to Robert Guiscard, Norman conqueror and duke of Apulia and Calabria.
43. Hethum I (died in 1271), ruled the kingdom of Cilicia from 1226 to 1270, founder of the Hethumid Dynasty. He abdicated in 1270 in favour of his son Levon and withdrew to a monastery.
44. Bohemond VI 'the Beautiful' (1237–75) ruled the remains of the duchy of Antioch and the county of Tripoli from 1251 to his death.
45. Edward I 'Longshanks' (1239–1307), English king from 1272. Due to his height and temperament, he struck fear into his opponents. He was a good warrior, governor and a man of faith.
46. Bohemond VII (1261–87) ruled the remains of the duchy of Antioch and the county of Tripoli from 1275 to his death. Most of his rule was spent at war with the Templars.
47. Jean I de Grailly (died in 1301), originally from Savoy, seneschal of the duchy of Gascoigne from 1266 to 1268 and again from 1278 to 1287, and of the Kingdom of Jerusalem from 1272 to 1276.
48. Amalric de Lusignan (1272–1310), constable of Jerusalem from 1289 and lord of Tyre from 1290.
49. Henri II de Lusignan (1270–1324), king of Cyprus and the Kingdom of Jerusalem from 1285.
50. Otto of Grandson (1238–1328), a knight from Savoy, long in service to the English crown, personal friend of Edward I.

Chapter Ten:
1. Shaizara Usama ibn Munqidh (1095–1188), professional warrior, writer and diplomat who served under Zengi, Nur ad-Din and Saladin.
2. Raymond Bertrand de Got (1264–1214), Pope from 1305 until his death. He was chaplain of Pope Boniface VIII, who appointed him archbishop of Bordeaux in 1297. He was elected Pope at the Conclave of Perugia as a neutral solution to the dispute over the election between the French and Italian cardinals.
3. Jacques Bernard de Molay (c.1243–1314), the last grand master from 1298 until the abolition of the Order. He was accepted into the Temple in 1265. He was in the Holy Land from 1270 until the fall of Acre, after which he went to Cyprus.
4. Anne Gilmour-Bryson, *The Trial of the Templars in Cyprus* (1998).
5. Louis I the Stubborn (1289–1316), son of Philip IV, king of Navarre from 1305 until his death. Like Louis X, he ruled France from 1314. He was the first to build a home tennis court and was recorded as the first tennis player ever known by name.
6. J.R.R. Tolkien, *Lord of the Rings*.

Bibliography

Barber, M., *The Trial of the Templars*, Second Edition (Cambridge University Press, 2006)

Chambers, J., *The Devil's Horsemen: The Mongol Invasion of Europe* (Cassel Publishers Ltd, London, 1988)

Davis, R.H.C., *The Medieval Warhorse* (Thames and Hudson Ltd, London, 1989)

Delbruck, H., *Warfare in Antiquity: History of the Art of War*, Volume I (Bison Book Editions, US, 1990)

Delbruck, H., *Medieval Warfare: History of the Art of War*, Volume II (Bison Book Editions, US, 1990)

Gilmour-Bryson, A., *The Trial of the Templars in Cyprus* (Leiden, Boston; Koln, Brill, 1998)

Gilmour-Bryson, A., *The Trial of the Templars in the Papal State and Abruzzi* (Citta del Vaticano: Biblioteca Apostolica Vaticana, 1982)

Hewitt, J., *Ancient Armour & Weapons* (Bracken Books, Random House, London, 1996)

Hyland, A., *The Medieval Warhorse From Byzantium to the Crusades* (Grange Books)

Maalouf, A., *Les Croisades veus par les Arabes* (J.C. Lattès, 1986)

Newman, S., *The Real History Behind the Templars* (Barclay Books, New York, 2007)

Nicolle, D., *Arms & Armour of the Crusading Era 1050–1350* (Greenhill Books, London; Stackpole Books, Pennsylvania, 1999)

Nicolle, D., *The Mongol Warlords* (Firebird Books, Poole, Dorset, 1990)

Ralls, K., Ph.D., *Knights Templar Encyclopedia* (Career Press, Franklin Lakes, NJ, 2007)

Read, P.P., *The Templars* (Phoenix Press, London, 2001)

Runciman, S., *A History of the Crusades 1: The First Crusade* (Penguin Books, London, 1990)

Runciman, S., *A History of the Crusades 2: The Kingdom of Jerusalem* (Penguin Books, London, 1990)

Runciman, S., *A History of the Crusades 3: The Kingdom of Acre* (Penguin Books, London, 1990)

Selwood, D., *Knights of the Cloister* (Boydel Press, Woodbridge, Suffolk, 1999)

Upton-Ward, J.M., *The Rule of the Templars* (Boydel Press, Woodbridge, Suffolk, 1997)

Urban, W., *The Teutonic Knights* (Greenhill Books, London; MBI Publishing Company, Minnesota, 2003)